NEW MONEY

LANA SWARTZ

NEW MONEY

How Payment Became Social Media

Yale

UNIVERSITY

PRESS

NEW HAVEN AND LONDON

Yale University Press books may be purchased in quantity for educational, business, or
promotional use. For information, please e-mail sales.press@yale.edu (U.S. office) or
sales@yaleup.co.uk (U.K. office).

Set in New Aster and Syntax types by IDS Infotech Ltd.
Printed in the United States of America.

ISBN 978-0-300-23322-3 (hardcover : alk. paper)

Library of Congress Control Number: 2019954706

A catalogue record for this book is available from the British Library.

This paper meets the requirements of ANSI/NISO Z39.48-1992 (Permanence of Paper).

10 9 8 7 6 5 4 3 2 1

For Eva Marigold

CONTENTS

NEW MONEY

1 THE COMMUNICATION OF MONEY

How Money Became Social Media

In June 2019, Facebook introduced Libra, its "global currency and financial infrastructure," which was slated to debut the following year.[1] The launch video opens with quick shots of historical communication technologies: a ticking rotary phone, someone licking an envelope, a tower radiating pulsing waves, a faintly discordant fax machine. "Remember when these were fast?" a reedy male voice-over asks. "Technology has improved the world around us," he asserts over images of a busy computerized stock-market trading floor, a soccer video game, and an advanced prosthetic arm. "So why is it simple to send one of these anywhere in an instant"—a man lays in a bathtub while text-message bubbles full of cute dogs (also bathing), a heart emoji, and a classic phatic "hahaha" pop up around him—"but not money?"

The voice-over continues, "What if we made money truly global" (a woman carrying what looks like a *quinceañera* gown through a warehouse), "stable" (a young couple riding a motorbike down a rural road lined with banana trees, the woman transfixed by something on her phone), "and secure" (a fisherman drags a small boat ashore as storm clouds gather). The video flashes to marketplaces, with vendors hauling flowers, fish, vibrant red peppers. "What if everyone was invited to the global economy? With access to the same financial opportunities?" A young woman takes a phone call in a brightly lit executive office; an older woman working as a janitor pauses to look at her smartphone on an elevator.

Why *doesn't* money move at the speed and scale of our communicative world? How can money be dependable and accessible to everyone? These are the questions of the Libra launch video. They are also the central questions of this book. Libra promises a utopian vision of everyday money that "works for everyone," that is "designed for the digital world." And in many ways, this vision, though vague, is aligned with concerns that this book will surface. But there are other questions that the Libra launch video obscures. What happens when a seemingly unstoppable Silicon Valley behemoth turns its attention to money?

This is a book about the communities produced by the form of communication that we call *payment* and whom these communities enable, permit, or force us to be. These communities and identities can determine the spaces we enter, the kinds of options we have access to, the ways we imagine ourselves; their tokens—credit cards, cash, or Bitcoins—live alongside the other identity materials we carry every day. How we pay is now part of who we are and where we belong. The consequences of exclusion—losing the "citizenship" of a transactional community—can mean life or death. Our transactional identities can overlap with our other identities—gender, class, line of work, language, geography—in complex ways. They organize space and our movement through it. They are technologies of belonging, inclusion, and exclusion. And we enact our transactional identities constantly, as we engage in any of the dozens or hundreds of transactions in which we participate every day.

Every year, Americans make billions of transactions.[2] Here are a few that you, depending on who *you* are, might make in one day:

> You might start your day with the Starbucks rewards app and end it by updating an expired card on Netflix.
> You might seamlessly tap a bus pass or fumble for coins.
> You might not even notice when your E-ZPass is pinged at an on-ramp or when your card is processed after a Lyft ride.

You might tell a homeless person that you don't have any cash. You might get cash from the ATM just to have some on hand. Once in a while, you might go into the bank for a crisp hundred-dollar bill for a special gift. You might use cash all the time. You might be a homeless person who accepts Square and/or Venmo—or a homeless person who doesn't.

You might pick up a tab with your fancy new titanium Chase Sapphire Reserve credit card and hope someone notices. You might pay with a debit card and not even think about what that might say about you. You might become embarrassed when the card "doesn't go through" and blame it on the new chip-enabled-card readers that no one seems to understand, even years after they were rolled out. You might find a prepaid card really convenient but be really sick of all the crazy fees.

You might get a Venmo payment from a friend to pay back her portion of that tab, annotated with emojis and an inside joke. Then, you might scroll through your Venmo feed, seeing what payments and emojis and inside jokes your friends have been sending to one another and wonder if you're missing out on something. Your Venmo account be frozen for some mysterious violation of terms of service, and you might not be sure why.

You might not be sure what Venmo is and feel miffed when your babysitter or dog-sitter or plant-sitter asks to be paid through it. You might also be annoyed to be stuck behind an older person who insists on writing a check at the grocery store.

The historian Fernand Braudel counted money as one of the fundamental "structures of everyday life."[3] This was true in the medieval world that Braudel described, and it is true today. The term "money" is a fairly broad one. When economists and other scholars interested in money study it, they rarely look at how it functions in everyday life: as a form of payment. The payment system is, as the anthropologist Bill Maurer puts it, the "plumbing of modern economies" and, as the Federal Reserve puts it, "highways of commerce."[4] It is, I will argue, a communication medium. We use its systems multiple times a day, every day.

Cash, cards, checks, and apps do more than transmit value. Our credit card, for example, says something about how we see ourselves and how powerful institutions see us. It says something about the nature of the transaction and the relationship between the parties involved. Transactions are embedded in and reflective of social, cultural, and relational meanings. These meanings shape and are shaped by the communication and media technologies—whether paper or electronic—that perform the transaction.

Transactions are also big business. Revenues in the global payments industry amount to nearly $2 trillion a year.[5] This is more than revenues of the global pharmaceutical industry, more than all media industries combined. While trading-floor wizardry is often seen as the star of the banking industry, payments are one of the largest and most important ways that banks make money.[6]

Yet the technologies of transaction often go unnoticed. A card is swiped, accounts are debited and credited sometime after, but what happens in between? Even though it is an essential information infrastructure and a huge industry unto itself, few of us notice it at all. As scholars of technology have pointed out, that's how we know an infrastructure is working well: as long as it's not broken, we don't need to understand how it works.[7]

And how payment works is changing, quickly. What was once a slow-moving and siloed sector of finance has been discovered and, of course, targeted for disruption by Silicon Valley. This too is big business: venture-capital investment in financial technology, or "fin-tech," is nearly $13 billion a year. Payment is increasingly assembled not as consumer financial services but as social media. This means a major shift, namely, from universal, interoperable systems like national currencies or the Visa/Mastercard network to niche platforms, each with its own design, vision for ideal use, business model, and governance system.[8] Money is becoming "social." What might this mean for the sociality of money?

Disruption in the payments industry is as much about big dreams as it is about big data. Even beyond the anarcho-capitalist cryptocurrency Bitcoin, many entrepreneurs make overtly political calls for private, extranational money, for direct and disintermediated economic communication, for either total privacy or total publicity in transactions. Even beyond the activists involved in local and alternative currency systems, many financial start-ups tout an attitude toward money that is "slow," "ethical," and rooted in "sharing" and other "values." Money has come to be seen as newly unstable, newly open to reinterpretation. Change the money, change the world. Alternatives to money-as-usual aren't just science fiction or utopian dreams. They're already all around us, being used every day.

This is a book about the cultural politics of transactional technologies. It offers a new way to think about money: as a communication medium dependent on particular technologies. In many ways, it is about the invisible: hidden payments, hidden infrastructure, and hidden people who are unable to access particular payment systems. It gives historical context to the "disruption" envisioned by entrepreneurs and demystifies the promises and perils of technological change. Each chapter takes up an essential mechanism of payment and explains how it works, how it got to be that way, how it's changing, and what implications those changes may have and for whom.

I am not the first scholar to suggest implicitly that money is a form of communication. One of the classic Aristotelian functions of money is to serve as *medium* of exchange." The philosopher Immanuel Kant found money to be "the greatest and most useable for all the means of human communication through things."[9] The sociologist Talcott Parsons described it as a "generalized medium of communication through the use of symbols given meaning within a code."[10] Karl Polanyi thought of money as a "semantic system similar to speech, writing or weights and measures."[11] But communication and media studies scholars, with key exceptions, which I will explore here, have largely ignored money.[12]

Money communicates value: I pay you $20; my account is debited and yours credited. How I pay you, the fact that I paid you, communicates something to you about our relationship. Money is communicated by media and infrastructures: paper, information systems, internetworks. These media communicate symbols of the entity that issues and authorizes them. Money is informational, symbolic, expressive, and mediated. It is communication, communicative, and communicated.

My focus, really, is not on money broadly defined but on money in its communication modality: payment. We often imagine the politics of money as economic: who has money, who doesn't, why. Payment technologies aren't just "economic"; they're circulatory. Their politics are communication politics: who gets to control and profit from communication infrastructure, who gets to access it and on what terms, what kind of traffic gets to travel over it. They involve questions of the public good and private interest, privacy and publicity. Payment is how we encounter money in everyday life; it is where the symbolic dimensions of money unfold. Maurer has persuasively argued that payment is an important and overlooked form in the theoretical study of money and in contemporary society more broadly.[13] In this book, I situate payment—as the communication and media of money—within communication and media studies.

I define communication, alongside theorist James Carey, as a "symbolic process whereby reality is produced, maintained, repaired, and transformed."[14] It is the sharing of information that produces shared meaning and, more generally, a shared social world. Communication is the very substance of social life. For Carey, as with John Dewey and other scholars in the American pragmatist tradition, communication doesn't just document and share documentation of the world; it is process through which the world is constructed.

In articulating this theory, Carey makes an influential distinction between the "transmission" and "ritual" views of communication. In the transmission view, communication is seen as the transportation of information across space, from sender to receiver, with the goal of control. At the time of Carey's intervention, transmission was the dominant approach to communication in the academy in the form of cybernetic paradigms that reduced all communication to the mathematical economy of the signal, telecommunications systems that managed people across distance, and mass media research that imagined audiences as receivers of messages that, in turn, had predictable effects on recipients. In the ritual view—Carey's own approach—communication is seen not as mere information transfer but as "the maintenance of society in time; not the act of imparting information but the representation of shared beliefs."[15]

In the transmission view, then, a newspaper is an "instrument that disseminates news and knowledge." In the ritual view, reading a newspaper is seen "less as sending or gaining information and more as attending a mass, a situation in which nothing new is learned but in which a particular view of the world is portrayed and confirmed." By seeing communication through the lens of ritual, by taking a "cultural approach" to communication, Carey argues that we can study the "actual social process wherein significant symbolic forms are created, apprehended, and used," which may, ultimately, "rebuild a model of and for communication of some restorative value in reshaping our common culture."[16]

Paper money, like all print media, conveys symbolic messages. All transactions are literally *trans-actions*: carryings across. The communication theorist John Durham Peters notes that "money, after all, is a kind of medium—and not only a medium of exchange, but a medium of representation as well."[17] The design of state currency tells us something about how nations would like to be seen. Banknotes produced in Massachusetts during the American Revolutionary War feature "a sword-wielding patriot holding an unfurled Magna Carta with the inscription, 'Issued in defense of American Liberty.'"[18] Early Canadian currency was decorated with the landscapes typical to the large country, depicted as "bucolic rather than heroic, mundane, not mythological."[19] Euro notes were designed to create a sense of shared but unspecific "Europeanness": imaginary bridges reflect a shared architectural past but exists nowhere.[20]

This imagery implies an "audience" for monetary media. The British Museum's paper money curator Virginia Hewitt therefore understands print money as offering "an unparalleled opportunity for officially-sanctioned propaganda, to color the recipient's view."[21] The historian David Henkin describes that in antebellum

New York, learning how to use cash was perhaps the most important form of "city reading" that often-illiterate Americans had to master, along with decoding handbills, street signs, and other forms of what the media scholar and practitioner Rekha Murthy calls "ambient street media."[22] The anthropologist Robert John Foster describes how Melanesians understand paper money as "the skin of the state—the site where [they] might look for news about relationships to the powerful forces brought by contact with white people and their institutions."[23]

There have been moments of popular pressure to use the medium of state currency to tell new kinds of stories. The Women On $20s campaign, launched in 2015, aimed to replace the image of President Andrew Jackson on the $20 bill with a woman.[24] The $20 was chosen both to mark the 2020 centennial of the Nineteenth Amendment, which gave women the right to vote, and because Jackson's legacy of Native American genocide seemed worthy of displacement. After an online survey, Harriet Tubman was selected.

Later in 2015, Treasury Secretary Jack Lew announced that a woman's portrait would replace Alexander Hamilton on the $10 bill, which was already scheduled to be redesigned. That decision was widely opposed, largely because the hit Broadway musical *Hamilton* had led to a surge in Hamilton's popularity (and in popular awareness of his role in establishing the US banking system). In 2016, Lew announced that Hamilton would stay on the $10 bill and Jackson would be replaced on the $20 bill by Tubman.[25]

However, in what felt like a blow to those who hoped that US currency could be used to value the histories of women and African Americans, the plan was scuttled under the Trump administration in 2017. Trump described his reticence to replace Jackson: "Andrew Jackson had a great history and I think it's very rough when you take somebody off the bill. Andrew Jackson had a history of tremendous success for the country. . . . I would love to leave Andrew Jackson and see if we can maybe come up with another denomination. Maybe we do the $2 bill or we do another bill. I don't like seeing it. Yes, I think it's pure political correctness. Been on the bill for many, many years and really represented—somebody that was really very important to this country."[26]

In 2017, Trump's treasury secretary, Steven Mnuchin, said, when asked about the fate of the Tubman $20 bill, "People have been on the bills for a long period of time. This is something we'll consider. Right now we've got a lot more important issues to focus on."[27] According to the former White House adviser Omarosa Manigault Newman, Trump's motivations were even simpler. He reportedly balked at the idea: "You want me to put that face on the twenty-dollar bill?"[28] The skin of the state indeed.

In 2018, the artist Dano Wall produced stamps designed to superimpose Tubman's face on top of Jackson's.[29] He sold the stamps and also provided resources for 3-D printing one's own stamp. Wall wrote of the project, "This country, and its government, have a serious problem with representation. Who we choose to honor as a society affects the moral attitudes that are baked into us as we grow up. The impact that seeing the face of Harriet Tubman staring back at you from a $20 bill should not be underestimated. This sort of representation can subtly but deeply affect someone's conception of themselves and their place in society. The slightly subversive nature of it being currency that's been hand-stamped by another human makes a discovery of one of these bills all the more joyous."[30]

There are precedents for "remixing" the media of paper money. English suffragettes struck pennies in the early 1900s with the slogan "Votes for Women" to spread the idea of universal suffrage to as many people as possible: the penny was used by all strata of society and was too small a denomination to be recalled for vandalism.[31] (It's worth noting that marking money today, as Wall's Tubman stamps do, is not illegal. US law does not prohibit stamping currency so long as the process does not obscure the denomination, render the bill unfit for circulation, or contain advertising.)[32]

The anthropologist Karen Strassler describes how the medium of state currency was "remediated," to use the term coined by the media studies scholars Jay David Bolter and Richard Grusin, in post-Sudharto Indonesia through stickers bearing the face of the opposition party candidate, Megawati Sukarnoputri, and designed to be placed on rupiah bills. This practice "transformed the state fetish of money into an 'artifact' of their critical and utopian

The stamp used to replace Andrew Jackson with Harriet Tubman on the $20 bill was based on an 1868 portrait held by the National Museum of African American History & Culture.

imaginings [and has] thus become an integral feature of contemporary Indonesian political communication."[33]

In these examples, across historical and cultural contexts, print money became the site of a media controversy, a drama over representation. Each of these examples shows how print money is not used merely to *transmit* value—although it certainly does that—but is used to produce shared social reality. In each example, money's audiences have tried to renegotiate its *rituals*, to re-create mass media as popular culture.[34]

But beyond the textual symbols money conveys, it is already highly expressive. The sociologist Viviana Zelizer has powerfully demonstrated how the social meaning of money is fluid. In order to accommodate this range of social meaning, we fashion "special monies."[35] Sometimes we make new money media forms—gift certificates for Mother's Day spa days, special red envelopes as in

Chinese New Year. Sometimes our "earmarking" is invisible, mental accounting: we are careful to allocate paychecks and baby gifts and gambling winnings differently.[36] As Zelizer writes, "camouflaged by the physical anonymity of our dollar bills, modern money is routinely differentiated."[37]

The social earmarking of monetary media is not only used to designate relations between people dyadically but—like the Tubman $20 bill, the suffragette penny, and the Megawati rupiah— among collectivities and institutions, not just with the goal of marking money to express different kinds of personal relationships but with the goal of telling new stories about the past, present, and future. This too can happen without decorating money or creating new money media. Today, US Sacagawea dollar coins are commonly used in Ecuador, where they circulate alongside Ecuadorian minted currency.[38] According to the anthropologist Taylor Nelms, Ecuadorians read the image of the North American Lemhi Soshone woman Sacagawea, pictured with a baby on her back, as particularly "Andean."[39] Sometimes we can see the ways in which monetary media become popular culture, and sometimes we can't.

Of course, it is not only paper currency that is communicative. Credit cards are designed to convey symbolic meaning—that the bearer is rich, a member of the Navy Federal Credit Union, or a fan of Hello Kitty—and they too can be used in ways that express a variety of social meanings. These symbolic, expressive dimensions, however, are only some of the ways that money communicates.

Indeed, Carey's distinction between ritual and transmission should not be seen as a neat, total, mutually exclusive dichotomy.[40] Holding too fast to the distinction between the symbolic and the nonsymbolic, the ritual and the transmission, means missing that, as the media scholar Jonathan Sterne notes, "social reality is made not only at the level of symbols. It is also built and organized, a world of motion and action."[41] We should pay attention to the ways that transmission itself has ritual dimensions, creates shared reality.

Money technologies involve *tokens* (the unit of currency, which may or may not take physical form), but they also involve *rails* (the infrastructures that make tokens move) as well as *ledgers* (the information systems that keep track of them). It is also important, then, to attend to the stuff of that transmission and accounting that are not on their face "symbolic." As the information studies scholar Leah Lievrouw articulates, drawing from Bruno Latour's 1991 description of technology as "society made durable," technology can perhaps better be understood as *communication made durable.*"[42] The media scholar Roger Silverstone describes the "double articulation" of communication technologies: they are at once tools for conveying meaning and meaningful things unto themselves.[43]

The media historian Carolyn Marvin argues that, in Carey's work, technology is often seen as opposed to ritual, as threatening to community. But Marvin shows all the seemingly nonsymbolic, transmissive technologies that go into ritual reading of that newspaper in Carey's example:

> The daily newspaper cannot be in the reader's hands without the delivery truck, the roads on which it travels, the printing satellite, the rocket that launched it, the reporters who make use not only of roads, telephones, and laptops, but pencils and notebooks. It requires a standardized technique for the transforming of and conveying language—the alphabet, and years of regimented training in its use. Newspaper reading is socially embedded in other technologically saturated settings as well—the house on Sunday, the subway ride to work, the automatic coffeemaker, and all the complex family, neighbor, stranger, gender, and class relations in which all these artifacts are also implicated, and through which their meaning is constituted. Newspaper reading cannot do without the artifact in a thousand forms patterned and textured in complex and meaningful ways among citizens in complementary, competing, and overlapping networks of association.[44]

Put another way, the rituals that produce shared social reality entail not only the production and interpretation of symbolic forms (or the encoding and decoding of messages) but the circulation (or transmission) of those forms and the infrastructure through which that communication occurs.

Susan Leigh Star, who playfully but accurately referred to herself and her collaborators as the "Society of People Interested in Boring Things," makes a case for the importance of large-scale shared technologies—infrastructures—and the classifications and standards that produce and are produced by them.[45] "Study a city and neglect its sewers and power supplies (as many have), and you miss essential aspects of distributional justice and planning power," Star writes. "Study an information system and neglect its standards, wires, and settings, and you miss equally essential aspects of aesthetics, justice and change."[46] Communication infrastructure is something that is "experienced," that shapes everyday life.[47]

Star cites Langdon Winner's classic example of Robert Moses, a New York City planner who made the decision that the bridges over the Grand Central Parkway would be low in height. These bridges were too low for public buses to pass through. Poor people were effectively prevented from traveling easily to and from wealthier Long Island suburbs, by design, not policy. Star writes, "there are millions of tiny bridges built into large-scale information infrastructures, and millions of (literal and metaphoric) public buses that cannot pass through them."[48] Infrastructures, as Paul Edwards argues, "act likes laws." He writes, "To live within the multiple, interlocking infrastructures of modern societies is to know one's place in gigantic systems that both enable and constrain us."[49]

It is true that city dwellers could not easily transport—or transmit—themselves to the suburbs, but the power of that infrastructural arrangement lay as much in ritual experience: it was about "knowing one's place." What low bridges are built into today's payment systems? How do they tell us whether we do or do not belong? Indeed, you also had to *buy* that newspaper. Did the kiosk newsstand take cards? Did it take *cash*?

The sociologist Nigel Dodd argues that "money is a process, not a thing: it *consists* of social relations."[50] But money is also a thing, a processual thing, as the philosopher Jane Bennet describes, a "vital" thing that has the capacity to act in the world.[51] Like other media technologies, it has materiality, and that materiality isn't threatened by digitalization; rather, it becomes newly material: wire and ether, servers and spectrum.[52]

These materials are developed and maintained by people. They are instantiations of labor: writing policy and contracts and code; laying wires and spooling receipt paper; cutting a silicon chip with a laser saw in a factory; and jiggling a card reader to get it to work in a café. The technology scholars Andrew Russell and Lee Vinsel illustrated this in a half-joking title for a hypothetical airplane-reading business book: *The Maintainers: How a Group of Bureaucrats, Standards Engineers, and Introverts Made Digital Infrastructures That Kind of Work Most of the Time*.[53] It's these maintainers who make payment systems, like infrastructures, work. They too are part of the ritual capacity of any communication apparatus.

A communication perspective also offers a way of understanding both meaning and power through mediation and infrastructure, both symbolic and material. Whereas Carey suggests that ritual communication produces not just a shared social reality but a deeper communion, the communication scholar Gretchen Soderlund demonstrates how this approach glosses over important ways that communication divides as much it coheres, oppresses as much as it uplifts.[54] Communication is often rooted in exclusion and hierarchy, promoting community among some people and fragmentation among others. It is often inflected with power, promoting certain representations and circulations at the cost of others.

This shortcoming of Carey's approach—its tendency to romanticize ritual communication and the community it is assumed to produce—is countered by media philosophers like John Durham Peters and Sybille Krämer, both of whom attempt to recuperate the transmission view of communication. For Krämer, the idea that we can fully come together, merge as one true community, is ultimately homogenizing.[55] From this perspective, the ritual view steamrolls difference: it excludes those who aren't experiencing what the "we" is experiencing. It demands affirmation and assent and obfuscates the domination and violence to which Soderlund pointed. True communion is impossible, and, insofar as it homogenizes, it may not even be desirable. As Soderlund suggests, "While communication and political theorists make lavish use of [the term 'community'], perhaps they should instead consider why it has come to index all that is desirable."[56]

Both Peters and Krämer take up money as a key example of transmissive communication. Peters argues that money is widely seen as distasteful precisely *because* it is a media form.[57] Money, like mediation and technology in general, is often treated with suspicion. It is a go-between between people and other people, between people and property, between people and labor. As Karl Marx put it, "Money is the pimp between need and object, between life and man's means of life."[58] It is seen as disrupting direct, dialogic communication and thereby distorting relations. Distrust of money, then, is a distrust of mediation, a fantasy of telepathy.

Krämer takes up what is often seen as the most destructive power of money—its ability to price things, to make them equivalent and comparable, to reduce quality to quantity—and marvels at it.[59] Money mediates difference, resolves conflict, and makes communication—in the form of exchange—possible. It might not be possible ever really to know another person, but it is possible, using money as a mediator, a medium, to "come to terms." Payment technologies are negotiators of communication despite difference, communication-in-difference.

Zelizer describes how in scholarship and everyday life, we tend to take one of two positions about money and relationships.[60] On the one hand, we tend to see money and relationships as occupying "hostile worlds": one necessarily pollutes the other, and so the two should never mix. On the other hand but sometimes simultaneously, we tend to see money and relationships as reducible to each other: family is "nothing but" an economic unit; businesses are "nothing but" nepotism. Zelizer offers a third way forward, which she calls the "differentiated ties" approach and which resonates with the approaches of Peters and Krämer. She shows how money is a tool to negotiate different relationships, different contexts, different selves. It can be used to create or dissolve social ties, as in courtship expenses and alimony, respectively, to manage and limit intimacy, and as in payments to therapists and sex workers, or to establish or maintain inequality, as in "women's wages." Both media in general and money in particular

are distrusted because they mediate, but they both afford communication—and difference—*because* of this capacity to mediate.

Payment is a form of communication, a way of transmitting information that produces shared meaning. Communication
through payment knits us together in a shared economic world:
a *transactional community*, by which I mean the set of relations
that are produced by transactional communication. In developing
the term "transactional community," I mean to partake of neither
the normative negative connotations of the word "transactional"
nor the normative positive connotations of the word "community."
Instead, I mean to show that transactional communities are made
up of what Zelizer would call "differentiated ties": they are made
up of acts of communication despite difference.

Transactional media show us their communities. There are
peoples, such as the Indo-Greeks who lived on the modern border
of Afghanistan and Uzbekistan from around 180 BC to AD 10,
who are only knowable as transactional communities, according
to the archaeologist Frank L. Holt.[61] The only real remaining evidence of them is the coins they left behind. Archaeologists map
where ancient coins are found to trace the geography of empire.
They divine political change from the tiny portraits of the kings
that turn metal into money. They read ethnicity in the number
systems that mark value. They understand the organization of
society through coin fabrication techniques. For these scholars,
numismatics is a way of uncovering lost civilizations. Coins, the
ancient payment technology, called the Indo-Greek civilization
into being and can be used to uncover it.

Modern state currency was designed to enact transactional communities that are the size and scope of the nation. Cash pulls people
together in a "national community of shared fate,"[62] and using it is
a ritual of citizenship. Like archaeologists searching for the lost
Indo-Greeks in their coins, scholars have read national identity into
the design of cash.[63] But all those who use cash need not be citizens
of a state; a transactional community is more inclusive than a state.

Sociologists and anthropologists often conceive of the relations between people who transact with each other as networks,

circuits, or spheres. The geographer Emily Gilbert writes that money "is not a totalizing social phenomenon but a changing and often ambivalent social network."[64] The sociologist Mark Granovetter has influentially described how economies aren't made up of abstract, idealized markets but rather should be understood as networks that are "embedded" in actual social circumstances.[65] Zelizer, whose approach is less structural and more relational than Granovetter's, describes how the connections we make through money ramify out into "circuits of commerce," which are characterized by shared economic activities that are marked by shared meaning and carried on by means of shared social relations.[66] And as the sociologists Liz McFall, Franck Cochoy, and Joe Deville point out, markets are only the "outcome of various arts and devices of attachment that work with the avid propensities of all entities to associate."[67]

In articulating transactional communities, I want to put communication, its media and its technologies, at the center of the collectivities formed through transaction. Transactional media call a community into being and trace its contours. If money is, as various scholars have asserted, like language, then transactional communities delineate who is able to talk to one another, to participate in the conversation.

What kind of "community" is possible through the communication of money? Communication—through the exchange of symbols, the experience of infrastructure, and engagement with other "vibrant matter"—produces a shared social reality. I am calling that shared social reality "community" because it is a way of being together that arises from communication, from countless transactions.

As Soderlund and many scholars, notably the feminist scholar Miranda Joseph, have pointed out, "community," insofar as it represents some kind of spiritual oneness, tends to be inflected with a positive valence, which is troubling because community is often a mechanism of exclusion and because oftentimes it is that very dream of oneness that reinforces an oppressive status quo.[68] Further, as Peters and Krämer articulate, that dream of oneness is just that, a dream: it is not possible to fully share experience.[69]

But the exchange of media—exemplified best by payment—creates a world in which oneness is impossible, difference persists, and yet communication occurs, community happens. A transactional community is one sustained by the rituals of communication-in-difference.

Members of a transactional community share imbricated senses of identity, geography, temporality, value, politics, and practice. Money, as communication media, performs a relation between people in a moment of transaction as well as relations between individuals and the larger imaginaries like "the economy" and "society." It is a creature of network effects: in order for it to "work," everyone has to recognize it as money. A transactional community is a community of shared belief.

We accept money—it is only valuable—because we have a sense of what institutions authorize it, who else will accept it and where, and that they will accept it tomorrow and the next day and the day after that. When we exchange money, we agree not just on its quantity but on its meaning. The technologies of money—which make it transactable and valuable—are mechanisms of maintaining these shared understandings. Gilbert calls state currency a "daily affirmation" of the nation-state, but all monetary exchanges are daily affirmations of a transactional community.[70]

There is a sense that we've moved from an era of mass media to an era of social media. The mass media era has been characterized by the unified, collective, passive experience of concentrated, unidirectional broadcast and print technologies. The social media era has been characterized by a participatory, peer-to-peer, globalized, but also surveilled experience of digital media. Similarly, what we're seeing now is a shift from *mass money media* to *social money media*.

The dichotomy between mass media and social media is vexed. Most critical scholars are uncomfortable with the very terms "mass media" and "social media."[71] There are problems with imagining that history happens in neat, discrete phases. Although it's useful to think broadly about the "mass media" and "social media" eras, reality is far messier. Even at the height of the so-called broadcast age, people still shared some of the most important information by word of mouth—over the back fence, through office memo—and received much of their journalism from overtly partisan newspapers. Today, social media itself has become a new form of mass media. Far more people use Facebook every day than tune into the Super Bowl: social media is more massive than the most massive of mass media events. And many of the links that are shared on social networking sites connect to mass media content producers. As Sonia Livingstone writes, "polarizations of the 'then' and 'now' kind, especially those that bracket history as 'how things were before now,' rarely enrich our understanding of social change."[72]

But payment is increasingly being *produced, practiced,* and *understood* as a form of "social media." I understand "social media" as an industry, a way of talking about a set of technologies, and a modality of norms and engagements. Social media is, as the technology scholar danah boyd puts it, "a phenomenon to be analyzed."[73] It is an object of study, a theoretical lens, not a coherent empirical truth.

So what is the implied "mass media" money form that is being "disrupted"? State currency—a universal, public, print media—is a mass media form. Virginia Hewitt described state-issued currency as "the most mass-produced objects in the world, painstakingly designed for millions of people to use."[74] Paper money may in fact be the most ubiquitous form of print media even today. Cash, as a transactional technology, is universal: it is, to quote the US dollar bill, "legal tender for *all* debts public and private" (emphasis added). It is both a "common economic language" and one of those big, public infrastructures of modernity, like the federal postal service or highway system.[75]

The term "mass media," with its one-to-many logics, tends to be used interchangeably with "broadcast," and there isn't a broadcast modality for money. As the communication scholar Josh Braun points out, the mass media era was marked by the logics of mass *distribution* as much as it was by a specific broadcast model.[76] Those networks are big, interoperable, and global. They are as mass a media distribution infrastructure as can be. And state-issued currency is still the primary value form that is communicated over these networks.

In recent years, the payments industry has become an object of entrepreneurial innovation. The industrial locus of the payments industry is shifting from Wall Street to Silicon Valley, from financial services to social media. And this makes sense. As the Facebook Libra launch video demonstrates, we need money that moves in the ways that our other communication moves. We need transactional communities that map our other lived communities.

In 2014, Facebook applied for a money transmitter license and the following year debuted a payments feature in its messenger program.[77] When this happened—six years before Libra was announced!—the London-based payments-industry guru Dave Birch wrote that he was surprised, "but only because it had taken so long for them to do it." Birch recounts the story of his teenage son's band's gig:

> There were five bands involved and the paying public arrived in droves, ensuring a good time was had by all. All of this was arranged through Facebook. All of the organisation and all of the coordination was efficient and effective so that the youngsters were able to self-organise in an impressive way. Everything worked perfectly. Except the payments.
>
> When it came to reckoning up the gig wonga, we had a couple of weeks' worth of "can you send PayPal to Simon's dad" and "he gave me a cheque what I do with it?" and "Andy paid me in cash but I need to send it to Steve" and so on. Some of them had bank accounts, some of them didn't. Some of them had bank accounts that you could use online and others didn't. Some of them had mobile payments of one form or another and others didn't. I can remember that at one point my son turned to me and asked "why can't [we] just send them the money on Facebook?"[78]

For Birch, Facebook money was, even in 2014, "overdue" because it was needed to keep apace with lives already lived through Facebook.

Silicon Valley is attempting to build money technologies that create transactional communities that work for our social media lives; they are doing so according to social media business logics. Many companies are hoping to harness the promise of transactional "big data" and put it into conversation with other "social" data sets. These new systems are governed according to practices native to Silicon Valley, such as click-through "terms of service" agreements. They are organized according to economic arrangements also native to Silicon Valley, such as venture capitalism. The goal of fin-tech is to "disrupt" payment by redirecting the flow of payment revenue and data through Silicon Valley's digital warehouses and toll roads.

Venmo—currently the most popular mobile payments platform in the United States—is overtly produced as a form of social media. Its primary innovation on other person-to-person payments like PayPal is a Facebook-like public "feed" of transactions. When one person pays another, the transaction becomes a "post" that is made visible to all of one's friends when they scroll through the stream. Users are required to annotate their transactions with notes. It's common to use emojis, like the martini glass for a round of drinks. You like or comment on your friends' transactions. Like many social media platforms, its privacy settings are "public" by default.

Venmo was designed to look and feel like a social media platform. It includes all the characteristics of a social networking site, as defined by the communication scholars danah boyd and Nicole Ellison in 2007: a public profile in the form of a Twitter-like "feed" of payments, a friends list, and the ability to view and traverse the connections and "posts"—in the form of annotated payments—of others.[79] It *looks* like social media. For one thing, its colors are Facebook blue and white. These familiar features and design elements instruct users that they are in the domain of the social rather than the merely financial.

The short history of Venmo follows the typical life cycle of a social media company: it started as a start-up, it came up through the star system of incubators and venture-capital funding, and it was ultimately acquired by the entrenched tech giant PayPal. Like many social media platforms, it has yet to turn a profit. Rather, as is customary in Silicon Valley, the goal has been *scale*: get as many users as possible, then figure out how to monetize the service—most likely with some kind of attempt to monetize data. Venmo operates like a social media platform: it is governed by terms of service and enforced by semiautomated moderation systems. As with other social media platforms, it has been hard to get the moderation right. There have been countless examples of accounts being suspended in error. As one user told me, "[Venmo] is like a bank with the customer service of Facebook."

People are practicing Venmo as social media. They use Venmo not just to transact but to create messages intended to be seen both by the recipient of that transaction and by a larger audience. They view and interact with these transactional traces, reading them as documentation of sociality. They come up with uses for Venmo that are native to social media. For example, it not uncommon to "penny poke" people by sending them a small amount of money to let them know you're thinking about them, not unlike the Facebook poke.

In dozens of think pieces, these practices are used to understand Venmo as a form of social media. It is described as "the next big social network," "the secret, hip social network you've never heard of," and "the ultimate social network for voyeurs and gossips."[80] It is implicated in all the familiar techno-panics associated with social media: cyberstalking, overshare, deception, fo-mo, trolling, inauthenticity, and danger.[81] Venmo is making us petty, ruining relationships, giving us "Venmo anxiety," rife with "scams and fraud," allowing us to harass political figures like Sean Spicer, and allowing our exes to stalk us.[82] In general, Venmo "really can be very dangerous."[83]

Venmo isn't the only form of social money media. There are countless other start-ups in this "space," each with its own set of repertoires. Most social networking sites—Facebook, Instagram, Snapchat, Google—have attempted to include a payment system in their platform offerings. There are also more radical attempts to rethink the sociality of money, like cryptocurrencies and community currencies. Payment is becoming social media. The social media industry is trying to do payment.

But just as the distinction between mass and social media is a tricky one, so too is the distinction between mass and social money media. The shift from mass money media to social money media is similarly not so neat or complete. Cash has never been truly universal. All kinds of other money tokens—foreign currency, coupons, checks, cards—have always been used alongside state-issued currency. This monetary media cacophony predates the universal state-issued currency, which didn't fully take hold in the United States until after the Civil War.[84]

State currency isn't going anywhere. Bitcoin and frequent-flyer miles are still denominated in dollars. Cash isn't going anywhere either, as studies of cash usage produced by the Federal Reserve Payments Study show year after year. The "cashless society" is as unlikely to be brought about by ongoing digitization as the "paperless office" is. Instead, we will continue to use cash for certain transactions, cards for some transactions, and, indeed, Venmo for other transactions. Some of us will use cash more and Venmo less. Even in the case of Venmo, the medium of money is layered: we pay a friend using Venmo, fund that transaction with a debit card, and denominate that payment in state currency, thinking in terms of "dollars." Similarly, the interface of many mobile wallets displays the image of a credit card on the screen of your phone. As Maurer notes, the story of payment innovation is one of addition, not progression. The technologies of payment are a palimpsest.[85]

Furthermore, just because Silicon Valley is discovering the "social" in payment doesn't mean that it is inventing it. As Zelizer writes, "Not all dollars are equal."[86] Indeed, money—like any media technology—is also a social technology. It is expressive and polysemous even in its most "mass" form. The payments industry sage David Birch has suggested that cash may even be *more* meaningful as it becomes "post-functional," that is, less central to our transactional lives.[87]

But as a social technology, payment can be designed in many different ways, to have particular affordances and constraints. As Maurer writes, "Just as technologies afford all kinds of uses for which they were never designed or intended, just as technologies can be hacked or tweaked or wired together with other technologies to create new assemblages that do different things, so too with money."[88] As a media technology, payment is being consciously redesigned—largely by Silicon Valley, largely in the image of social media—right now. Money has always been social; money has always been media. Right now, we're reconciling it as a form of "social media."

As money is redesigned by Silicon Valley, the question of control emerges. New communication technologies are often imagined as bringing about new freedoms but in reality bring about just as new constraints. Cash, though a technology of the state, has low barriers to use, is hard to control, and is hard to surveil. The same cannot be said for the new media of money, especially since they are being built in the model of social media. Who controls these new rails? Who watches the traffic that flows through them?

In order to understand the stakes of the shift from mass money media to social money media, we have to understand how new

The Girl Scouts now take cards, thanks to platforms like Square and Venmo.

payment forms create new transactional communities and, within them, transactional identities, transactional relations, and transactional power. So this shift from mass money media to social money media is also a shift from mass transactional communities to social transactional communities. With what implications?

A new kind of social difference is emerging, one that goes beyond nation-state (dollar, pound, or peso) and status (cash or platinum rewards credit card) and includes anything about us made measurable by social media data. We can see things about how these systems have been working, ubiquitously and invisibly, because we see them breaking or being transformed or replaced or interfered with or gamed. This means that this book is also about the past and the possible futures of these communities in which all of us are involved. This also means that this book reveals the "territory" of transactional communities and identities: the infrastructure, the businesses, the surveillance and risk assessment, the laws and public institutions—how the machine works, starting with transactional media, from credit cards to cash and coin.

2 TRANSACTIONAL PASTS

A Very Short History of Money as Communication

D EE Hock, who founded what would be become Visa, had by
the late 1970s developed a strange vision for credit card
networks. He defined money as information socially "guaranteed"
to be valuable, and he believed that there lay tremendous power
in its digitization and transmission. As he describes, "Money would
become nothing but alphanumeric data in the form of arranged
energy impulses. It would move around the world at the speed of
light at minuscule cost by infinitely diverse paths throughout the
entire electromagnetic spectrum."[1] Writing of his experiences of
the early days of Visa, Hock sounds a lot like today's Bitcoin enthusiasts. It seems that whenever money is revealed to be a form
of communication, when its wires are exposed, things start to look
odd. Suddenly it's easy to see, as Hock did, that money is both
much simpler and more complicated—and somehow even more
powerful—than we imagined.

I would like to start with a very short, very partial, and largely
synthetic communication history of money.[2] The goal is to tell a
story that foregrounds transactional communities. Like other
forms of communication, transactions don't happen telepathically.
Instead, they are enacted through media and infrastructures,
which are always instantiations of meaning and power relations.
This is by no means intended to be an exhaustive or authoritative
history. Rather, it is a provocative one: it offers a way of looking

across time to see money as a communication technology. It is also meant as a corrective to some of the breathless futurity that tends to surround new money technologies and technology more broadly.

What we think of as the technologies of money have long tracked alongside what we think of as the technologies of communication: print, telegraph, mainframe computer, information networks, mobile phones. The repeating themes in the history of money technology are communicative, circulatory, as are its politics. The history of payment bears traces of ongoing conflict: between space and time, ephemerality and permanence, individual identity and collective accountability, private control and the public interest.

Paper money is one of the most ubiquitous and one of the most overlooked forms of print media. Cash is perhaps overlooked *because* it is ubiquitous. But state-issued paper money is actually a relatively new technological achievement. Before the nineteenth century, the media of money was fragmented and stratified. As print currency was standardized, it became a form of mass media. Like the nation itself, national currency was buoyed by innovation in printing technology in the nineteenth century.[3] Like other forms of print culture, such as the newspaper, print currency was both instrumental to and an instrument of the emergence of the nation-state as what Benedict Anderson calls an "imagined community."[4] State currency mapped the nation as an economic territory with a common economic medium.

Print currency is literally a form of media in that it is covered with messages that tell stories about a shared past, present, and future. It is as much a "medium of representation" as it is a medium of exchange.[5] When nation-states were new, paper currency was an important way to distribute official histories to the populace before universal education became common.[6] Even in the present, the US dollar might be one of the only ways that most Americans encounter the federal government on a daily basis.

In the United States, national currency was not fully consolidated until after the Civil War. Prior to that, foreign currencies,

This one-dollar bank note was issued by the Northern Bank of Kentucky in Lexington in 1856. It was printed by Toppan, Carpenter, Casilear & Company of Philadelphia, which was well known for printing both currency and stamps during the 1850s. The note depicts George Washington, as well as an allegorical image of Progress with a pastoral scene, a railroad, and skyline, in the background. The note is signed by the bank's cashier and president. Before 1863, banks issued their own currency. These notes were usually backed by the bank's reserves and used locally. But banks often made too many notes, and many went bankrupt when financial panic struck, particularly in 1837. Currency from these failed banks are known as "broken bank notes."

private bank notes, and scrip produced by railroads, insurance companies, and other private businesses circulated alongside currency issued by the US Treasury. The historian David Henkin describes how, in cities where lots of different kinds of money circulated, everyday spending required street smarts, knowing how to navigate a messy, complex monetary media environment.[7] Bills may have come from a failed or fictitious bank or may have been a counterfeit copy of a note from a functioning, real bank. Money was "part of the mystery of the city that could only be decoded by connoisseurs."[8] As this monetary cacophony gave way to the comparative order of state-issued paper money, immigrants from both the hinterland and other parts of the world could more easily assimilate—economically—into the modern American metropolis. Georg Simmel describes how modern print currency allowed people to transact, to live as strangers, freed from the old bonds of long-term economic entanglement inherent in rural patriarchy and feudalism.[9]

Before the emergence of state currency, money technology was, in most of the world, highly stratified. The poor used low-value petty tokens like bronze or copper coins, and the wealthy used bills of exchange and kept track of their obligations through accounts. As the political scientist Eric Helleiner describes, "The result was a tiered monetary order rather than a coherent national one, in which economic 'communication' between rich and poor was inhibited by the existence of a fluctuating and unclear 'exchange rate' between the respective forms of money used by these two classes."[10] State-issue paper money unified these classes into an economic polity with a "common economic language," whose members would, at least, do business with each other, engage in commerce if not always conversation.[11]

In an economy the size of a nation, paper money had to move across a territory the size of a nation. "Communication" was once synonymous with "transportation": to communicate a letter meant to carry it through networks of road, rail, and canal.[12] The US postal system, which transported newspapers and messages from afar, bound the country together and forged a national imaginary from a loose confederation of states.[13] The mail also functioned as an infrastructure for the movement of monetary value. Before the twentieth century, checking accounts were common only among the wealthy, so when most people wished to send a payment long distance, they "put their money into an envelope, sewed the envelope shut, . . . sealed it with wax," and then mailed it.[14] Like state currency, the US mail service was a "daily affirmation of the nation state."[15] Postmasters were the most widespread representatives of the federal government.

Some of the largest payment companies—notably American Express and Wells Fargo—began not in the financial services industry but in the communication industry. They competed with the US Postal Service to transport "gold dust, bullion, specie, packages, parcels, and freight of all kinds" from coast to coast via stagecoach, courier, ferry, and engine.[16] These origins can be glimpsed in the vestigial stagecoach that gallops across the Wells Fargo logo.

A Well Fargo Express Company horse-drawn wagon carrying bullion and mail, Deadwood, South Dakota, 1890.

The competition between the private shipping industry and the federal post office demonstrates an important tension in the management of communication infrastructure: between *universal service*, the expectation of basic capacities to all, and *common carriage*, the expectation of fair, nondiscriminatory service. The US post office lacked the resources, and the infrastructure, to provide universal service to the entire nation. In general, the federal system prioritized slowly developing reliable infrastructure over speedy delivery.[17] The private shipping company, in contrast, "went everywhere, did almost anything for anybody, and was the nearest thing to a universal service company ever invented"; indeed, private express shipping was often "the first thing established in every new camp or diggin's," especially in the Gold Rush West, where there was lucrative work to be found in transporting bullion.[18] But these benefits came at a price. The private expresses were cartels that avoided competition, engaged in price fixing and freight discrimination, and were in general hard to hold accountable.[19]

By the turn of the century, the US Postal Service had developed a sophisticated network that met the needs of more Americans. In 1898, it instituted universal Rural Free Delivery; in 1913, it began to offer improved parcel post services.[20] In 1917, as part of the war effort, the United States nationalized its railroad and private express mail services. This effectively ended that era of competition between the public and private posts to move not just mail but money.

In the history of communication technology, the telegraph is often described as "informationalizing" communication, as separating the movement of mass from the movement of information. It wasn't until after the advent of the telegraph that the term "communication" came to primarily signify the transmission of information rather than the conveyance of matter.[21] Like the mail before it, the telegraph was expected to transform geography through communication and thereby "make one neighborhood of the whole country," as its inventor, Samuel Morse, hoped.[22]

Today, Western Union, once the great American telegraph monopoly, brands itself as "the fastest way to send money" and has taken pains to present itself as a pioneer in payments, but the telegraph was not used as a payment system on any large scale until the twentieth century.[23] Indeed, until the 1980s restructuring, money transfer services never accounted for more than a small share of the company's revenues.[24] The movement of value became "telegraphic"—that is, communicative over long distances, through information, and divorced from its direct physical movement—not through the telegraph but through analog networks of paper engineering: documents that directed exchange like money orders, traveler's checks, and bank checks and the networks of settlement and clearance necessary to fulfill them.

These networks built on the existing infrastructure of the post, public and private. The US postal system, following the British system, had long experimented in postal money orders but began issuing them regularly during the Civil War to allow money to be sent between Union soldiers and their families without the increased risks of sending currency through the post during wartime.

By 1893, one observer wrote that "cases have been known, and, it is believed, are not rare, in which persons permanently abiding in locations where there are no reliable banks, have, for security, invested their savings in money orders issued upon application made by themselves in their own favor."[25] In the era before national currency was fully developed, postal money orders functioned as a form of state-issued paper money for some Americans.

By the time the post was nationalized at the start of World War I, private shipping companies had already moved on to new ways of making money by moving money without having to ship anything, in the form of first money orders and then traveler's checks. Indeed, by this point, a large swath of the private expresses had consolidated under the brand of the largest company: American Express, which was already leaving behind the postal industry and was well on its way to becoming a modern financial services firm.

American Express began issuing money orders in 1882. Unlike postal money orders, American Express's system did not require filling out extensive forms, so users did not have to be literate in English or any other language. American Express money orders were used to send value within the United States as well as for immigrants to send value abroad. Its immigrant user base grew along with the immigrant population in the United States. Unfortunately for early users, these money orders could not always be cashed abroad because American Express had not yet developed a robust network of international correspondent institutions willing to honor them. Eventually, because of the large number of immigrants to the United States from Ireland and Italy, American Express developed an especially large network of correspondent banks in those countries. By the late 1880s, American Express was transacting millions of dollars in foreign money orders per month to both countries.[26] Dollars mapped the territory of the United States, but American Express money orders mapped a transnational territory of kinship and community.

American Express soon offered a payment technology marketed to the elite: the traveler's check. According to company lore, the idea for traveler's checks emerged when American Express president J. C. Fargo made the grand tour of Europe. At the time, international travelers carried letters of credit from banks in their home country. Letters of credit had existed more or less unchanged since the Renaissance: they vouched deposits that the bearer could draw on at corresponding banks abroad. When Fargo returned from his trip, he complained that his letters of credit had been a huge inconvenience. They had to be verified at each bank in a cumbersome process, and once he was outside major cities, they were of "no more use . . . than so much wet wrapping paper."[27]

The new American Express traveler's checks were low-denomination coupons that travelers could give to merchants, who would in turn cash them at any of the many correspondent banks that American Express had cultivated through its trade in foreign remittances made by immigrants. American Express traveler's checks were widely referred to as "blue paper money."[28] As opposed to national currency, the private paper monies issued by American Express were classed and differentiated.

Although American Express charged fees for both its payment products, these fees were not its primary source of revenue. Soon after beginning to offer money orders, in part because of the large number purchased by immigrants that went uncashed in the early years, American Express executives began to notice that the company always had a large surplus of cash on hand waiting to be redeemed. As long as that surplus (or "float," as it would come to be called) could be tracked and predicted, American Express could use it to fund investments. This combination of fees and float remains fundamental to the business models of payment companies today.

As useful as the postal and private money orders and traveler's check systems were for transporting value across distance without actually having to ship money through the mail, they were far from a mass-scale infrastructure for settlement and clearance. The Federal Reserve, established in 1913, and its network of check clearinghouses, was an important communication infrastructure for the "telegraphic" movement of informational money across the United States.

Bank checks were not uncommon, particularly among the upper classes, in the nineteenth century, but cashing checks between banks was often a complicated process. A check that was issued by one bank and cashed at another often had to travel through a byzantine system of correspondence banks and physical clearinghouses before being returned to the bank that issued it. The early twentieth-century banker James Graham Cannon tells the story of a representative but particularly well-traveled check that was drawn on the Peconic Bank of Sag Harbor, Long Island, deposited in a bank in Hoboken, New Jersey, then traveled from the Hoboken bank to a New York City bank and then to banks in Boston, Tonawanda, Albany, Port Jefferson, Far Rockaway, New York City (again, but a different bank), Riverhead, and Brooklyn, before finally arriving at its final destination, the Sag Harbor bank, where it was cleared.[29]

Because it was costly to physically transport checks, for example, zigzagging all over the eastern seaboard through correspondent banks, many banks didn't cash checks for their full amount.[30] Some banks were well connected with many correspondent banks and offered par clearance. In some states, nonpar banking was prohibited. But rural people often had to settle for discounted checks, sometimes paying quite a bit for their checks to be cleared. As with money order and traveler's checks, this system was socially stratified, in this case, geographically.

In 1915, the Federal Reserve established a national check-clearing network with a centrally managed, hub-and-spoke-style clearinghouse system.[31] Instead of being shipped along a circuitous path through banking relationships, checks would be settled and cleared all within the Federal Reserve network, of which all banks were members. The justification for nonpar banking—the costs of authorization and clearance, of communicating checks and currency throughout the country—was eliminated. Under the Federal Reserve system, money was already becoming less tied to physical mass and more instantiated as socially guaranteed numerical value. Conceptually, check clearance happened instantly across space and was, in this sense, "telegraphic."

Crucially, without the Federal Reserve system, it would have been difficult to move currency itself, to provide clearance, in the

far-flung reaches of the country. Whereas American Express offered a private system to perform this service, the Federal Reserve
offered a public one. The development of the Federal Reserve
check-clearing system was part of a larger long-term effort to
create a public utility for the movement of money nationwide.
The federal clearinghouse system would become the basis for the
twentieth-century electronic Automated Clearinghouse, which
still provides the basis for most check, debit, and direct-deposit
money transfer today.

In 1963, Matty Simmons, executive vice president of Diners Club,
the first charge card company, wrote a newspaper editorial that
he described as an "obituary" for cash. In it, he declaimed that
cash would soon be dead "everywhere" because it "simply hadn't
become modern." For Simmons, cash's fatal flaw was that it was
not able to "keep up with the fast-moving world."[32] Diners Club,
Simmons implied, would be cash's heir because it was designed
to interoperate with the networks of rapid and physical and informational mobility that were, at midcentury, beginning to be
assembled. Interstate highways, personal automobile financing,
rental cars, motels, democratized jet travel, teletype reservation
systems, corporate business trips: these were all mid-twentieth-
century inventions.

For the first time on a mass scale, people moved much faster
and farther than their money could. The US banking industry was
comparatively fragmented, and banks were mostly small and local
entities.[33] The speed of mobility had outpaced the federal clearinghouse system: out-of-town checks took days to clear, so many
merchants refused to accept them; and it was difficult for a traveler to withdraw cash away from home.[34] As a contemporary writer
put it, "the traveler—the man who needed it the most—was cred-
itless," because "unless he went around with pockets full of money,
he was unlikely to find a friendly face in a strange town."[35]

Diners Club was not a credit card but a charge card. A cardholder would present the card to merchants, who would send a
bill to Diners Club, which would in turn send an itemized bill of
all transactions to the cardholder. Diners Club sought out these

The comedian Marty Allen shows off his collection of credit cards, 1960.

corporate accounts in large part because they represented sig-
nificantly less default liability than individuals, and the cards were
attractive to businesses because they helped manage travel expenses.[36] The cashless society, along with the perfectly bureaucra-
tized luxury it offered, had become as much a part of an idealized
modern near future as the jet pack. It was a novelty: there are
reports of crowds gathering just to watch someone pay with a
card.[37] A book of traveler's checks had come to seem like just
another old-fashioned wad of paper.

American Express and banks attempted to compete with Diners Club throughout the 1960s, but neither brought card products permanently to market until the end of the decade, when Diners Club quickly lost its market dominance. American Express took over the high end of the market, using its nearly century-old reputation as a trusted purveyor of traveler's checks and other nonbank financial services to offer universal charge cards to the elite. Banks offered something for everyone else: lines of rotating credit. Consumer financing had been available through banks and merchants like department stores for a long time, but BankAmericard, offered by Bank of America, then a regional bank in San Francisco, was the first product to connect it to a universal payment card.[38]

By the 1970s, banks nationwide became interested in offering their own credit card products. In order for the system to work across the country, there needed to be a large and geographically dispersed network of both cardholders and merchants. Because of federal restrictions that were not repealed until the 1990s, banks could not expand across state lines, so banks needed a way to enable these cardholders and merchants to transact with those who held accounts from other banks. Although Bank of America could not issue cards to consumers outside California, it could license its BankAmericard program nationally. This system, which later became the independent bank membership organization Visa, was a computer network that standardized messages to create "open loop" payments without the need for a centralized clearinghouse. Economists cite Visa as a founding example of "coopetition," an unusual market arrangement in which firms create a shared, cooperative infrastructure on which to compete.[39]

To Dee Hock, the company's lead inventor and chief executive, Visa was primarily a novel networked information system: it was not in the business of consumer debt but in the business of "electronic value exchange": sending standardized messages that moved the information known as money.[40] By understanding money as information, we can, as Hock did, understand payment as transmission: the movement of that information from one place, person, or account to another. In Hock's view, transactions were transmissions, acts of communication. Perhaps for this reason, Visa, headquartered in San Francisco, developed stronger collaborations within the technology and data-processing industry than it did within banking. It was developed in collaboration first with DEC, a leading hardware and software producer, and then with IBM.[41]

Hock believed that anything that could be transmitted through a system like Visa could serve as money and that banks and governments would soon lose their monopolies on the transfer and even issue of currency.[42] Of course, Visa would not turn out to be quite as revolutionary as Hock thought that it might be. But it did create a reliable, international, open-loop system of seamless communication, which has had more impact than many other so-called technological revolutions.

With the growth of the internet came a new spatialized market imaginary: not only global but translocal, peer-to-peer. Many early internet users saw themselves as building, as Howard Rheingold put it, a "virtual community" where people could "homestead on the electronic frontier."[43] But if Wells Fargo had been a fixture at any new settlement on the frontier of the American West one hundred years before, no such simple system of electronic value transfer was yet available in its "electronic" counterpart. It was difficult for small businesses to accept card payments long distance and was nearly impossible for individuals. Payment cards—unlike money orders and checks—were only designed to pay merchants, not other people. In order to conduct commerce online, individuals and small businesses had to ask buyers to write checks, send them in the mail, and then wait several days for them to clear before the seller could send merchandise. Peer-to-peer money did not move at the pace of peer-to-peer communication.

Through the 1990s, there were various attempts to enable person-to-person digital payments. In the late 1990s, a cluster of different start-ups merged to become PayPal. PayPal emerged in the context of the Silicon Valley tech industry and its "Californian ideology," which links values of anticorporatism, social autonomy, and cultural bohemianism with the seemingly paradoxical value of marketism.[44] Many tech entrepreneurs imagined networked computers as vectors of personal liberation, as well as virtual and alternative forms of community and social life.[45] The PayPal political project was not just about the free flow of information but about unfettered access to global currency markets. PayPal's originary vision was not just one of a global community connected by peer-to-peer commerce but of a global market untethered from nation-states.[46]

Ironically, PayPal's business model was only possible because of its use of the automated clearinghouse, or ACH, established in the 1970s and partially operated by the Federal Reserve. Descending from the Federal Reserve clearinghouses, the ACH was developed as a utility to ensure par clearance of checks for banking customers. It charges no fees, keeps no float, and therefore has no direct revenue. In order to circumvent the card networks, and the costly fees associated with them, PayPal asked its customers to link directly to their checking account and then used the ACH transaction code to draw money from the customer account. PayPal effectively created a private on-ramp to an existing semipublic infrastructure. Nevertheless, it enabled people to access that infrastructure as both senders and receivers of money, to engage in commerce at the scale of their communication. Although the new

An M-PESA mobile money agent, Nairobi, Kenya, 2016.

payment systems offer different value propositions, arguably more do not deviate substantially on the back end from PayPal.

The years 2007 and 2008 marked the beginning of a historical moment ripe for rethinking money technologies and the transactional communities they form.[47] Global financial crises undermined the legitimacy of governments and financial institutions. M-Pesa, the first successful large-scale mobile money system, was launched. With the release of the iPhone and then much-

A Bitcoin ATM, 2018.

less-expensive Android phones, much of the world's population was carrying networked computers in their pockets.

The years since have been marked by what my collaborators and I have called a "Cambrian explosion" in payments, conjuring a period approximately 541 million years ago when suddenly all sorts of complex creatures began to appear on Earth.[48] There's Bitcoin. There are a thousand things that claim to be "the next Bitcoin." There's the rise and fall of the "sharing economy" and its more honest rebrand: the "gig economy."[49] China is said to be building a "Social Credit System" that will compel all citizens to surveil their neighbors and report on their trustworthiness.[50] In 2018, Crypto-kitties, a blockchain-based game that involves arbitrage on virtual pet cats, raised $15 million from several top venture-capital firms.[51] Money has always been strange, and when we take a moment to collectively look at it, it gets strange again.

But few of these new money forms have penetrated daily life, and cash and credit cards have yet to be displaced. The "cashless society" is always around the corner.[52] The chaos and uncertainty of the Cambrian explosion has more to do with a sense that we are living in a world in which chaos and uncertainty are warranted than it does with actual changes to our monetary repertoires. How might this chaos echo the chaos of currency in the antebellum American metropolis? How might it be even more chaotic?

Nevertheless, the forms and functions of everyday money are changing, but in ways that are more mundane than flashy in their disruption and yet harder to see. These changes are familiar in the history of payment and other infrastructures: infrastructures accumulate and ossify, they mediate circulations in ways that distribute harm unevenly, and they serve the public good but are always caught up in these struggles for control and enclosure.

3 TRANSACTIONAL IDENTITIES

Paying with New Money

O N August 23, 2016, JPMorgan Chase announced the launch of the Chase Sapphire Reserve credit card. The new card promised to "reinvent the luxury card category."[1] This was not your typical credit card launch. The online buzz, particularly on travel blogs, was intense. When a link to the application went live a week ahead of schedule, thousands of people applied for the card before it was even officially announced.

Weeks later, early adopters were proud to show off their cardholder status. In a genre of YouTube videos usually reserved for high-tech gadgets, cardholders uploaded "unboxing" videos, removing the Chase cards from elegant blue packaging—no skinny, unmarked envelope or chintzy activation sticker in sight—and wishing others good luck with their own applications.[2]

In fact, application volume reportedly so exceeded Chase's expectations that the company ran out of the materials to make the physical cards. A shortage of titanium alloy—the deep azure of Princess Diana's (now Kate Middleton's) engagement ring—forced Chase to issue temporary plastic cards.[3] As the *New York Times* observed, "It's not often that a card goes viral."[4] So what was so special about this particular credit card?

The Chase Sapphire Reserve's $450-a-year member fee shocked many casual observers, but those accustomed to "the luxury card category" argued that the card more than paid for itself with its lavish schedule of benefits. First, there were the rewards. In addition to points on all purchases, it offered triple points on travel, dining, and "sharing economy" (such as Airbnb and Uber) purchases and an unprecedented signing bonus of one hundred thousand points. These points could be redeemed for 50 percent more on travel purchases through Chase's booking portal and could be transferred to most other airline and hotel loyalty programs. The dollars-to-points exchange rate wasn't fixed, but savvy users could usually get 1.5 to 2.1 cents per point. There were the cash reimbursements: cardholders could be reimbursed $300 a year for travel purchases and $90 a year for application fees to Global Entry or TSA Pre-Check. The card also offered other ways to skip lines and gain access to hidden realms: airport lounges, special hotel and rental-car privileges, opportunities to buy tickets to the hit Broadway sensation musical *Hamilton* at face value and backstage passes to music festivals, and of course a 24/7 concierge phone number. And once cardholders were in those realms, their card promised other perks, like no foreign exchange fees.

Leaders at American Express, pioneer of ultrapremium cards, were reportedly unsettled by the success of the Chase Sapphire Reserve. One American Express executive, according to intercompany lore, admitted that even he was tempted by Chase Sapphire Reserve: "An Amex says you're rich, but this says you're interesting."[5] (In a bid to perhaps court more "interesting" cardholders, American Express soon began offering perks like "NBA Jersey Assurance," which replaced any jersey purchased should an NBA player switch teams.)[6] What does it even mean for a credit card to "say you're interesting"? What *does* a Chase Sapphire Reserve say about you, and why were so many people eager for this payment-conferred identity?

Financial institutions have always been concerned with the identities of their customers. The media studies scholar Josh Lauer has shown that the concept of "financial identity" emerged centuries before any YouTube unboxing videos.[7] Alongside state-issued records of identity, such as the passport and birth certificate, credit bureau reports made modern people into "legible economic actors."[8] Long before social media, credit bureaus of the nineteenth and early twentieth centuries formed sophisticated surveillance networks, gathering all sorts of stories and information about people that extended well beyond their debts and payment history, including any detail that could paint a picture of a potential borrower's moral character. These records disciplined people, in the Foucauldian sense, to be "good" consumers of debt. Today, three major credit-reporting agencies track your lending accounts, producing an aggregate record of financial identity: the credit report.

Over time, as Lauer documents, credit bureaus began to be more quantitative and aspired to be more "objective." Today, credit reports track your lending accounts, such as credit cards, auto loans, and mortgages; the date you opened the account; your credit limit or loan amount; the account balance; and your payment history.[9] They track every time you or someone else inquires about your credit, for example, to apply for new accounts. Credit reports also include delinquencies, collections, and bankruptcies. It's worth noting what doesn't go into your credit report: regular rent payments, regular bill payments, steady employment, savings, and many other things that might also be predictive of financial responsibility but do not require entering into indebtedness. A collections notice can appear as a demerit on your credit report, but decades of on-time payments of utility and phone bills will not.

Using the information compiled in these reports, each of the three major credit-reporting agencies uses its own system to assign a credit score. In spite of the industry's pursuit of "objectivity," however, the financial identity produced by a credit report is a distorted reflection of who you are. This disembodied second self is a version of what the legal scholar Joshua Nichols calls a "data double."[10] And the "reputation" of that double is codified by your credit score.

But the "interesting" identity conferred by Chase Sapphire Reserve is only partially dependent on the financial identity produced through credit reporting. In short, flashing a Chase Sapphire Reserve card says that you have good credit. Perhaps surprisingly, though, it does not say that you have *exceptionally* good credit. Chase doesn't publish information about who gets approved for the Chase Sapphire Reserve, but according to most reports, would-be cardholders need a FICO score—which ranges from 300 to 850—of at least 700, which was the average credit score in the United States in 2018.[11] They need to self-report a yearly income of at least $50,000, about $5,000 higher than the US median income.[12] There are other factors that might cause an application to be denied, such as having too many credit cards, recently applying for too many credit cards, or having a short history with credit cards. For those who do get rejected, there is a phone number to call to be reconsidered.

Indeed, the Chase Sapphire Reserve card is more accessible than its "ultrapremium" branding would suggest. This financial identity isn't elite because it represents fabulous wealth. Rather, Chase Sapphire Reserve credit card holders are a privileged class not necessarily because they have better credit but because they are particularly well disciplined by credit scoring; they are, as the sociologists Wendy Espeland and Michael Sauder put it, eager to "react" to these systems; and they have enough wealth and time to participate in them.[13]

There has been some backlash to the democratization of luxury that Chase Sapphire Reserve hath wrought: in 2018, the *Wall Street Journal* reported that airport lounges were overrun by cardholders and were now, according to longtime first-class travelers, "a total zoo."[14] Were those who were allowed entrance to lounges because of their credit card "too interesting" for such genteel spaces?

If not for sheer wealth and spending power, then how, as one of many ultrapremium credit card products, does a Chase Sapphire Reserve say that you're *interesting*? On the one hand, it symbolizes a particular lifestyle. It says that you eat out, take Uber rides, and book flights often enough to benefit from earning extra points on these *interesting* categories. It says that your life is flexible enough to make use of travel-related benefits, that you'll actually use these points instead of letting them lie fallow. *It's so easy to make back that $450 fee*, Chase Sapphire Reserve fans insisted, *that you almost get there with just the $300 travel reimbursement and $90 TSA Global Entry or Pre-Check reimbursement!*[15] As if everyone has a lifestyle that affords yearly travel and demands expedited screenings, as if everyone were annoyed by things like the high cost of foreign exchange fees.

Beyond lifestyle and taste preferences, Chase Sapphire Reserve also suggests that you—the *you* who is perceived as *interesting* by an American Express executive—partake of a particular definition of what it means to be a financially literate person today. For the most part, rewards credit cards lose their value if you carry a balance, so they aren't intended to be used for rotating short-term loans—for necessary expenses or living above your means—but as a tool for attaining rewards and other benefits. As dozens of think pieces have suggested, Chase Sapphire Reserve also says that you have a relaxed, modern, distinctly "millennial" attitude toward credit cards. Unlike previous generations of careful consumers, you know not just to compare interest rates on savings accounts and dutifully store money away but how to, as a *New York Times* article put it, "turn your renovation into a vacation" by putting such big expenses on credit cards that offer travel rewards.[16] Unlike the previous generation of anticonsumerist tastemakers, who were, at least in the popular imagination, wary of big corporations and credit card debt, you see credit cards not as a symbol of debt bondage but as a vehicle of access and privilege.

Or, at least, that's what it tries to say. What cards "say" can usually only be heard by those who exist in proximate economic subject positions: the audience for the Chase Sapphire Reserve is the same as for the think pieces about the Chase Sapphire Reserve. To everyone else, it may be notable for its heft and deep-blue color—dark and hefty enough to, in the right lighting, be mistaken for an American Express "Black Card"—but the details of its reward program and membership structure are invisible. Outside of its milieu, Chase Sapphire Reserve is just another swipe, albeit one that ramifies difference, even if imperceptibly.

But Chase Sapphire Reserve is not just a credit card; it's a whole lifestyle. Or more precisely, it's a branded product specially designed to both produce and convey a whole lifestyle. A relatively elite financial identity—defined, as Lauer does, in terms of credit score—is of course necessary for being approved for a Chase Sapphire Reserve, but the card performs a *transactional identity* that says that those who use it are "interesting" beyond their credit score: to the card issuer, Chase, which wants their payment business; to merchants who seek their swipes; to businesses that partner with Chase to make their lucrative offers; to other people who know what a Chase Sapphire Reserve is. This transactional identity persists beyond the creditworthy approval process. It exists at the moment of payment and continues through the vacation "earned" through that aggregation of payments.

Every payment produces and performs a transactional identity. While Chase Sapphire Rewards gives triple points for eating out, most EBT (electronic benefit transfer) cards used by welfare recipients can't be used to buy warm rotisserie chicken. Hot chicken is usually a loss leader for grocery stores, meant to attract customers and priced lower than raw chicken. But EBT cards can be used to buy *cold* rotisserie chicken that has been placed in a store refrigerator. Every card is a lifestyle. Every card says something about you.

While Chase Sapphire Reserve offers extra points for eating out, EBT cards used by welfare recipients disallow certain categories of purchases, such as warm food. Indeed, every card is a lifestyle. Every card conveys and performs a transactional identity.

The transactional identities performed by payment shape how other people see us. According to the personal finance blog *Budgets Are Sexy,* how your dinner date picks up the tab is an important source of information in any modern romance.[17] In a world where credit card programs compete for the best consumers by offering rewards, both those who don't qualify for these rewards and those who can't be bothered to take advantage of them are undesirable partners. Be suspicious of cash, the blog post warns. The only reasons to use it are "recently filing for bankruptcy" or "trying to get rid of piles of illegally obtained cash." A debit card indicates someone who is a "former debt-a-holic or just lazy." On the other hand, beware those who flash the American Express "Black Card," which, according to the post, comes with exorbitant fees but impractical benefits. The only reason to carry it is to demonstrate that you qualify for a card made of metal, not plastic, a "titanium rectangle of elite douchebaggery." The Chase Sapphire Reserve had not yet been introduced at the time of this blog post, so it's hard to know if "interesting" titanium cardholders are as objectionable as those who are just "rich."

What's a desirable card for a suitor to carry? The post suggests perhaps "amazing rewards cards" from "unsexy brands" like Discover Escape or Costco. These show that "this guy is more concerned about saving money than his image." The post suggests, "There's a good chance he's looking forward to fatherhood . . . if that's your thing." Lothario or family man, criminal or loafer, debtor or "douchebag": the method of payment is, we're told, a valuable clue about someone's true identity. These variations are an index of modern masculinity, a range of possible transactional identities.

Our payment cards open access to the money—actual or potential, checking account or line of credit—that we're allowed to access. They live in our wallets, alongside the documents that explain who we are, and open up access to the places we are entitled to go. There is a reason why payment-card fraud is commonly called "identity theft."

Cash—in the form of state-issued currency—is aligned with the economic territory of the state that issues it. But cash can be used to perform a variety of identities. A 2012 post on the blog *The Hairpin* suggests the following indicators: "Handing crumpled bills from your pocket: You microwave eggs"; "Using a $100 bill: You have a weirdly sparse condo. A lot of beige in there."[18] As the anthropologist Clifford Geertz points out, "the difference, however unphotographable, between a twitch and a wink is vast."[19] So is the difference between "'Getting rid of some ones': You have a Roth IRA" and "'Sorry about the ones': You constantly struggle with the decision to buy skinny jeans. You wonder if this is forever."[20] Being part of a transactional community means knowing the difference but not necessarily noticing that you know the difference.

The transactional identities expressed by payment are, crucially, not individual but relational. How we pay tethers us to institutions that authorize our economic life. It is an indicator that provides insight into our traditional financial identities. "I'm too anxious to watch my credit card score very closely, but I try to pay attention to credit card junk mail I get every week," one thirty-something American woman told me. "If suddenly I'm getting these 'fix your credit' type of cards, I'll try to check. If I keep seeing preapprovals for decent-looking cards, I know I'm probably in okay shape." Payment cards are an interface between institutional and lived selves. Payment cards are the visible, physical markers of the otherwise deeply private and taboo institutional realms.

Like any other money technology, cards produce transactional communities, networks of relations united by a common payment method, and therefore common sense of identity, geography, and value. Transactional technologies knit people together into a shared economic world and also enforce the boundaries of membership in that world. State currencies mark their users as members of the transactional community of the nation-state, if not citizens. This is no less true for Chase Sapphire Reserve cardholders than it was for the Indo-Greeks, described briefly in chapter 1 of this book, who left no trace of their civilization behind other than the coins they used.[21] When payment forms—such as cards—disintermediate state currencies, a range of new transactional identities are produced.

But what makes a Chase Sapphire Reserve different from the coins used by the Indo-Greeks or that crisp or crumpled cash is the industrial ecosystem that sustains it as a transactional community.[22] How we pay is also an industry. In the payments business, the banks that provide and manage cards are called *issuers*. So, if you are fortunate enough to have a Chase Sapphire Reserve, JP Morgan Chase is your issuer. All issuers do basically the same thing: issue cards, extend credit, and facilitate payment. But in recent decades, the issuing business has become increasingly competitive. Issuers are now designing card products to attract niche consumers, which, in turn, creates new, niche transactional identities that make up a transactional community characterized by niches.

Today, in the United States at least, most people pay at least some of the time with some kind of card product. Cards are branded and designed to give some indication of their prestige, but for the most part, they all basically look the same. They all have to use the same infrastructure, be slotted into or swiped by similar machines. They are, indeed, mandated to more or less look alike by the International Organization for Standardization and International Electrotechnical Commission.

But under the surface, different cards are imbricated in different infrastructural, economic, and discursive assemblages.[23] They are part of different industrial histories and future trajectories. Some cards pay people back for using them; some cards charge people usage fees. Some cards are expensive for merchants to accept, and some have low, regulated fees. Our economic agency is determined not just by how much money we have but by the form that money takes—and the business model underlying that infrastructure. Relations enacted by transactional identities are not just between you and your money or you and a payment infrastructure but between you and other payers, whose inequality is created, sustained, and invigorated by payment itself. Hierarchy, difference, and communication are fundamental to the architecture of the modern card network.

The potential of a single mechanism—the swipe (or tap or insert)—to enact different transactional identities is a by-product

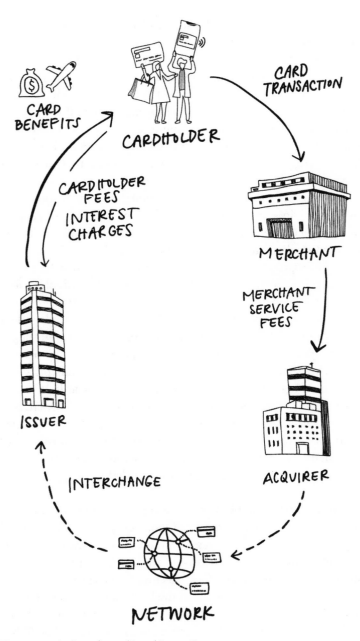

CARD BENEFITS

CARDHOLDER

CARD TRANSACTION

CARDHOLDER FEES INTEREST CHARGES

MERCHANT

MERCHANT SERVICE FEES

ISSUER

ACQUIRER

INTERCHANGE

NETWORK

The communication of a credit card transaction.

of the "open loop" networks such as Visa and Mastercard that connect merchants and banks. With their logos on both consumer cards and merchant cash registers, open-loop networks do not represent particular banks but rather networks of cooperating banks. Unlike "closed loop" systems that only work with one bank or merchant, an open-loop network ensures compatibility among many participating banks, merchants, and cardholders. All merchants who are part of the Visa/Mastercard network are compelled by network rules to "honor all cards," meaning that they must accept all credit, debit, and prepaid cards as long as they bear the Visa or Mastercard logo.[24] The transactional community produced by the open-loop card networks is defined by its capacity to enable distinction between transactional identities while still facilitating transactional communication across that difference.

At every moment of payment, the Visa/Mastercard network responds to the transactional identity of each cardholder and configures itself accordingly. Indeed, from one customer card to the next, a single point-of-sale terminal may call forth countless configurations. Different pathways are opened and closed throughout the global financial infrastructure, and different algorithmic agents are set to work rectifying account balances, tallying interest, generating fees, and—for some—producing rewards. Whereas cash treats all payers as equals, the open-loop network enables endless variation and differentiation in the transactional identities of its users. All of this difference is submerged: all cards are accepted, no distinctions—other than those intentionally conveyed by the market of the card itself—are revealed.

When the Chase Sapphire Reserve card was announced, many people were shocked by its $450 annual fee. One *New York Times* story from the press blitz read, "Value-Seekers Warm to a $450 Annual Credit Card Fee."[25] Most of the online comments on the story debated the "value" of such a card. Some called it a "scam" or reminded fellow readers that "the house always wins." Others defended the fee and attempted to explain how it was indeed possible to beat the system. Most commenters seemed to know that card issuers make money by charging interest on the lines of credit they extend, as well as other fees for late payments, cash advance, and so on, but they did not have the full picture of the business of paying. What is the underlying business model of rewards cards? How are they able to profit from offering these services? To understand how open-loop networks came to dominate everyday payments in the United States, it is necessary to examine how money is made within the payments industry.

In general, merchants pay to be paid. Card networks like Visa serve as a platform for connecting two sides—the merchant side and the cardholder side. In most such "two-sided markets," one side is willing to pay a premium to access the other side. In payment, the merchant side has been willing to pay to access the cardholder side. Card issuers charge a fee to merchants' banks, called "acquirers," for "supplying" their merchants with customers. This fee is called *interchange*. Technically, merchants do not pay interchange directly. Rather, they negotiate and pay a "merchant discount" to their merchant services acquirer that is typically calculated as a percentage per transaction and includes interchange. The acquirer pays the card network, and then the card network pays interchange to the issuer.

In the card-issuing industry, cardholders are described as "revolvers" or "transactors."[26] Revolvers use their cards primarily as a line of rotating credit and pay off their balance as they are able. Issuers make money off revolvers through interest on these loans. Transactors use their cards primarily as a mode of payment—to transact—and pay their balance in full every month. Issuers attract transactors using member benefits, and they make money off their business by charging merchants higher interchange, some of which is used to fund the member benefits. Both groups are valuable to issuers; but some issuers specialize in one or the other, and all issuers segment and create differentiated products to attract each group.

So, if I swipe my Chase Sapphire Reserve at Target, Target pays a merchant discount fee to its acquirer, Bank of America Merchant Services, which in turn pays an interchange fee to Chase.[27] There are many costs that go into supplying me to Target. Setting aside reward points and portals for *Hamilton* tickets, Chase provides me with a line of credit, a physical card, customer service, billing, fraud prevention, and so on. Chase recoups the cost of all of this by charging the interchange fee to Bank of America Merchant Service, and Bank of America Merchant Services recoups the interchange fee by charging the transaction fee to Target. Target recoups the transaction fee by charging me a bit more for my box of Wheat Thins.

Indeed, merchants not only pay to be paid but pay *more* to be paid by the "best" customers. When a merchant swipes a Chase Sapphire Reserve or other premium card, it pays a little bit more to receive the payment than it does for a standard credit card. Interchange pricing is set by the card networks and determined according to a complicated set of rules, but the standard fee for a regular credit card is about 1.51–1.80 percent, for a traditional rewards card about 1.65–1.95 percent, and for the highest-end rewards card about 2.10–2.40 percent.

If I go shopping with a friend, and we both buy $100 worth of makeup and school supplies and toilet paper at Target, and I use my Chase Sapphire Reserve and my friend uses her regular nonrewards University of Virginia Credit Union card, Target makes as little as $97.60 from my sale and as much as $98.49 from hers.[28] These sound like fairly small differences, but to issuers like Chase that make money off interchange—and the merchants like Target that pay it—it adds up fast. The interchange on a debit card is regulated and is lower.

Interchange fees have been controversial in the payments industry. Merchants argue that interchange fees represent price fixing by card-network cartels. In order to accept any card that runs on the cooperative Visa/Mastercard network, merchants agree to accept *all* cards that do—prepaid, debit, and rewards. A merchant cannot selectively turn down Chase Sapphire Reserve and accept the UVA Credit Union card. Open-loop card networks and issuing banks see these fee schedules not as collusion but as an efficient means of "coopetition," of organizing an infrastructure shared by many different competing parties. American Express is a closed-loop system without discrete issuers and acquirers, runs its own network, and continues to demand high fees from merchants. Merchants may choose not to accept American Express, but it's not possible for them to avoid other high-interchange luxury cards that run on the Visa and Mastercard networks. (Merchants that do accept American Express do so for the same reason they initially accepted any card: because those who pay with it tend to spend more money.)

Because merchants' costs increase to account for interchange, some merchants and customers argue that, ultimately, rewards cards lead to higher prices, so customers wind up paying for their own rewards—or for others' rewards. Some consumer advocates argue that customers who don't use rewards cards wind up subsidizing the cost of those who do. So my friend who swiped her UVA Credit Union card is helping to pay for my vacation with that extra eighty-nine cents that Target made off her, and customers who use cash wind up subsidizing both of us. A 2010 study by researchers at the Federal Reserve argued that on average, each cash-using household winds up "paying" $149 to card-using households, and each card-using household winds up indirectly receiving $1,133 from cash users every year.[29] The study has been critiqued, but most researchers agree that while it's hard to measure the big-picture effects of interchange, the current fee structure is most likely inefficient and may not positively impact all consumers and merchants.[30] How we pay—the way it marks us, who pays or gets paid for it—is relational and unequal.

As the anthropologist Bill Maurer has pointed out, this system doesn't exactly fit the picture of the capitalist economy or always operate according to its principles. For one thing, the economics of interchange make little sense according to traditional market logics because it's one of the rare situations in which competition, on the part of issuers competing for the "best customers," drives prices up—for merchants, acquirers, and potentially consumers.[31]

Payment cards, the interchange they produce, and the rewards that interchange funds quantify the hierarchical relationship between various transactional identities. Interchange creates a market in which some people's business costs more to accept than others'. Maurer notes that interchange looks and feels more like a tribute—a fealty acknowledging rank, gratitude, and protection—than like a price set by the logics of supply and demand in a capitalist system. From this perspective, everyday transactions are made strange: merchants pay more for the privilege of receiving the business of certain people, and then those people are paid in the form of rewards.

Payment cards that can be used at all merchants, not just the one that issued it, and that are managed by a third-party company are relatively new, a late twentieth-century innovation, as are the differentiated transactional community they produce.[32] Chase Sapphire Reserve is the latest sensation in a long line of payment products that produce transactional communities. First, charge cards like Diners Club and American Express brought paying through a card offered by a third party to the American elite. These early charge cards overtly functioned like membership organizations and offered a range of services along with payment to members. Then bank-issued credit cards made payment through a card common, but these cards mainly supplied a line of credit and did not include the range of services that charge cards did. Finally, competition in the issuing industry led to the development of a wide range of credit card products, some of which catered to the elite and provided benefits that rivaled charge cards, some of which targeted the middle class and poor.

Early progenitors of the payment card were Charga-Plates, first issued in the 1930s by department stores, gas station chains, and other large-scale merchants. These merchants had long extended credit to regular customers, and the Charga-Plates made it quicker and easier to access and bill accounts. Small metal rectangles, the Charga-Plates looked like military dog tags and were embossed with the account holder's name, address, and other relevant information. This embossed information could be quickly imprinted onto a paper "charge slip." This sped up transactions and reduced errors.

The Diners Club card, which emerged in the early 1950s, as described in chapter 2, was the first universal third-party payments card. Unlike Charga-Plates, it was not limited to one particular merchant and was a third-party company in the busi-

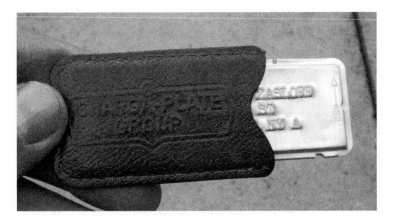

The Charga-Plate is the ancestor of the credit card.

ness of facilitating payment. Although the terms are sometimes used interchangeably, the Diners Club card was not a "credit card" but a "charge card." In fact, it preceded the credit card by at least fifteen years. Unlike credit cards, which came later, the Diners Club card was not tied to an account of revolving credit. It did not allow members to carry a balance. Its revenue came from its annual membership fee, transaction fees charged to the merchants, and advertising sold in the magazine it sent to its members.

Most Diners Club memberships were corporate accounts. This was beneficial for all parties: corporations were less likely to default than individuals, employers paid cardholder fees, the itemized billing effectively outsourced the accounting of travel expenses, and merchants could host pricey business dinners. Once members began to use the card for work, they often ordered additional accounts for personal use. In 1958, Diners Club started a "Women's Division" to cater to wives and the emergent class of professional women.[33] Although for most people, "putting it on the card" began as a business practice, it became a part of everyday life.

The Diners Club was, indeed, like a club. The elimination of "vulgar cash" added a "pleasant, club-like feeling that comes from walking into a beanery and paying with a card instead of cash."[34]

It marked its members as an elite group to whom "country-club-style billing" (as the practice of receiving a folio bill later was commonly called) was available at an expanding number of merchants. The feeling of being known and trusted was no longer limited to a particular shop or club in a particular city but spread out wherever the Diners Club was accepted. Its network of merchants grew to include most US cities, highway corridors, and international tourist locales.

The norm of merchants paying to be paid was set early with Diners Club. Diners Club was a closed-loop system: it could only be used at merchants who signed up to participate in the system, and its infrastructure constituted a closed loop between the merchant, the payment provider, and the customer. There were no card issuers or merchant acquirers, just Diners Club in the middle, facilitating payment. Merchants paid a fee directly to Diners Club in order to access its members. In order to convince merchants to be part of the network, Diners Club advertised a (probably pseudoscientific or wholly fictional) psychological study that showed that payment cards give customers "a feeling of inexhaustible potency" that makes them more willing to part with their hard-earned money.[35] It was certainly true, of course, that Diners Club members had more money to spend, whether their own or that of their employers. Either way, charge card companies were able to convince merchants that in order not to lose out on business dinners and elite leisure travel, they needed to be part of the invisible geography of the "club." Paying a little bit more per transactions to attract the "best" customers would, in the big picture, pay off.

By the end of the 1960s, American Express overtook Diners Club for these elite customers. In the early years, American Express cards were quite difficult to obtain, more so than today's "ultrapremium" rewards cards. Like Diners Club, American Express cards were closed-loop charge cards that did not extend a line of credit.[36]

As American Express continued to grow during the 1970s and 1980s, its marketing strategy remained largely unchanged. Carrying American Express was like belonging to an exclusive club. For example, in the 1970s, the company's "Do You Know

Me?" campaign featured famous, successful, but largely unrecognizable people whose American Express card granted them the recognition they deserved. For example, a 1971 television ad featured Mel Blanc, who asked, "Do you know me? Would you believe I am Bugs Bunny? I am also the voice of many other cartoon characters. But in here they don't care if I am Elmer Fudd. So I carry an American Express Card." A 1978 ad in the same campaign featured Francine Neff, the first woman US treasurer, serving from 1974 to 1977, who asked the same question, "Do you know me? I was treasurer of the United States, so many people know my name but not me. That's why I carry the American Express card. It's welcome all over, and that makes me welcome all over. Sure, it's super to have my signature on $60 billion, but for traveling and entertaining, it's a lot better to have my name right here."

In the 1980s, American Express followed up with the "Membership Has Its Privileges" campaign. One typical television ad explained, "One word distinguishes the American Express card from the others: member." Indeed, American Express did not use the term "cardholder" and instead preferred "cardmember." The privileges of membership, as depicted in the ad, included no preset spending limit, so you could take a helicopter to reach the best ski slopes; fourteen hundred offices worldwide, so you would have no need to worry if you found yourself stranded in China having lost your cash and passport; wide acceptance at all the important places, so you can buy your grandson that lion plush toy he fell in love with at FAO Schwartz; and concierge travel help if a business opportunity requires you to leave for Bangkok, today.

A 1988 ad demonstrated that the privileged cardmember need not choose between work and family. In it, a handsome businessman in his midthirties is sitting in what looks like an interminable board meeting. He turns to the man next to him and whispers, "I've got to leave *now*, or I'm going to miss my flight." At the airport, he sees that his flight has been canceled. A courteous airline representative tells him that there is one seat on a flight leaving in twenty minutes; it's in first class. "I'll take it," the businessman says, and he hands over his American Express card. Upon landing, he stands huddled in the rain with other travelers trying to hail a taxi but then sees a town-car driver, who, it turns out, is also happy to take his American Express card. Finally, he makes it to his destination on time: a spot in a darkened theater, next to his sophisticated, blond wife, just in time to see their young daughter perform as "second potted plant." The message was that American Express will take care of those who travel under its auspices, for their business as well as their familial obligations. One of the privileges of membership, then, is the privilege of family.

American Express had made its name when, at the outbreak of World War I, it was able to honor traveler's checks held by Americans marooned in Europe. If, as Cicero described, Romans were able to travel freely and were afforded special treatment throughout the empire simply by declaring, "Civis romanus sum," the same was true for American Express cardmembers. The card was like a passport issued by a private nation. This idea is invoked by the American Express Centurion Card, which debuted in 1991. Membership has its privileges—in some transactional communities more so than in others.

While American Express outpaced Diners Club among elite cardholders, beginning in the late 1960s, bank-issued cards offered a card for everyone else: not charge cards but *credit* cards attached to lines of rotating debt. Consumer financing had long been available through banks, but BankAmericard, offered by San Francisco's Bank of America, was the first product to connect it to a payment card.[37] Eventually, this system was licensed to other banks and became the Visa network. Unlike Diners Club and especially American Express, bank credit cards were easy to obtain. At first, BankAmericard did not even require an application, and unsolicited cards were sent out by mail in massive drops, a practice that was ultimately prohibited in 1970.[38] Even after, most Americans could be approved for some kind of credit card, with high interest rates for those with the lowest credit.

In addition to allowing customers to carry a balance, the bank-issued credit card system also did away with the pretense of exclusivity. Whereas Diners Club and American Express were closed-loop systems that connected member cardholders with member merchants, open-loop systems like Visa and Mastercard acted as intermediaries among many different banks, merchants, and cardholders. As the historian of technology David L. Stearns demonstrates, "opening the loop" was the key innovation of the bank card system.[39] The Visa network (and later the Mastercard network) was an information system that allowed individuals to pay with a card issued by their bank at a merchant that had an account at a different bank. This was absolutely essential for credit cards to function at any scale, as banks were prohibited from operating across state lines and, in most states, from operating more than a few branches.[40] Diners Club and American Express had no such restrictions because they were not banks.

Bank-issued credit cards expanded the range of merchants that accepted cards. Yes, membership might offer the privilege of buying a luxury dinner, an expensive toy, or an emergency first-class plane ticket, but in the early decades, there were many things that couldn't be bought with an American Express or Diners Club card. The credit cards issued by banks were intended to be used for more mundane purposes. In early BankAmericard advertising, would-be cardholders were asked not to imagine that they were members of an exclusive club but simply to imagine how much easier their lives would be if they could easily pay for things with a line of credit. "Think of It as Money," a major campaign encouraged. One 1972 ad showed a man holding newborn triplets: "Think of it as money. For the unexpected." Another ad from the same year showed a man painting a wall: "Think of it as money. For the home." Unless you bought diapers and drop cloths at Bergdorf's, it would have been difficult in 1972 to put these expenses on an American Express.

Between 1970 and 2001, the percentage of households with credit cards more than quadrupled, while the percentage with charge cards—restricted to the elite and therefore never high to begin with—dropped.[41] Charge cards introduced Americans to the idea of paying through a third party and made it seem desirable, but bank-issued credit cards made it common. While banks offered varied credit limits and different interest rates for credit cards, they did not offer the range of services that charge cards did—no concierge service, no international offices. You were a customer of your bank—you probably had a savings account there as well—but you weren't a *member* of an elite international transactional community.

Soon the issuing business began to change, resulting in an ever-growing array of payment-card products, offering new features and reaching new consumers. Beginning in 1978, regulations against interstate banking were eroded, and banks participating in open-loop networks started to compete to issue credit cards on a national level. Issuers began to devise new cards that reflected market segmentation. Cards became more expressive of, designed for, and designed to exploit a greater variety of transactional identities. By 1987, one American woman who did not have a credit card of any kind told the *Los Angeles Times* that she felt like a "non-person."[42]

Bank issuers began to compete in earnest with American Express for elite cardholders by yoking their credit cards to airline loyalty programs. Airlines had offered internal frequent-flyer rewards programs since 1979, when the airline industry was deregulated.[43] These programs mirrored many of the qualities of Diners Club and American Express. They created a "club" that codified "business class" as a distinct upper strata of the middle class.

As with charge cards, membership in the club was made possible through affiliation with a corporation. Although most rewards were earned through business travel paid for by the passengers' employers, they were linked to the passengers' individual identities and could be redeemed for pleasure: travel with partner airlines and nights at partner hotels, upgrades to first class, specialty customer service, and benefits at partner destinations, like ski resorts. Frequent-flyer programs converted business activity performed on behalf of an employer into luxury consumption experiences for individual members. In 1987, Citibank, one the largest credit card issuers, brokered a deal with American Airlines, which had one of the largest frequent-flyer programs, creating the first airline-miles card. American Express followed suit and began offering "Membership Miles" to its cardmembers in 1991.

The 1990s saw what the economists David S. Evans and Richard Schmalensee have dubbed the "issuer brawls," in which the newly consolidated big issuers—no longer local or even regional banks, most with names that are still recognizable today: Citibank, MBNA, First USA/Bank One, Chase Manhattan, Capital One, and Bank of America—along with American Express, developed new card products to compete more fiercely for cardholders, both revolvers and transactors alike.[44] They also began to offer features that felt more like the benefits American Express had promised its elite "members": purchase protection, rental-car insurance, travel rebates, and concierge services.

Because these new credit cards did not require payment of the full balance at the end of every month, as charge cards did, they could be offered to a much larger, if somewhat lower status, market segment than American Express. In the late 1980s, Visa took aim at American Express with an advertising campaign that described all the places American Express was not accepted: its transactional community was exclusive, perhaps, indeed, too exclusive.[45]

The new card products of the 1990s inherited the discourse and mechanics of membership from charge cards and the accessibility of credit cards to perform a variety of qualitatively different transactional identities. Some offered differentiated menus of fees—an annual fee but low foreign exchange rate, for example, or a relatively high interest rate but an interest-free grace period. Large companies like General Electric, AT&T, and General Motors issued cards that used the Visa and Mastercard networks. These cards offered rewards such as, in the case of the General Motors card, points that could be used toward car rebates. Banks began offering "Affinity Cards" that were cobranded with nonprofit organizations. For the first time, credit cards could be used as an overt instrument of self-expression: cardholders could demonstrate their passion for the Sierra Club or make clear to which university alumni associations they belonged, and they could also make a small donation to those organizations in lieu of rewards points.

By the first decades of 2000s, the credit card market was differentiated enough to perform a wide range of transactional identities. During the Great Recession, banks had relatively limited money to loan, so issuers focused on transactors with high credit scores. They designed cards with ample perks that could lure these transactors into swiping but made those cards difficult to attain. As lending money became more available, more people began to expect perks with their credit cards—online "churner" communities committed to gaming the system and maximizing points emerged—and what had previously been "ultrapremium" card packages became more common.

The Credit Card Accountability Responsibility and Disclosure (CARD) Act of 2009, part of the wave of consumer finance regulation passed after the financial crisis, created some restrictions on issuers. It prevented them from excessive marketing to people under age twenty-one, restricted fees on low-balance cards for people with bad credit, created transparency measures around interest rates and rules around late fees, and prohibited sudden interest-rate changes.

These protections only apply to consumer cards, not business cards. As a result, business cards are aggressively marketed to small business owners, freelancers, and the self-employed. These come with high credit limits and attractive rewards packages, including perks that are designed for small businesses. For example, the Chase Ink Business Preferred credit card grants additional reward points for purchases made on shipping, internet, and phone bills and on advertising on social media sites and search engines.[46] Small business cards serve an accounting role, as they can be used to avoid commingling personal and business expenses.[47] They provide a line of working credit that can be impossible to get otherwise.

But the lack of regulation means that issuer practices that would not be allowed in consumer cards can negatively impact the small business cardholder. Small business owners may be offered much-higher limits than people with their credit history would be able to access through an individual, rather than small business, card. Small business cardholders with bad or limited credit may find themselves faced with skyrocketing interest on variable-rate cards, similar to the predatory adjustable-rate mortgages that preceded the 2008 housing bubble. Some cards have exorbitant late fees and other, sometimes hidden, penalties.

Chase Sapphire Reserve has become, like avocado toast, an accessory of the stereotypical entitled millennial, but real millennials, along with a growing number of the general population, may find themselves occupying a transactional identity that looks more like that of a business credit cardholder. New forms of work are emerging, and people are being asked to envision themselves not as employees but as businesses that deliver services. As the anthropologist Mary L. Gray and the computer scientist Sid Suri put it, on-demand freelance "gig work" is "unraveling the typical job."[48] A 2016 study found that 94 percent of Net jobs created between 2005 and 2015 were in the form of "alternative work arrangements," that is, freelancers, contractors, and on-call and temp-agency workers.[49] The "1099 economy"—so called because freelancers do not receive a W-2 Wage and Tax Statement from their employers but instead use 1099 forms to report miscellaneous earned income—is also on the rise because of labor performed through platforms like Uber and Airbnb.

In this context, the business credit card becomes an indicator of precarity, a tool to manage it, and an encumbrance that deepens it. It is purpose built for a life in the 1099 economy, a life in which being savvy about credit card rewards isn't just about "turning a renovation into a vacation" but a way of gathering money and quasi-monies that, together, make up a livelihood, a life in which the blurred line between the personal and the professional needs to be traced. The lines of credit attached to these cards smooth over income volatility but make their bearers vulnerable to potentially insurmountable indebtedness.

The 1990s also saw the proliferation and popularization of new kinds of payment cards, each with different transactional identities and different underlying business models: debit, prepaid, and secured credit cards. Emblazoned with the logos of Visa or Mastercard, these new cards simply worked everywhere that accepted payments on the open-loop networks. Merchants had no choice but to accept all of the new cards. And when these cards are swiped, they invoke or hail different transactional identities and activate different communicative infrastructures.

Debit cards competed not so much with charge or credit cards but with checks and, indeed, were originally marketed as "check cards" to avoid confusion between the words "debit" and "debt." Checks don't generate interchange. One of the public services that the Federal Reserve provides is to absorb the cost of check settlement and clearance. Debit cards, however, do elicit interchange, which is a source of income for debit card issuers. It is, however, lower than credit card interchange, due to regulation aimed at keeping the cost of debit transactions down, particularly the Durbin Amendment of the 2010 Dodd-Frank Wall Street Reform and Consumer Protection Act, which capped debit interchange. In practice, this regulation can actually hurt credit unions and small community banks that primarily serve debit card users and can't compete with big issuers to offer competitive rewards cards.

Over the years, banks have experimented with offering debit card rewards, hoping to lure the "best" customers in the same way that premium credit cards do, but the relatively low interchange has made this strategy undesirable to issuers. Compared to charge cards and credit cards, debit cards, in the United States anyway, remain relatively undifferentiated from each other in their branding and cultural meaning.

Many people who prefer debit cards think of credit cards as an instrument of debt, which they seek to avoid. Debit cards may not say that you're "rich" or "interesting"; rather, they say that you simply wanted to pay with a card without being entangled in systems of rotating credit that were, and remain, a source of anxiety and moral weakness. A 1993 article in the *Chicago Tribune* described debit cards as "perfect for the 1990s spirit of deficit and debt reduction."[50] Similarly, in the United Kingdom, *The Guardian* reported in 1994 that "shoppers are rejecting the 'buy now, pay later' mentality of the 1980s," which was "reflected in increased use of debit cards . . . among those who have surrendered their credit cards."[51] Debit cards were associated with discipline over indebtedness.

Debit cards offer lower guarantees of consumer fraud protection than credit cards do. Whereas consumer fraud protection for credit cards is regulated under the Fair Credit Billing Act, debit cards are regulated under the Electronic Fund Transfer Act. The names of these laws indicate the different business models and infrastructural arrangements at play: credit card customers are being *billed* for debt they owe, and debit card customers are using a service that *transfers* their funds.

With credit cards, the acquirer pays the merchant, the issuer pays the acquirer, and the issuer bills the cardholder. If there are fraudulent charges, the cardholder can refuse to pay them. In this case, the issuer has to get its money back from the acquirer, who in turn has to get its money back from the merchant.

With debit cards, the funds for a transaction come out of the cardholder's checking account directly. When the debit card issuer works to get this money back, it is trying to get *your* money back, not its own. Under the Electronic Funds Transfer Act, the loss to the customer for fraudulent charges is limited to $50 if the bank is notified within two business days and $500 if the bank is notified within fifty-nine days. If customers wait until sixty days to report the fraudulent charges, they risk losing all their money and being held responsible for any overdrafts and related fees that might occur.

In the past decade, a whole industry of so-called fringe financial services has developed around serving those who are not well served by those traditional banks.[52] For payment, this has meant reloadable prepaid cards. Prepaid cards are immensely common. The economic lives of many Americans are not well served by credit cards. Debit cards, by nature, require a checking account, and nearly 27 percent of US households, 33.5 million people, are "unbanked" or "underbanked."[53] Prepaid cards transform those who primarily use cash into cardholders, to pull them into participation into the open loop of card payments, while maintaining distinctions among transactional identities.

Prepaid cards solve the industry puzzle of how issuers can make money off customers who are neither revolvers nor transactors and who don't use a checking account: charge many small fees. Prepaid cards function like any card on the open-loop network, are regulated like debit cards, and have similar interchange-fee structures. Instead of issuers being paid circuitously via the processes of interchange and rewards for every swipe, prepaid cardholders are nickel-and-dimed, but these charges occur in dollars, not cents. They pay a transaction fee every time they swipe—along with a monthly fee, a cash reload fee, a balance inquiry fee, an inactivity fee, and on and on, including a fee when they close their accounts.[54]

For example, a card issued by Green Dot, one of the largest prepaid-card companies, would come with the following fees: up to $1.95 to initially purchase the card, a 3 percent fee for every transaction, a monthly service fee of $7.95 (which might be waived if $1,000 or more were loaded onto the card in the previous billing cycle), up to $4.95 to reload money onto the card, $2.50 for cash withdrawal, $0.50 for a balance inquiry, $5.00 to replace a lost card.[55] This schedule of fees is fairly standard. Some prepaid cards, such as the Movo Virtual Prepaid Card, have no initial, monthly, or transaction fees. Other prepaid cards, such as the Commerce Bank mySpending Card, charge $0.50 to call automated customer service and $1.50 to speak with a live agent.[56] As the legal scholar Mehrsa Baradaran points out, "One of the great ironies in modern America is that the less money you have, the more you pay to use it."[57]

These fees might seem absurd to those who primarily use premium credit cards, who are excited to use their card and reap the frequent-flyer miles. But as the economic-development expert Lisa Servon demonstrates, the reality is that these fees for prepaid cards are more predictable and easier to live with than those assessed by banks for credit and debit cards. For example, Servon tells the story of a young single mother who accidentally overdrafted on her debit card by $10 and was unexpectedly hit with a cascade of penalties and fees that ultimately amounted to $300.[58] Being caught off guard by fees is common, especially when banks use "debit resequencing" software to maximize overdraft fees by taking out larger withdrawals first and then smaller withdrawals for which there would have been sufficient funds and then charging a fee on every transaction.

Prepaid issuers are well aware of this aspect of the transactional practice of their cardholders. The packaging of the Green Dot reload prepaid card makes the value proposition clear: "No overdraft fees, ever." Similarly, its website describes offering "the power to control your money."[59] Bluebird, American Express's prepaid-card product, which it produces in partnership with Walmart, explicitly describes itself as an "alternative to banking" and as having "all the benefits of banking without the fees."[60] For those who pay with a stored-value account like debit or prepaid instead of on credit, the question is not whether they will have to pay to pay but whether they can reliably anticipate and control these fees.

Prepaid fees are often comparable to those of storefront check cashers, but prepaid cards may be preferable to check cashers for a variety of reasons.[61] Increasingly, prepaid cards are much more than cards: they are being "appified" to offer a full spectrum of mobile-phone-based money-management services for the unbanked. Most newer prepaid-card products accept direct deposit into an account. Many employers incentivize the direct deposit of paychecks, and the federal and most state governments similarly prefer to direct deposit benefit checks and tax rebates into some kind of an account because it reduces costs.[62] Reloadable prepaid cards, then, are designed to take the place not only of payment cards but also of checking accounts.[63] This has allowed prepaid issuers to make claims that they offer "financial inclusion."

Indeed, it is hard to be fully "included" in present-day transactional communities without being able to shop or pay bills online, all of which require some kind of payment card. In fact, Green Dot was originally founded as a way for teenagers, who typically don't have a card in their name, to make internet purchases. Today, many prepaid-card products are paired with a mobile app or online portal that allows customers to monitor their balances and make online payments. To reach customers who prefer to do this kind of quasi-banking in person, many prepaid-card issuers have partnered with chain retailers like Walmart to offer in-person loading and withdrawal services.

These accounts, unlike checking accounts, offer no interest. And they don't allow cardholders to build a credit history. There have been attempts to try to change this. In 2012, the personal finance guru Suze Orman launched the Approved Card.[64] The card had relatively low fees and a few additional benefits such as access to credit reports, but Orman claimed that she was most excited about the potential for the product to shift the paradigm around prepaid cards and credit reporting. TransUnion, one of the big-three credit bureaus, had provisionally agreed to examine data from Approved Cards to determine if it might be included in some future credit-scoring method. Many people were skeptical. The hip-hop producer and entrepreneur Russell Simmons had previously tried and failed to attract the interest of credit bureaus to his RushCard. Indeed, nothing came of the agreement with Trans-Union, and the Approved Card was discontinued in 2014.[65]

Like charge and credit cards, prepaid cards are often heavily branded to confer particular transactional identities. These tend to correspond with the largest user groups of prepaid cards, which are African Americans and older white men and increasingly Latino users.[66] Many of the celebrities who endorse cards, including Magic Johnson, Tom Joyner, and Russell Simmons, are African American. American Express Bluebird features primarily black and Latino actors in its advertisements. Green Dot offers the NASCAR Reloadable Prepaid Visa, emblazoned with checkered flags.[67] Netspend, another major prepaid issuer, offers a card in partnership with Major League Baseball that allows cardholders to brand their card with their favorite team.[68] Univision, the US-based Spanish-language broadcast television network, also offers a card.

In addition, there are prepaid cards that are designed not only not to look like prepaid cards but to look like premium rewards credit cards: gold cards, platinum cards, black cards. Before the Kardashian family found their niche selling branded lipstick kits, they attempted to sell a branded prepaid card, the Kardashian Kard, in 2010. The venture was abandoned after less than a month because of a backlash to the card's high fees. Connecticut's attorney general at the time, Richard Blumenthal, sent a letter to the issuer, University National Bank, that stated, "Among the prepaid debit cards now on the market, the Kardashian Kard is particularly troubling because of its high fees combined with its appeal to financially unsophisticated young adult Kardashian fans. Keeping up with the Kardashians is impossible using these cards."[69] The major misstep seemed to be targeting young women and girls, a population frequently understood as worthy of protection, rather than the fees themselves, which are fairly standard in the prepaid industry.

Regardless of the transactional identity that the card branding conveys, the underlying business model and infrastructural arrangement differs little from prepaid-card product to prepaid-card product. The NASCAR card does not differ from other Green Dot cards, including its Spanish-language offering, apart from its physical branding. This may be changing. The prepaid-card market—along with other alternative financial services geared to those who don't use traditional banking institutions—is a lucrative and growing industry. The total dollar amount that consumers put on general-purpose reloadable prepaid cards grew from less than $1 billion in 2003 to nearly $65 billion in 2012, and this is expected to nearly double to $116 billion by 2020.[70]

As prepaid cards are becoming more commonplace, there seems to be a move away from obvious visible branding and toward varied underlying business models that cater to varied transactional identities. For example, in 2016, Green Dot and Uber announced a partnership to create a prepaid-card product for Uber drivers.[71] The product would enable Uber drivers, who may or may not have a checking account, to get access to their earnings faster than they would if they chose to use a different kind of disbursement. In general, low-wage and gig-economy employers are increasingly adopting prepaid cards for payroll.[72]

Instead of prepaid cards, some financial advice books, websites, and gurus recommend other kinds of products, such as secured credit cards. Like prepaid cards, secured credit cards are designed for people with little or no credit. Issuers extend rotating credit to "subprime" cardholders but require them to secure that line of credit with an up-front cash deposit.[73] So, if you are approved for a secured card with a credit limit of $1,000 with a secured deposit of $250, you pay the issuer $250 up front. That $250 is held by the issuer in a special deposit account. You are then free to use that $1,000 line of credit as you see fit. You are expected to pay at least the minimum repayment to the issuer every month, plus interest, plus annual fees. These interest rates and fees vary from product to product, with some manageable and some downright predatory. The issuer only uses your secured deposit—that $250—as a last resort for nonpayment. You can also only access it if you close your account. With secured credit cards, cardholder spending and repayments are reported to credit bureaus, so if you make regular purchases and pay them back on time, you'll build credit. Some cards even offer a process to upgrade to a standard, even a rewards, card, if your credit sufficiently improves.

Nevertheless, prepaid cards offer some advantages that make them more desirable. For many people, it can be burdensome not to have access to large chunks of money—$250 can be a lot, and many secured cards demand higher initial deposits. For the debt averse, it can be unsettling to transform $250 in cash savings into $1,000 credit with 24.99 percent interest. Whereas reloadable prepaid cards are heavily marketed and branded to appeal to and convey a variety of transactional identities, secured credit cards tend to be unmarked by difference one way or the other. Unlike prepaid cards like the RushCard, secured credit cards don't also function as an account into which paychecks and other funds can be deposited. In addition, if a secured cardholder doesn't repay as stipulated, the issuer will take the secured deposit, and the cardholder's credit score will be further damaged.

Consider the Uber driver choosing between a prepaid card issued by Green Dot and a secured card. Because of the partnership between Uber and Green Dot, his wages, which are irregular and varied in amount, are deposited into the prepaid-card account more quickly than they would be otherwise. The card associated with the account can be used anywhere any Visa or Mastercard can be used. For anything that requires cash, he can make a withdrawal at Walmart. There are fees, but he can anticipate them. On the other hand, if he wanted to build his credit score with a secured credit card, he would have to open a checking account, get paid by Uber into that checking account, pay an up-front amount to secure that credit card, regularly use the secured credit card, pay off the credit card on time every month or risk accruing interest, and carefully check that account or risk unpredictable fees. In everyday practice, the choice between a prepaid card and a secured card isn't always so clear.

Despite prepaid cards being designed to appeal to a variety of transactional audiences—from those who follow Suze Orman to those who follow the Kardashians, Russell Simmons, or NAS-CAR—and to fit financial practices common across a variety of economic lives, popular critique of users of prepaid cards has been racialized. As the communication scholars Carolyn Hardin and Armond Towns argue, prepaid cards are often leveraged as evidence that African Americans lack financial literacy and are insufficiently rational in their economic practice. But Hardin and Towns argue that because prepaid cards do not produce indebtedness and are otherwise disentangled from the traditional banking system, they are "one mode through which black consumers engage in the plastic economy with a measure of control over their historical relation to capitalism—a position that has rarely been available to them in the past."[74] Instead of calls for financial literacy education that ask black people to reject prepaid cards in favor of a banking system that serves them no better, Hardin and Towns insist that "better alternatives must honor black economic life and the wisdom it carries."[75]

Instead of prepaid or secured credit, many consumer advocates have recommended a return to a payment system aligned with communicative infrastructures: postal banking.[76] Such a system, which provides access to financial services through post offices, is currently operated in 183 countries including the United Kingdom, France, Italy, Japan, Brazil, and India.[77] The United States Postal Savings System operated from 1911 to 1967, and at its peak in 1947, the system held almost $3.4 billion in deposits.[78]

The postal banking system of tomorrow, as imagined in a bill introduced in 2018 by Kirsten Gillibrand, Democratic senator from New York and 2020 presidential primary candidate, would leverage existing postal infrastructure to provide not just savings and loans but a range of "transactional services" such as debit cards, online checking accounts, and mobile banking.[79] Instead of paying high fees to direct deposit a paycheck into a Green Dot account and then pay for groceries with its associated reloaded prepaid card, a postal banking customer would pay comparatively low fees to go through services developed by the US Postal Service. Instead of making cash withdrawals at Walmart, a postal banking customer would make withdrawals at one of the nation's thirty-one thousand post office branches. Even beyond postal banking, there are various ways to think about public options to pursue the public interest in payments. The much-lauded cashlessness of Sweden is dependent on its central banking system and national ID program.

The transactional identity marked by postal banking would—like cash—evoke the nation as a transactional community. But payment cards issued by the US Postal Service could be as varied as its stamps, which have included images of working military dogs; the first woman astronaut, Sally Ride, and the first African American astronaut, Guion Bluford; Marvel as well as DC superheroes; and Elvis Presley (issued in 1993 and still the most popular commemorative stamp ever issued).[80]

Nevertheless, as Hardin and Towns point out, it is important to consider how any national payment technology will confront historical, present, and future racial injustice. The open-loop card network honors all cards; how can new payment forms facilitate transactional communities and honor all transactional identities?

By the turn of the twenty-first century, payment cards were ubiquitous. By 2004, over 90 percent of Americans had a payment card.[81] Point-of-sale terminals for accepting card payments are ubiquitous in many parts of the world, and open-loop networks allow cardholders to swipe even when far from home. Today, almost every American uses some sort of noncash payment technology—debit card, credit card, prepaid card, charge card, check, mobile app—to pay. According to the Federal Reserve, Americans make billions of card transactions valuing trillions of dollars every year.[82]

Some of these cards open up invisible networks of privileged access; some of them only look like they do. For example, the Magnises card, brainchild of Billy McFarland, organizer of the ill-fated Fyre festival—which made headlines in 2017 for scamming aspiring "influencers" in search of a luxury Instagrammable experience—was simply a luxurious-looking metal card onto which one could graft the magnetic stripe of any card, credit, debit, or prepaid.[83] Indeed, the payments industry is a system of social categorization and distinction, of membership and exclusion. The market segmentation of the issuing industry—the business of paying—creates a mass media transactional community that organizes the world into hierarchical transactional identities. Its open-loop architecture enables communication among and across these hierarchies, all the while maintaining them.

So what does your payment card say about you? If you were to open your wallet right now and dump everything out, what kind of story would you piece together? What networks of affiliation might you be able to access? Where are your payments accepted? What rewards or fees are accrued and to whom when you pay? How much is your business worth? Are you *interesting*? To whom? And how?

Every single one of these instruments is just the visible tip of a vast infrastructure and the industry that powers it. Different cards configure you in different ways: as supplicant, as customer, as member. Cards are used in different ways and have different meanings for the people who carry them. Some people see their card as a lifeline, some as source of shame, some as an instrument of power and privilege. Our transactional identities are individuated and intertwined.

4 TRANSACTIONAL POLITICS

Getting Paid and Not Getting Paid

In 2014, Eden Alexander had a severe reaction to a common medication. She was covered in blisters, and, as she put it, her "skin was peeling off like paint."[1] Dismissed by urgent-care workers and referred to a dermatologist and a psychiatrist, she soon developed a secondary MRSA infection. By the time a hospital admitted her, Alexander was in myxedema coma, a rare condition with a very high mortality rate.

During Alexander's recovery, she and her friends set up a crowdfunding campaign using GiveForward, a platform specifically designed to raise money for medical costs. But soon, Alexander was notified that her campaign had run afoul of terms of service and would be canceled, all donations refunded. What had gone wrong?

In the initial email, GiveForward notified Alexander that WePay, GiveForward's underlying payment service provider, had "flagged her account" as in violation of WePay's terms of service, which stated that it could not be used "in connection" with pornographic services. Eden Alexander is an adult performer. On her Twitter account, she described herself as a "multiple award nom'd Adult, Fetish, Bondage +Alt Model, FemDom, CamGirl. Teazeworld Girl! (Ultimate)Grand Supreme. Feminist Porn & BDSM director."[2] The GiveForward campaign, however, made no mention of her job and focused entirely on her medical expenses.

Alexander posted a screenshot of the email on her Twitter account.[3] Immediately, there was a flurry of tweets, blog posts, and news coverage criticizing WePay. Two days later, in response to the growing uproar, WePay published a post on its company blog, stating that its system had detected that Alexander had retweeted other supporters who'd offered adult material in exchange for donations to her crowdfunding campaign.[4] This was, according to the WePay blog, "in direct violation of our terms of service as our back-end processor does not permit it."[5] Alexander had indeed retweeted two supportive pornography companies: a studio that had offered a free video clip to anyone who donated $50 to Alexander, and a website that had offered a set of pictures to anyone who donated $20 or $50 and a year's membership to anyone who donated $100.[6]

In the blog post, WePay wrote, "Upon further review, WePay suspects Eden may not have been aware of the terms of service and we are offering her the ability to open a new campaign for further fundraising."[7] WePay did not enable her to restart the same campaign or collect any of the funds that had already been donated, nor did it explain the limits or scope of its social media monitoring. CrowdTilt, another crowdfunding site serviced by a different payments provider, Balanced Payments, offered to host Alexander's campaign, and she quickly raised over $10,000.[8]

WePay had originally made its name as the preferred payments processor of the Occupy movement, vowing not to surveil or freeze accounts associated with the protest movement the way that PayPal and the card networks had done to WikiLeaks.[9] Previously, staffers from WePay had criticized PayPal's notoriously opaque and inconsistently enforced terms of service by pranking the 2010 PayPal Developers Conference. They dropped off a six-hundred-pound ice sculpture filled with five-dollar bills that directed people to the WePay site UnfreezeYourMoney.com.[10] According to WePay, this stunt increased its user base by 225 percent.[11] At the time, WePay founder Rich Aberman described his company as the "anti-PayPal," in large part because of its better customer service around confusing account freezes.[12] In another ironic twist, WePay's origin story involves its founders splitting the costs of a friend's bachelor party, an event that, as many of Alexander's supporters pointed out, would have probably included activities outside the bounds of its present terms of service.[13]

Many supporters of Alexander saw WePay's actions as overt discrimination against sex workers. The blogger and feminist porn star Kitty Stryker argued, "Because Eden is a cam girl, I guess she doesn't deserve fundraising." Stryker also noted that the WePay terms of service prohibited "adult or adult related content, including performers or 'cam girls.'" This wording, to Stryker, implied that Alexander had violated WePay's terms of service, "not by raising money FOR porn, but *by being a cam girl at all.*"[14]

The Twitter hashtag that supporters of Alexander used was #whorephobia, a play on "homophobia," implying that WePay was afraid of the mere association with someone in Alexander's profession. There is plenty of evidence that such whorephobia exists and indeed is alive and well. As of 2018, the sex-worker activist Liara Roux has documented dozens of examples of financial service companies discriminating against sex workers.[15]

Others, such as civil libertarians concerned with privacy and freedom of information flows, were more concerned about the implications of WePay's surveillance-based business model. One poster on Reddit wrote, "My worst fear wasn't realized (that there is a sex worker blacklist being distributed by banks and money exchangers), but my second to worst fear was: they actively monitored her social media for an excuse to ban her (and used a retweet as the excuse)."[16] That there could be some sort of a "blacklist" for exclusion from payments was disturbing, but so was the prospect of private social media surveillance that would effectively accomplish the same thing.

In WePay's blog post responding to the uproar, the company argued that it did not take a moral stance against pornography or sex workers and that it had successfully managed crowdfunding campaigns for other pornographic performers in the past.[17] WePay cofounder and CEO Bill Clerico explained on Twitter that WePay had to follow the "rules set by banks, Visa & Master-Card." He also emphasized that WePay was "required to monitor customer websites and social media [because] we have to, not [because] we want to."[18]

All of these reactions need unpacking. Alexander's supporters and others who were outraged at WePay's poor stewardship of payments were right that, in effect, it was a case of "a white tech bro deciding it's his place to take away money from a porn performer who needs medical care."[19] But Clerico was also right that Alexander was in violation of WePay's terms of service, which were embedded in multiple interlocking systems. But neither provides a satisfying explanation of how or why this happened.

Like many critical infrastructures, the systems that enable us to get paid are mostly invisible: we only notice them when they stop working.[20] When the systems of getting paid go wrong, it usually comes in the form of an account freeze. Those who face account freezes usually don't have a good sense of how or why it happened. Even when explanations are given, they may not be clarifying. As one observer put it, "The same as always: The 'system' has 'detected' an 'unusual' amount or frequency of money transferred. So they closed it for 'security reasons' and it will take days, if not weeks to reopen it again."[21] The technologies through which people get paid feel like black boxes to most users. The case of WePay not working for Eden Alexander when she needed it most provides an opportunity to move past the hot takes and figure out what went wrong and why.

Eden Alexander is not alone. Every day, countless people and organizations, for a variety of reasons, suddenly and unexpectedly find themselves cut off from the infrastructures of getting paid. And, as in Alexander's case, the consequences can be dire.

The power—and politics—of not getting paid is well illustrated by the controversy around "Operation Choke Point," a 2013 partnership between the US Department of Justice and the multiagency Financial Fraud Enforcement Task Force. Established by President Barack Obama after the 2008 financial crisis, the task force targeted fraud and consumer predation in financial institutions by constraining merchants' ability to get paid. As one Justice Department official described it, "We are changing the structures within the financial system that allow all kinds of fraudulent merchants to operate," with the intent of "choking them off from the very air they need to survive."[22] The first major action under Operation Choke Point came against a North Carolina bank that had processed payments for Ponzi schemes.

Immediately, Operation Choke Point was met with opposition from Republican lawmakers and certain sectors of the financial services industry. California Republican representative and head of the House Oversight Committee Darrell Issa stated that the "true goal" of Operation Choke Point was not to combat fraud but to "'choke out' companies the [Obama] Administration considers a 'high-risk' or otherwise objectionable."[23] He held up as evidence task force documents that described gun and ammunition sales as "high risk." On the other hand, supporters contended that the goal of Operation Choke Point was to shut down criminals, predators, and fraudsters. They argued that the allegations of a political motive were baseless and that the gun and ammunition documents were totally beside the point, part of long-standing FDIC best practices guidance and not related to Operation Choke Point at all.

What both proponents and critics of Operation Choke Point could agree on was that payment intermediaries wield tremendous power. Being able to be paid, by whom, and how define the terms of existence for organizations and people alike. In the metaphor of Operation Choke Point, money is like "air": those who are denied it can be "choked off."

Another striking illustration of the power of not getting paid came in 2010, when WikiLeaks began releasing thousands of classified US State Department diplomatic cables. A range of information intermediaries, seemingly in response to a memo by the Department of State, stopped providing services to WikiLeaks.[24] These included Amazon, which provided cloud storage, and EveryDNS, which hosted its website domain name. In addition, the accounts of the German foundation accepting donations for WikiLeaks were frozen by PayPal, Mastercard, Visa, and Bank of America.

As a *Wired* magazine blogger noted, there was an "element of theater" to WikiLeaks' struggles against censorship by its data and domain-name service providers, because all of that information was mirrored elsewhere, including on more secure servers, but the attack on WikiLeaks' money flow was, in contrast, "the real deal and [had] the potential to genuinely impact the organization."[25] According to WikiLeaks, the payment embargo "blocked over 95% of our donations, costing tens of millions of dollars in lost revenue."[26] Indeed, the legal scholar Seth F. Kreimer points out that not being able to receive funds through payment intermediaries is perhaps the most effective form of "proxy censorship": it can actually shut down an organization.[27]

In today's "network society," power over the infrastructures that move around information, materials, or, in this case, value has become more potent than force, coercion, and other forms of overtly despotic power.[28] The stakes of not getting paid can be equally high even when there is no overt political agenda. If deprived of the "air" of payment, individuals and families can be "choked off" in the same way that Ponzi schemes and hacktivists can.

In 2015, there was a software "glitch" that resulted in thousands of reports of paychecks not being deposited by customers of the RushCard.[29] The RushCard, discussed in chapter 3, was started by the hip-hop mogul Russell Simmons and could be used to make payments and to receive direct deposits. The card wasn't linked to a bank account and didn't require a credit check or credit history; it was intended to provide financial services to those who would otherwise be "unbanked." Unlike many other prepaid cards, customers were encouraged to keep a kind of savings account by getting their paychecks direct deposited into their RushCard account. One customer complained on Twitter, "@rushcard it's been a whole week without money, it's hard out here. Single mother no help. I work hard for my money and now I can't get it."[30] Thousands of similar complaints are available through the Consumer Financial Protection Bureau's Consumer Complaint Database.

Then there is the case from one of my college students, whose Venmo account was recently suspended. He had purchased $400 worth of supplies for his fraternity's Super Bowl party. He was then paid back that $400 through Venmo by the fraternity's social chair, who added the caption "Super Bowl." The next day, he went out to dinner with a friend and paid for his half of the meal through Venmo, adding the caption "Bet," a term that in current slang means "agreed" or "settled." According to the young man, his Venmo account was then frozen, with Venmo explaining that, between the large "Super Bowl" payment and the "Bet" payment, it had been flagged for gambling, an activity prohibited by terms of service. He said that he called Venmo and tried to explain, but his account remained closed, with some of his funds inaccessible. Everyone else in his fraternity uses Venmo, and most of their social transactions, both official and unofficial, are conducted through Venmo. Even as one of the most privileged members of our American society—a white, male student at an elite university—he is cut off from the dominant form of payment aligned with his transactional community, his communicative world.

To be a full member of any transactional community, to fully participate in a modern economy, and, indeed, to survive, you have to get paid. You have to have access to some kind of payment system, be it cash or electronic. And those systems have to work, reliably. A system that suddenly and unexpectedly cuts you off from money can be as perilous as not having access to any system at all.

Being able to get paid is perhaps *the* fundamental requirement for "citizenship" in a transactional community. Take the case of national currencies. It's fairly easy to be a tourist and use the local money to pay, but it's much harder to receive payments. This is often quite intentional: one of the myriad ways that boundaries and borders are invisibly enacted. Not being able to get paid means you don't quite belong.

Payment is communication, the transportation of information from one place to another. But money is, uniquely, information that is socially guaranteed to be valuable. It's the information that allows you to provide "operating expenses" for a business or for a family—to keep the heat on, to have enough to eat, and to pay your rent. Getting paid is an act of communication that can mean life or death.

But getting paid often goes unnoticed. In part, this is because getting paid is backgrounded, a predictable, regular beat in the

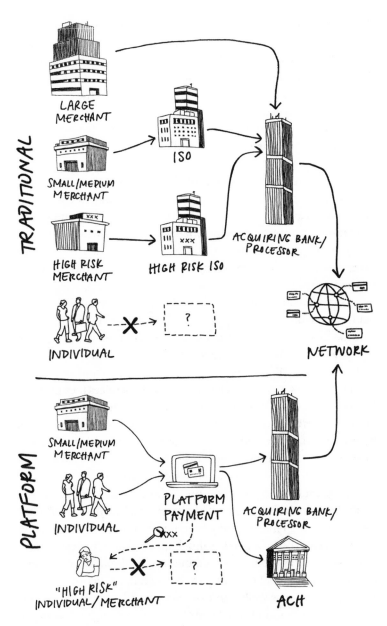

Getting paid with traditional and platform payment systems.

rhythm of our financial lives. For most people, getting paid happens less often than paying. Even those of us who live paycheck to paycheck mostly get paid, indeed, through paychecks, usually direct deposited into bank accounts. The problem is *usually* being able to earn enough money, not getting access to the money we have already earned. And yet when the systems we rely on to get paid stop working, the result is the same as not having earned enough money in the first place and can be devastating.

Getting people and businesses paid is an important part of the modern payments industry. Even for people in the industry, card payment "acquiring"—as discussed in chapter 3—is one of the least familiar aspects of the payments industry because there are many subtly different varieties in how it might be conducted.[31] There can be many layers, many middlemen, many different parties to your payment.

As described in chapter 3, merchants—or whoever is getting paid—pay to be paid. They pay their acquirer fees every time a card is swiped, as well as for information processing, leasing point-of-sale equipment, and so on. Acquirers themselves pay fees to credit card issuers for "providing" the customer. They then pass these fees along to merchants, plus additional markups for the services they provide. Card networks like Visa and Mastercard act as intermediaries between issuers and acquirers. They set rules and conduct payments by sending standardized messages between member banks, and they operate the computer networks that send these messages, as well as operating the information systems that process them.[32]

Large merchants usually connect directly to a large acquiring bank. Large merchants usually have internal teams tasked with managing payments and may even develop their own payments software, so they don't need as much information processing and other services as smaller merchants might. Smaller merchants usually don't connect directly to acquirers. Large acquirers—like JPMorgan Chase or Wells Fargo—don't typically provide merchant customer services, and small merchants don't bring enough scale to get competitive pricing. Instead, smaller merchants get paid through an independent sales organization, or ISO. ISOs are essentially payment service wholesalers. They buy acquiring services in bulk from acquirers and then resell them to merchants.

ISOs are often referred to as the "feet on the street" for the acquiring industry.[33] They provide ongoing customer service to merchants, such as data processing, software, and hardware like point-of-sale terminals. There is a lot of variability among ISOs. An ISO could be one person or a very large company. Some ISOs specialize in a particular industry or type of business. There can be multiple ISOs in between a merchant and the processor, each of whom gets a cut of the fees that the merchants pay. Pricing by ISOs is highly variable, depending on the merchant's industry and the kind of services the ISO provides.

So, when I buy a $2.10 coffee with my UVA Credit Union Visa card at a Starbucks first thing in the morning, it may seem like the money is moving only in one direction: my card issuer, UVA Credit Union, pays (via the Visa exchange system) JPMorgan Chase (which is Starbucks' acquiring bank); and JPMorgan Chase credits Starbucks with the money for my coffee.

But money also moves in the opposite direction: Starbucks pays a transaction fee to its acquiring bank, JPMorgan Chase.[34] JPMorgan Chase pays UVA Credit Union an interchange fee for supplying my business. Because Starbucks brings a high volume of transactions, it is charged relatively low, fixed rates. Starbucks has developed custom hardware and software to manage points of sale and has a variety of different internal corporate roles that ensure that it is able to be paid for the millions of cups of coffee it sells every day.

Conversely, it wouldn't make a lot of sense for my local independent coffee shop to do business with JPMorgan Chase directly. Instead, my regular café—let's call it C-Ville Joe—works with a small ISO—let's call it Commonwealth Merchant Solutions—that resells payments from Wells Fargo. The ISO does for my regular café many of the things that Starbucks' internal team does: manages point-of-sale equipment, ensures compliance to both legal and industry data standards, provides service when things go wrong.

In addition to selling payment services, acquirers also sell risk. When a merchant accepts a card payment, its acquirer temporarily

Sometimes merchants, like this veterinarian in Logan, Ohio, 2017, make the costs of card acquiring obvious to their customers.

fronts it the money paid. When I swipe my card for that cup of coffee, JPMorgan Chase effectively loans Starbucks $2.10, minus interchange, for my payment. Then UVA Credit Union settles with JPMorgan Chase for all the aggregated payments it owes. Finally, Chase bills me for that $2.10, along with all the other payments I made, plus interest.

If for some reason I dispute that $2.10 charge, citing fraud or dissatisfaction, UVA Credit Union initiates what is called a "chargeback." When a chargeback occurs, the acquirer is responsible for refunding the money to the issuer, which in turn refunds the customer. Then, the issuer has to recoup that money from the merchant. UVA Credit Union gets that $2.10 back from JPMorgan Chase, which gets that money back—plus additional fees—from Starbucks. That liability travels through the food chain of acquiring. If I want my money back from C-Ville Joe, UVA Credit Union collects it from Wells Fargo, which collects it from Commonwealth Merchant Solutions, which collects it from C-Ville Joe. Part of the acquirer's job—part of the service it charges merchants for—is to "hold the risk" for the merchant. Every act of getting paid is also, temporarily, a loan.

Ideally, customers never want their money back, and if they do, merchants readily refund that money to their acquirers. In reality, however, it can be difficult for an acquirer to recover money from a merchant. For example, a merchant may face a cluster of chargebacks simply because its product is terrible, and it may go out of business for the same reason and be unable to repay its acquirer. And what about the case of actual fraud? The acquirer can try to recover that refunded money from the merchant, but if the merchant is a competent scammer, it will have already evaporated, leaving the acquirer holding the bag.

For acquirers, this risk is a business opportunity. ISOs serve as the middlemen for risk just as they serve as the middlemen between merchants and payment acquiring services. They take on the risk of the merchants they service for the acquirer. These merchants are sorted into risk categories: those that have a similar probability of chargebacks are priced similarly. Different ISOs have different "risk appetites." Some ISOs specialize in "high-risk" payments, and they charge merchants higher fees. The price of getting paid, in addition to scale, is tied to risk and, specifically, risk of chargeback. In the acquiring business, it is often said that "risk pays."

For ISOs that specialize in high-risk merchants, the ideal customer is one who is considered the riskiest—and therefore can be charged the highest prices—but who doesn't actually generate that many chargebacks and, crucially, is not actually doing anything illegal. In general, the industry standard for chargeback risk is a 1 percent rate of chargeback transactions in relation to total sales transactions, and staying under 2 percent allows merchants to contract with a standard "high-risk" ISO; but risk—and the fees associated with higher risk of chargebacks—is highly variable.

Any legal merchant, no matter how "risky," can accept payment cards if it is able to find an ISO that will take it on—and if it is willing and able to pay the fees that the ISO sets. The ISO may ask the high-risk merchant to presecure the account, require personal financial guarantees from business owners, or implement other policies to mitigate loss. If a merchant has an increase in charge-backs, it is in the best interests of the ISO to put the merchant on an improvement plan or raise prices before cutting it off as a client.

Certain industries are categorically defined as high risk for chargebacks and outright fraud. These include those that sell products that are borderline illegal, such as counterfeit luxury goods and herbal drugs; those that are controlled in some states but not others, such as firearms; those that sell products that customers are likely to be unsatisfied with, such as psychic read-ings and get-rich-quick schemes; those that engage in deceptive marketing, such as diet pills and vacation time-shares; and those that sell products that customers might later be embarrassed to admit they ordered, such as pornography and gambling wagers. It's also common knowledge in the industry that chargebacks go up after the holidays, when consumers realize they've overspent. Whether rooted in embarrassment, regret, or just a desire to get something for nothing, this kind of chargeback is known as "friendly fraud," and it's built into the price of payment.

Acquirers can only go so far in charging high prices for risky business. In addition to managing risk, acquirers are also respon-sible for compliance with "know your customer" (KYC) regula-tions. This means verifying the identity of those on whose behalf they accept payments, demonstrating due diligence that these clients are not engaged in money laundering, funding terrorism, or otherwise engaged in illegal activity. If acquirers are found to be out of compliance, they can face heavy fines. In fact, the list of industries that so inflamed critics of Operation Choke Point was really just long-standing guidance from the FDIC regarding due diligence for risk management and KYC regulations.

The notion of a "chargeback" demonstrates how payment is a technology used to manage risk. According to the sociological theorist Georg Simmel, modern money—that is, state-issued cash—allowed us to transact as strangers in the modern metropolis and to have an anonymous economy untethered from the bonds of family and patronage.[35] A key part of this is temporality of the transaction: in villages, exchanges were done mostly on credit, and everyone knew you were good for it because everyone knew where to find you; but in cities, you exchanged cash, and that was it. There was no need for a continued relationship. People getting paid didn't trust the person paying them, nor did they have to. They just had to trust in the cash. But cash, on its own, doesn't enable chargebacks. So, for those who exchanged their cash for goods or services, it was buyer beware. The card system, in allowing cardholders to revoke payment through chargeback, stretches out the temporality of the transaction. The card issuer becomes a guardian and a steward of the cardholder's financial interests.[36]

In recent decades, the acquiring business—the business of getting paid—has been changing in important ways. In the 1990s, high penetration of the World Wide Web promised a peer-to-peer economy, but there wasn't a way for people to pay each other using cards. The acquiring business was designed for merchants to get paid, not people. Payment cards were developed in the mid-twentieth century, for an economy that clearly delineated between buyers and sellers, and their design did not anticipate the geographically dispersed, person-to-person communication system and, crucially, economy of the internet era. Ordinary people aren't merchants, so they can't access acquirers the way merchants do. They don't have merchant services accounts, they can't be assessed for risk the way businesses are, and they aren't accustomed to paying high fees to be paid.

In the 1990s, new payments providers emerged with the goal of enabling people to receive payments from each other electronically. These new systems were an overlay on existing infrastructure, a clever hack (or hasty kludge) that bridged old and new technologies and policies. The first and probably still the most successful service for people to get paid electronically was PayPal. The value proposition of PayPal, then as now, was to offer person-to-person payments in an online setting. In this context, there aren't clear "merchants" and "cardholders." Instead, there is parity between users, who sometimes buy and sometimes sell. In the industry, PayPal and other intermediaries like it are referred to as payment service providers, or PSPs.

In order to gain customers and make a profit, PayPal had to offer payment services at a lower rate than the existing payment system. This would have been difficult, if not impossible, in the traditional ISO model. PayPal would have been just another, additional middleman in the chain. PayPal's primary innovation, then, was to bypass the traditional acquiring system entirely. This newer approach to acquiring began with PayPal in the 1990s and continues to be the dominant model for emergent PSPs coming out of the tech industry, such as WePay, Square, Venmo (now owned by PayPal), and most payment systems embedded in social media platforms, such as Snapchat Snapcash and Facebook Messenger Payments.

PayPal bypasses the traditional acquiring system by keeping money inside its closed loop for as long as possible. When one user pays another through a PSP, the PSP records a transfer on its internal accounts, debiting the account of one user and crediting that of another. This is called a "book transfer." It is most advantageous to a PSP when the money never leaves the PSP's accounts and just goes continuously back and forth between users as book transfers. In this scenario, the PSP can charge fees of users without paying out fees to external systems. It can also make interest from the reserve of money held in users' accounts, or "float," as it's called in the payments industry.

When prompted by the user, the PSP uses a separate system to withdraw the funds from the paying user's checking account or credit card and deposit the funds into the receiving user's checking account. If a checking account is used, PSPs usually use the automated clearinghouse (ACH), a nonprofit network for bank-to-bank transfers. The ACH, which was established by the Federal Reserve in 1975, was intended to function as a utility for financial institutions and charges very low fees. By riding the rails of the ACH, PSPs can avoid paying fees to the card networks, so PSPs encourage users to use their checking accounts.

If a credit card is used to fund the payment, PSPs enter the acquiring ecosystem not as an ISO but as a merchant that is operating on behalf of other small merchants. In the industry, this is called being an "aggregator" or "master merchant." As a master merchant, the payment service can then negotiate directly with the network, processor, or acquirer to receive custom, large-scale pricing, the same way a big box store would. It cuts out most of the middlemen, instead serving as the primary intermediary itself. When customers want to use their credit cards, PSPs usually pass the interchange fees onto them. Some PSPs are actually incorporated as ISOs, which means partnering with an acquirer, following particular rules, and meeting particular standards.

PSPs are often embedded inside a platform that facilitates marketplace transactions. For example, PayPal was a subsidiary of eBay for most of its existence, and while it can be used to pay in many different contexts, its initial function was to power the eBay economy. In the traditional ISO model, the interests of cardholders are represented by issuers, and the interests of merchants are represented by acquirers. In the platform model, the true client of the PSP is the platform, not the parties on either end of the transaction.

PSPs were originally envisioned as a way for people to get paid by other people when they couldn't contract with acquirers. Today, ISOs—seen as old-fashioned and overpriced—are a target for disruption by Silicon Valley. Traditional ISOs are rapidly losing ground to start-ups for merchant business as well. These payment-facilitation platforms might function like PSPs but also might be registered ISOs of a large acquiring bank. These offer an array of value-added merchant services, like loyalty points, analytics, and bookkeeping.

For a long time, ISOs were the only connection that small- and medium-sized merchants had to the card payments ecology. Like most middlemen, they are frequently unpopular among their merchants and seen as price gougers. Today—at least in Charlottesville, Virginia, where I live—it's hard to find an independent coffee shop that uses a traditional ISO instead of a start-up. The tablet, equipped with software, a card reader, and a stylish swivel stand, is becoming more ubiquitous than the clunky point-of-sale terminal that ISOs lease to their clients.

The shift from traditional ISOs to start-ups has been accompanied by an important shift in the way that risk is managed. It is a shift in what sociologists call "riskwork"—the ordinary and mundane practices of imagining and managing risk—that produces payment failures for people like Eden Alexander and for college students with overly canny Venmo captions.[37] To manage payment is to manage risk, and to manage risk is a way of doing politics.

In the traditional acquiring system, there is a market for risk. Any legal merchant can get paid if it's willing to pay the rates

A traditional point-of-sale system next to a tablet with platform payment software.

commanded by a high-risk ISO. In new payment start-ups, risk is managed not through a market but through a mechanism native to tech-industry platforms: like other forms of social media, participation in these payment systems is governed by terms of service. Unlike traditional ISOs, which usually negotiate custom contracts with merchants, PSPs don't have direct vendor-client relationships with their users. Instead, all users are subject to the terms of service, which they agree to (but usually don't read) when they sign up for an account and which are subject to change at any time.

Transactions that would be considered "high risk" in the market model are simply banned. This is because PSPs access acquiring banks as master merchants, and in order to qualify for the lowest rates, PSPs must guarantee that all the transactions they conduct will be low risk for chargebacks. There are long-standing lists, provided by regulatory and industry groups, of high-risk merchant categories: time-shares, home-based charities, herbal remedies, and so on. Most payment start-ups simply take these lists and drop them into their terms of service as explicitly prohibited. Whereas in the traditional model, an acquirer had some sort of direct relationship and personalized contract with merchants, in the platform model, terms of service flatten these relations and, as the sociologist Robert Castel writes, "dissolve the notion of a *subject* or a concrete individual, and put in its place a combinatory of *factors*, the factors of risk."[38]

Like other social media platforms, these person-to-person payment systems use surveillance and automation to enforce these terms of service and to deal with the problem of risk. In addition to banning transactions that are considered "high risk," they increasingly use machine learning to monitor the social media presence of those who receive payments to catch such transactions as they happen.

PSPs that are designed for use by merchants, rather than people, are also governed by terms of service. Instead of merchants contracting with an ISO and paying fees tied to factors like their chargeback risk, they agree to the PSP's terms of service and pay a flat rate. For example, in the traditional model, a merchant who sells love spells would be charged higher fees by its ISO to cover the risk of chargebacks from customers who find that the spell didn't beguile the object of their desire. In the new model, the sale of love spells would be banned entirely by terms of service. In fact, Square explicitly bans "occult materials." According to the founder of the Pagan Business Network, many of its members have grown weary of changing and inconsistently applied policies from PSPs and have instead sought out costly high-risk accounts with traditional ISOs.[39] Indeed, for the most part, traditional high-risk industries remain in the market model, accessing the payment networks through ISOs.

But this option—simply contracting with a high-risk ISO— isn't available to individuals, community groups, or other entities not incorporated as businesses. Neither the old nor the new model of acquiring was designed for "high-risk" categories of person-to-person or informal transactions. Face-to-face or online, people may try to use payment start-ups for purposes not approved by the terms of service, but they do so at their peril. They are likely to have their accounts frozen or even permanently suspended. Although PSPs endeavor to replace cash, they expressly prohibit the sort of flexibility that characterizes the person-to-person cash transaction. Because these policies provision who can receive payment, fundamental to participation in an economy and even survival, they are inherently political.

When Eden Alexander retweeted her supporters' offer of free pornographic pictures and videos to anyone who donated to her crowdfunding campaign, she unwittingly stepped into a gap produced by the misalignment of an older model of risk adopted by a new model of infrastructure. Unlike a traditional merchant, Alexander was not the client of the payment provider WePay; the crowdfunding platform GiveForward was.

Pornography, according to regulatory and industry guidance, is a "high-risk" industry. Merchants are subject to extra scrutiny because, it seems, transactions for pornography do present a high rate of chargebacks. According to some industry estimates, the rate of chargebacks in relation to total sales transactions for adult-services merchants can be as high as 4 percent. In comparison, a low-risk business usually has a less than 1 percent rate of charge-backs in relation to total sales. It is widely accepted that people tend to ask for their money back for pornography. Some of these chargebacks are due to what payments-industry professionals refer to as "It wasn't me!" friendly fraud claims: because pornography is taboo, if purchases are discovered by a spouse or an employer, cardholders may be inclined to say that they did not authorize the transaction. Some of these chargebacks might be due to legitimate fraud. Perhaps also because pornography is taboo, many websites distributing pornography use deceptive tactics, such as misleading subscription pricing and spam. Pornographic sites have also been used as a trap to capture and illegally use credit card information.

So, in general, pornography is banned by terms of service from payment start-ups—including WePay—both for person-to-person payment and for merchant services. This industrial arrangement leaves out anyone who may not be able to develop a long-term relationship with an ISO, including individual pornographic performers. As Chris Mallick—who claims to have invented online payments when, in the 1990s, he started the first ISO that specialized in online pornography—put it, pornographers "had two jobs: taking pictures, and collecting cash. It turned out that they were really good at one of those things, and really bad at the other."[40] Mallick's vision of the "pornographer" as the one who "collects the cash" and "takes the pictures" rather than the person, say, who is *in* the picture is telling.

The systems of getting paid replicate long-standing imbalances of power within the sex industry: individual performers are imagined as commodities, not entrepreneurs, compelled to remain dependent on managers who have access to the infrastructure through which money flows. This usually takes the form of "payroll" checks from websites that have contracted with a high-risk ISO to receive payments or, of course, cash. While many industries have been radically changed by the internet's person-to-person economy, pornography—at least insofar as money and power are concentrated among middlemen managers—has not been one of them.

When Alexander was banned from getting paid, she wasn't just banned from receiving payments for pornography; she was banned from the system entirely. It wasn't just the donations that were motivated by the offer of pornography that were refunded—and, in fact, we have no way of knowing whether *any* donations were motivated by this offer. All the donations were refunded and the entire campaign was shut down. If Alexander had had another crowdfunding campaign, say, for a creative project, and had additional funds not related to the medical GiveForward campaign, she would probably have lost access to those funds as well.

During public uproar over the suspension of Alexander's crowdfunding campaign, the various platforms involved were eager to displace the blame. GiveForward blamed the terms of service of WePay. WePay blamed the policies of its payment processor, Vantiv. Risk was governed by a matryoshka doll of rules. Vantiv expects low-risk payments and therefore bans "high-risk" industries like pornography. This in turn determined WePay's terms of service, which in turn determined GiveForward's terms of service. Alexander agreed to all of this when she signed up for WePay. Whether or not Alexander was actually "selling" pornography and whether or not any chargebacks would have ever accrued became irrelevant.

People who happen to work in pornography, like anyone else, may seek to participate in online economic activity, but when terms of service are enforced by social media surveillance, the mere fact that they participate in the sex industry in ways evident on social media may be enough to exclude them entirely. It may be difficult for them to get paid at all: the ISOs exclude them from receiving payments because they are individuals, and PSPs exclude them because they are associated with high-risk industries.

The adoption of "high-risk" merchant categories by PSP terms of service, which are then surfaced and enforced by automation and machine learning, represents a misalignment of two different paradigms of risk and risk management. "High risk," as it was determined in the traditional acquiring model, was never meant to be a mechanism for exclusion. Rather, it was meant to create market categories for pricing. What was, as the sociologists

Marion Fourcade and Kieran Healy put it, a "within-market classification" used to create differential pricing becomes a "boundary classification" used to exclude certain transactions entirely.[41]

This moralized experience of payment is not limited to the moment of transaction itself. danah boyd has described how social media platforms often unintentionally create "context collapse," when one social domain suddenly comes crashing into another.[42] For example, neither my undergrad students nor I want to run into each other out on a Friday night, but if we become Facebook friends, we run the risk of seeing pictures of just those activities, which are clearly meant for an entirely different audience. A particularly dire context collapse occurs when the ability to get paid is lost because social media activity in one area of life (identity as a pornographic performer) crashes into another (crowdfunding for a medical emergency). These moments of context collapse make evident the problems of boundary classifications and the politics of risk management in payments.

In addition to agreeing to GiveForward's—and WePay's and Vantiv's—rules, Eden Alexander also agreed to be monitored for violations of these rules. Those terms of service were algorithmically enforced, and when Alexander hit that retweet button, she was caught in the dragnet.

Jillian C. York of the Electronic Frontier Foundation wrote on her Twitter account, "What someone does in their free time isn't [WePay's] business to monitor."[43] While porn was Alexander's job, not her "free time," York's point was that WePay's surveillance had unfairly conflated aspects of Alexander's life. She also tweeted, "Wow, do they follow me around SF too to make sure I don't accidentally strip?"[44] Instead of pornography being treated like a high-risk *transaction*, pornographic performers are being treated like high-risk *people*, even when they're not working.

In 2013, the year before Alexander's campaign, WePay launched Veda, an "intelligent social risk engine." Veda asks users for five pieces of information—first name, last name, name of business, email address, and phone number—and then uses its proprietary systems to mine additional data from social networks such as

Facebook, Twitter, and Yelp. Using algorithms, Veda analyzes "social signals" to measure risk and to make a decision about whether WePay will offer or continue to offer payment services. As WePay founder Bill Clerico put it, "Veda's intelligent brain is the new, smarter way to assess risk." Through Veda, WePay promised "no risk of fraud" through application of sophisticated machine-learning algorithms.[45]

In practice, WePay seemed to offer primarily increased detection of violations of terms of service by mining social media data for indicators of high-risk, prohibited behavior. Because WePay, like most PSPs, accessed its acquirer, Vantiv, as a master merchant, it was able to cite Veda as an innovative way to guarantee low-risk transactions and, therefore, undoubtedly lower its rates for transactions, which WePay was able to pass on to its platform clients, increasing scale of adoption, which would have no doubt pleased its venture-capital funders.

When Eden Alexander retweeted offers of pornography as an incentive for donating to her crowdfunding campaign, the transactions related to the campaign became, at least in the eyes of Veda, transactions for pornography. Even to GiveForward, a platform meant to mitigate the costs of health care, Alexander could not be treated with care but was, rather, as the legal scholar Pat O'Malley puts it, an "actuarial entity," statistically knowable, who had been surveilled and "diagnosed" with "risk," specifically risk for a chargeback that is unlikely to ever occur but nonetheless must be guarded against.[46]

Within the traditional payments industry, the important service that high-risk acquirers provide—and the substantial profits they can turn—are well understood. Vantiv, founded in 1971 as Fifth Third Bank, is one of largest and oldest merchant transaction acquiring processors, and it works with ISOs that serve numerous industries, including higher-risk merchants. Rather than blame Vantiv's "policies," it may have been more accurate for WePay to point to the specific contract that Vantiv had negotiated with WePay, which no doubt hinged on WePay's ability to guarantee low risk in terms of both chargeback and fraud.

Surveillance scholars have described how the power of surveillance lies not just in watching and recording but in identifying, classifying, and assessing that which is surveilled.[47] Surveillance, then, is a form of "social sorting." As David Lyon writes, "Surveillance today sorts people into categories, assigning worth or risk, in ways that have real effects on their life-chances."[48] Payment systems like WePay work much like surveillance operations in the criminal justice system: they collect information to identify and classify individuals according to their risk of terrorism, criminality, or, in this case, violation of terms of service.[49] As Fourcade and Healy point out, the "classification situations" produced by the wrangling of "big data" are "presented, and experienced, as moralized systems of opportunities and just deserts." They "have learned to 'see' in a new way and are teaching us to see ourselves that way, too."[50] Indeed, when WePay froze Eden Alexander's account, it was one of the leading PSP start-ups that made extracting insights from social media data in order to manage risk its primary value proposition—and the basis for most of its venture-capital funding and ultimate acquisition by Chase in 2017.[51]

In theory, the tech industry should be keen to develop systems that, like ISOs, are able to profit from varied "risk appetites." Online lenders like Wonga, Lenddo, and Lendup are able to make loans—at high interest rates and other fees, most likely—to "digital subprime" borrowers, that is, borrowers who are, based on thousands of data points ranging from browser search history to Facebook friends, found to be at high risk of nonpayment.[52] But these probabilistic methods inherit a model of risk from an older model of payment, and they import it without adjusting it for a new context. Castel's description of the model of risk used to predict psychological deviance applies here: "A risk does not arise from the presence of particular precise danger embodied in a concrete individual or group. It is the effect of a combination of abstract *factors* which render more or less probable the occurrence of undesirable modes of behavior."[53]

In recent years, there has been a shift away from clear-cut risk categories in the payments acquiring business and toward probabilistic modeling and monitoring. While most platforms manage risk by applying blanket prohibitions of "high-risk" transactions, there is now a move to use data collection and machine learning to model, identify, and control risk. But a shift away from lists of banned activities doesn't mean that account freezes have decreased or become less mysterious. In fact, there are countless examples of users unexpectedly not being able to get paid through leading person-to-person payment systems. Venmo accounts have been frozen over transaction descriptions that reference Cuban food, the name Ahmed, and weird jokes like "iced coffee obama nsa inside job syria," as well as actual donations to Syrian refugees.[54] Users have found that their accounts, and therefore their ability to receive funds, have been blocked when they try to raise money for charity, crowdfund without going through a crowdfunding platform, or receive an unusually large amount of money.

The shift away from clear-cut risk categories in the payments industry has come at the same time as the rise of predictive analytics in the tech industry. WePay, as we have seen, pivoted from being the "anti-PayPal" and the "unofficial payment system of Occupy Wall Street" to offering an "intelligent social risk engine" to "hit a moving target" in a world where "fraud doesn't stand still."[55] Predictive analytics systems, by their very nature, are always experimental. They are always being retrained to identity new attributes that correlate with unwanted risk—risk of chargebacks, risk of KYC violation—and to disregard attributes that do not correlate with these risks.

When Venmo accounts are suspended because of, say, using the term "Cuba" to annotate a transaction, users are told that they may have run afoul of the US Department of Treasury's Office of Foreign Assets Control and are asked to explain themselves.[56] In theory, every time a user submits an account of a night of drinking rum and coke or eating ham sandwiches or watching *Dirty Dancing 2: Havana Nights*, the system "learns" what not to flag. Eventually, it is hoped, Venmo's predictive analytics will get better at recognizing "real" violations and will no longer bother with these false positives.

These account freezes should not be seen as mistakes: they are evidence of the way machines learn, the way they are "supposed" to work. These systems—like most outputs of the tech industry—are allowed to live in "perpetual beta," in which products are never really finished but are instead "developed in the open, with new features slipstreamed in on a monthly, weekly, or even daily basis."[57] While some kinds of "high-risk" transactional activities may no longer be overtly banned, surveillant systems may be less reliable because it is difficult for users to predict what kinds of transactions and activity—related or unrelated—will result in suspension of services. It's a question of how much "perpetual beta" users are willing—or are compelled—to tolerate.[58] Perpetual beta—to use the language of deconstructive democratic theory— creates a horizon of possibility in which machines are able to learn but not one in which humans are able to live.[59]

As risk-management systems have become more experimental, they have also become more opaque. WePay's Bill Clerico compared Veda's machine-learning capacities to credit scoring: "A traditional credit score only shows a sliver of who you are, but an online profile allows us to assign our users a more accurate 'WePay credit score' based on their personal history of verified, social data."[60] On the surface, a "WePay credit score" does not seem very different from a traditional credit score. They both use data points; WePay just uses more and different kinds of data. There is also a similarity with regard to how they are used for getting paid: an ISO uses a traditional credit score to price payment services for a merchant. But, again, a key difference lies in opacity and opportunity for recourse. The 1970 Fair Credit Reporting Act was intended to ensure that no secret databases were used to make decisions about Americans' financial lives and that Americans would have the right to see and challenge any such information.[61] No such regulations are in place for social media analytics.[62]

Nevertheless, variable risk remains incompatible with platform payments, where growth and scale often trump even profit and contractual relationships are governed by terms of service, which are blanket rather than bespoke.[63] The result is that some transactions—and some people—are banned entirely. Nowhere is this seen more clearly than in the adult-entertainment industry.

The "interlocking of intentionalities" and the challenges and failures of the payments industry to serve people working in pornography reflect the larger set of interconnections among risk-management systems, governance by terms of service, surveillance-based business models, and access to economic infrastructure—conditions that may increasingly shape how we are all paid.[64] Any person who wants to get paid electronically is beholden to systems governed in ways that are inconsistently enforced, experimental, and opaque and offer little recourse for contestation.

Terms of service, across all kinds of platforms, tend to be inconsistently and confusingly enforced. This is no less true for platform payments. Kitty Stryker, in her blog post supporting Eden Alexander, noted several examples of successful GiveForward campaigns that seemed to directly violate WePay's terms of service.[65] WePay prohibits "weight-loss programs," but GiveForward had hosted a campaign to pay for someone to go to a weight-loss clinic and another for someone to have weight-loss surgery. WePay prohibits "magic, enchantment, sorcery, or other forms of yet-to-be-explained science," but GiveForward had hosted a campaign to accept "love gifts or love donations for psychic readings." WePay prohibits "hate, violence, racial intolerance, or the financial exploitation of a crime," but GiveForward had hosted a campaign that promised to reveal "the evils of the homosexual agenda."

Stryker's assertion that WePay was inconsistent at best and hypocritical at worst seemed confirmed when, less than six months after Alexander's campaign was closed, GoFundMe, another crowdfunding platform, partnered with WePay to host a campaign to support Darren Wilson, the Ferguson, Missouri, police officer who fatally shot the unarmed teenager Michael Brown.[66] Many people accused GoFundMe and WePay of violating their own terms of service, particularly the language about "hate, violence, racial intolerance, or the financial exploitation of a crime."[67] Backers of the campaign had posted statements like, "You deserve a medal, not a trial by jury" and "Thanks for giving that gorilla what he deserved."[68] Ultimately, the campaign raised $500,000 for Wilson.

There are perhaps reasons—which aren't totally obvious and don't necessarily make a lot of sense to the casual user of platform payments—that the campaign to benefit Darren Wilson was left open but the campaign to benefit Eden Alexander was closed. Foremost, no one offered racist materials to anyone who donated to the campaign, or, at least, no one organizing the campaign or benefiting from it retweeted such an offer. WePay did not respond to concerns about racist language on the campaign's page, but GoFundMe wrote a blog post defending itself against the "misinformation" surrounding the campaign. It argued that while there were many people on social media stating racist and hateful content in connection with the campaign, and even making comments on the GoFundMe page for the campaign itself, the organizers of the campaign were not responsible for the actions of others. Furthermore, the campaign's organizers had "repeatedly acknowledged and apologized for any offensive comments left by others and manually removed the comments from appearing on the campaign."[69]

WePay apparently draws very careful boundaries around what kinds of online behavior impact the transaction and violate terms of service. During the backlash following Alexander's account closure, a blog post from WePay claimed, "We have worked with other adult entertainers who use our service and abide by our terms of service without any issues."[70] A crowdfunding campaign may be supported by racists because they see it as a racist cause, but precisely when does the donation constitute a racist transaction?

In recent years, as racist groups have become bolder and sought to collect money for overtly racist goals, many have found that PSPs are unwilling to collect payments on their behalf. Hatreon—named as a portmanteau of the crowdfunding platform Patreon and the word "hate"—an explicitly alt-right crowdfunding platform, was embargoed by the card networks in 2017 before it could gain real any traction.[71] Cut off from payment, these racist groups have instead turned to Bitcoin wallets.[72]

As the internet researcher Tarleton Gillespie points out, platforms of all kinds routinely make these seemingly arbitrary calls about what is and is not acceptable, what does and does not violate terms of service.[73] The lines they draw are confusing and inconsistent. Racists and trolls are good at figuring out how to come right up to the edge of but not technically break a rule and knowing how and when to avail themselves of alternative systems. But for most people, including people who happen to be adult entertainers, these lines are hard to walk. And it's harder than you might think to know what is and what is not "adult entertainment": in 2018, many platforms reclassified ASMR videos—in which performers, mostly women, whisper and make other sounds in order to trigger in listeners a tingling feeling, sort of like the opposite of nails on chalkboard—as pornography.[74] YouTube demonetized the videos, and PayPal blocked ASMR's practitioners. A failure to anticipate and, as the science and technology studies scholars Wendy Espeland and Michael Sauder put it, "react" to unpredictability is experienced as a moral injunction and a loss of access to payment.[75]

What happens when you fall on the wrong side of terms of service? Or are flagged by predictive systems as a violator or as an opportunity for a computer to learn? In the traditional model, merchants are the client of the acquirer, but in platform payment systems, there is often little means of recourse to users. While platform payment systems tend to offer more avenues for complaint than other social media services do, users usually face a byzantine and ineffective process, with little choice but to comply and wait.

One method that seems to be effective is public shaming of the offending companies. One blogger saw WePay's offer to restart Alexander's campaign as an offer "to make an exception for her, because people complained."[76] If Alexander had not been a popular member of a vocal and visible online community, WePay would probably not have felt the need to publicly offer her the opportunity to start her campaign over, and CrowdTilt would probably not have publicly stepped in to offer her assistance. As an MSNBC blogger wrote of another high-profile account freeze by PayPal, "If you ever find yourself under the thumb of a corporate monolith, make sure you have an army of Internet followers to back you up."[77]

At one point in the course of my research for this chapter, I was tweeting a lot about how hard it was for sex workers to get paid.[78] A representative from a feminist sex-worker organization direct messaged me to find out if I had suggestions for a payment system that her group could use to collect entrance-fee donations for its annual conference. The representative explained to me that, on the one hand, she wanted to avoid companies that "actively discriminated against sex workers," but, even more importantly, her organization would be crippled if its account were suddenly frozen without timely recourse. She contacted several payment service providers and asked about what precisely would trigger a violation of terms of service. After all, she was organizing a conference *about* sex work, not paying or getting paid for sexual services. But she was considering paying honoraria to speakers, some of whom were sex workers. She didn't feel confident in any of the providers after hearing their answers.

And she had good reason to doubt any assurances. Indeed, there are plenty of stories from people in totally nonstigmatized situations: a blogger collecting money for Christmas toys for needy children and a game developer selling forum subscriptions that would finance completion of the game had contacted PayPal in advance, only to find that their accounts were frozen anyway.[79] Even as platforms embrace machine learning and automation in their fraud-detection strategies, sex work remains on the prohibited list. Indeed, in 2017, Gab, a social media platform popular among neo-Nazis for its lack of hate-speech moderation, was dropped by its payment processor, Stripe, for pornography.[80]

I struggled to give the organization representative a good answer. "Sexually oriented materials or services" are prohibited by the terms of service of most leading payment service providers, including PayPal, Square, Venmo, and Amazon Payments. Most of the payment service providers that are designed for use by sex workers aren't designed for individuals. For example, Verotel, one of the payment service providers cautiously suggested by the blog *Sex Worker Helpfuls*, specializes in payment processing for high-risk websites.[81] It is not clear how an individual sex worker, or a group organizing a conference, would be able to accept payments using it. Another company listed described itself as "the ultimate payroll solution for the adult entertainment industry" and was an e-wallet for managing paychecks from adult-entertainment companies. There seemed to be nothing that guaranteed reliable payments for sex workers.

It seems unlikely that the financial services industry will better serve sex workers anytime soon. In 2017, the End Banking for Human Traffickers Act passed the US House of Representatives and was introduced to the Senate by the strange bedfellows Marco Rubio and Elizabeth Warren. The legislation would, in a similar manner as Operation Choke Point, pressure banking and payment intermediaries to close accounts associated with suspected human traffickers.[82] Many advocates worry that such a law would do nothing to thwart "human trafficking" and instead would only hurt cam girls, porn performers, strippers, and other individual sex workers, making them even more vulnerable to an already unstable ecosystem.[83]

There were only two systems I could recommend to the woman with absolute certainty: cash and checks. Both, of course, were largely inappropriate for her purposes. It's unrealistic to expect a group to organize and promote a conference online, attract attendees from all over the world, but only accept donations and registration fees by mail. Paper payments alone—whether in the form of cash or check—simply can't move at the speed and geography of the internet era. They aren't able to keep pace with the way most of us live our lives today. The digital has become ordinary, and there seems to be no way for an independent individual also associated with the sex industry to *reliably* accept ordinary payments over digital channel, for any purpose. Porn performers and other sex workers have to choose between payment channels that are totally unreliable or totally inappropriate for the communicative reality and transactional community.

The technology of money has long tracked alongside the technologies that are used for communication more generally, and these technologies have created a shared geographic, temporal, and communicative lived experience: paper currency, like other forms of print culture, gathered people together under the auspices of the imagined community of the nation-state; postal expresses shipped currency and other forms of value alongside other forms of mail to further pull together far-flung regions into a communicative and economic whole; in the mid-twentieth century, electronic payment cards were part of an ecology of communication technologies, such as teletype, the highway and personal automobile, and democratized jet travel, which enabled people to travel with greater ease.

Today, people communicate electronically, quickly and across great distances. Internet access, at least according to the United Nations, is a human right, but what about access to payment systems that operate at the speed and scale of the internet?[84] Our economies, like our communicative worlds, are electronic: We expect to text message our roommates and Venmo them rent. We expect to be able to get paid by a friend, relative, or employer in another state. In addition to access and reliability, a fully functional form of getting paid should also be aligned with the reasonable communicative expectations of our transactional community.

Plenty of Americans receive payments in cash, and while they are often assumed to be dodging paying taxes, they may also simply be availing themselves of the only payment system that is self-clearing, immediate, and truly reliable.[85] Cash can't get caught up, lost, or diverted by the infrastructure. Unlike company scrip, Walmart vouchers, or Amazon gift cards, cash is, as is printed on US dollars, "legal tender for all debts public and private." Cash may not be, as a Diners Club executive put it in 1963, sufficiently "modern" because it "can't keep up with the fast-moving world"; but it *works*, and it generally works for everyone.[86]

Getting paid becomes a bit more complicated when we try to develop systems for getting paid that both "keep up with the fast-moving world" *and* actually work, for everyone. Since the 1990s, payment professionals have dreamed and developed ways for people to get paid electronically, something that previously only merchants had been able to do. But we still haven't gotten it right, not for everyone and not all of the time. The task for those who hope to design how we get paid in the future is to figure out how to maintain all the things cash gets right.

5 TRANSACTIONAL MEMORIES

Social Payments and Data Economies

IN a 2017 *New Yorker* comic, Olivia de Recat presents a series of hand-drawn Venmo transactions and decodes what they really mean.[1] Venmo, currently the most widespread person-to-person payment app in the United States, allows individuals to pay their friends directly. According to reporting in the business press, Venmo is unusually popular among "millennials," who use it to divvy up shared monthly expenses among roommates or settle up restaurant tabs when dining in a group in which no one has cash and the server is reluctant to split the check.[2] People can invoice their friends for money, as well as send it to them. Venmo includes a "social feed" of payments: when one person pays another, the transaction is made visible to all of both people's friends, not unlike a Facebook news feed or Twitter stream. Users are obliged by the platform to annotate their transactions with notes. For example, a user might add martini-glass emojis when paying a friend back for a round of drinks.

In de Recat's comic, the feed of transactions starts out innocuous: "Susan paid Kim"—*light bulb, electrical plug*—and the explanation, "Susan is paying her share of the electric bill." Then things take a turn for the heartrendingly personal: "Your ex"—the comic addresses its reader in the second person—makes an appearance, and "you" can't look away. Through a series of emoji-annotated transactions, you can see that your ex has gone out for beers with a work friend he once claimed to hate, that he's "being a martyr" by insisting on paying his roommate back some small amount of money, that he's going out for coffee with a mutual friend and there's no doubt they've "talked about how bad you're doing."

And then you see it: Chloe has paid for your ex and captioned the transaction with *sushi* and *smiley face*. The evidence is clear: "Your ex is having sex with some girl named Chloe." You click on Chloe's feed. She charged your ex for John Mayer, indicating that he took her to the concert with tickets you bought him for his birthday! But wait a minute. Chloe is also doing all sorts of things you find kind of cool. She paid her friend Samantha for "Lichten-stein at the Broad Museum," an exhibit you've been meaning to check out. She paid Austin for "poetry reading." You wonder, "Maybe she'll be at the pop-up show this weekend and you'll meet really organically."

You do indeed meet, "really organically" of course. These days, you're paying Chloe—*palm tree, sunshine*—because "You went to the beach and discussed how weird your ex's feet are, how he never fully washes his dishes, and how his relationship with his sister is kind of unsettling." And your ex is getting paid by some new girl named Piper—*hamburger, heart*—and you know what that means. And then the comic comes full circle: "Chloe paid you"—*light bulb emoji, electrical plug emoji*—and the explanation, "Chloe is paying her share of the electric bill."

Breaking up, starting new friendships, moving into new apartments. Venmo is a scrapbook, a shoebox stuffed full of receipts and stories. A scroll back through a Venmo feed reveals a thousand memories, silly, shameful, and precious. The narrator of Marcel Proust's *In Search of Lost Time* nibbles a madeleine dipped in tea and is taken on a journey through his own past, a flight of nostalgia that constitutes his vast novel series, which is itself a medita-tion on memory and modernity. Today's "Proustian moment" might be triggered instead by a Venmo transaction: "You paid Aunt Léonie for Starbucks"—where, conveniently, both madeleines and tea are currently sold.[3] Sadly there is no madeleine emoji to use on Venmo.

Venmo, it is clear, is a technology of memory.[4] It is an example of what the sociologists Alya Guseva and Akos Rona-Tas call the "new sociability of money": the ability of digital money technologies to "preserve the details of economic transactions, to capture our geographic movements, to infer our tastes and routines."[5] As Nigel Dodd writes, "a device for *remembering* cannot be divorced from the criticism that it is also a vehicle for political and commercial *surveillance*, above, as long as the technology involved is controlled by corporations and states."[6] What happens when transactional memory, once private, becomes materialized and surveilled by friends and frenemies, states and corporations?

The memories that Venmo records *seem* like they'd be only interesting to you—they're the mundane details of your own life. It's the same quotidian overshare that critics of social media regularly lampoon, but even more so. No one really tweets about what they ate for lunch, but they do Venmo about it. Venmo makes these otherwise-private memories—this wad of receipts—public and connected, a form of social media. Venmo doesn't just connect us dyadically—whom we paid and who paid us—but enables us to traverse the memories of the financial lives of others by making transactions visible, transforming them into a social stream.

For example, in a 2014 episode of the technology and culture podcast *Reply All*, Chiara Atik tells of the prurient pleasures of the peek that Venmo offers into the financial lives, the financial memories, of others.[7] In the podcast, Atik describes how she found a series of transactions from one of her acquaintances, "Melanie," particularly compelling. First, Atik noticed that Melanie was billing her long-term live-in girlfriend for a lot of things, such as a chandelier and "half a couch." It looked to Atik like an acrimonious breakup in which Melanie and her (now ex-) girlfriend were divvying up their belongings. Then Atik noticed that Melanie seemed to be on the rebound, charging and paying her friends for "Pizza night with the girls." These gave way to dating transactions for "Taxi, dinner, drinks." Then, Melanie seemed to have found love again, demonstrated by airplane emojis designating weekend getaways. It's the same story as in de Recat's comic. It's the same story as a thousand other stories. The crucial difference, however, is that Atik isn't telling her own story. Now, thanks to Venmo, it has a viewer, a third-person narrator.

In recent years, there has been something of a miniature moral panic around Venmo. In a fairly steady flow of think pieces, it is blamed for bringing money into relationships, making them pettier and more transactional.[8] It said to produce FOMO, or fear of missing out, among those who peruse their friends' feeds, convinced their friends are all having a good time without them. Venmo is, users are scolded, another example of how voyeuristic, how "addicted" to social media, we have become.

And yet people seem to love Venmo. It's the "best social network," and its social feed is its "secret sauce."[9] As the reporter Samantha Cole put it on Vice Motherboard in 2018, Venmo feels "a little scandalous, another baby step toward the deep end of eroding online privacy. You know, in a fun way."[10]

And even beyond mere voyeurism, people find ways to express a range of socialities through Venmo. Users "penny poke" their friends, sending a small sum of money or, say, the exact price of their favorite coffee or beer, to cheer them up.[11] Venmo has been used to connect with celebrities: fans of the *Bachelor* contestant Becca Kufrin sent her money for wine after she was eliminated from the show, and frustrated Americans trolled then–White House press secretary Sean Spicer, requesting, for example, that he donate to victims of the "Bowling Green Massacre," a fictitious event that the counselor to the president Kellyanne Conway used to justify the executive order banning travel and immigration from seven majority-Muslim countries.[12] Usage continues to rise, reviving the person-to-person payment sector, which had been seen for a long time as both crowded with competitors and failing to gain traction among users. One industry consultant told me at a 2017 fin-tech event, "Who knew that all it would take would be to add emojis and make it more like Twitter?"

Person-to-person payment technology, the message was, needed to figure out how to become social media, and it seems like it has. Recent headlines in the tech press declared both that payment apps like Venmo are poised to become "the next big social network" and that "social media apps have become payment apps."[13] In the past five years, there have been attempts by nearly all major social media (and social media adjacent) platforms—including Google, Apple, Facebook, Instagram, and Snapchat—to roll out payment services, with varying degrees of ambition and success.

Payment has not yet become fully embedded into social media platforms—and payments innovators have been claiming that it will, soon, for at least a decade—but it makes sense that these predictions will prove accurate sooner rather than later. Payment is an important part of our communicative worlds, which are aligned with our transactional communities. Consider WeChat, the "everything app" that is ubiquitous in China. For WeChat's nine hundred million daily users, everything that can be done on the mobile phone, on the internet itself, is done through the WeChat platform. On WeChat, you can arrange to meet a friend for lunch, locate a nearby restaurant, book a table, place your orders, and pay the tab.

At the 2017 Money2020, the largest and most influential fintech trade show, WeChat was on everyone's minds. Which industry actors—or combination of industry actors—could bring a WeChat-like experience to the US market? Crucial to this vision, of course, was payment. As we live more of our lives through social media, payment becomes an essential feature of any full communication environment.

Becoming social media is not only about adding emojis. Rather, it means that payment instruments must adopt the underlying logics of social media systems, how they configure social relations, structure the flow of communication, and allocate value.[14] Social media and money are both technologies of memory, and both are part of what the media scholar Jordan Frith has called "a new memory ecology" assembled on mobile phones.[15] Whenever we write an email or take a selfie with a friend, we create a small artifact of our lives that lingers on, extending our private memories into the domain of data.[16] And as our personal archives grow, they shape how and when we encounter the past, a novel way of knowing ourselves that the media theorist José van Dijck describes as a "multimodal" form of remembering.[17]

Today, many of us entrust our mediated memories to social media systems. On a platform like Facebook, the artifacts of our pasts swirl together, flowing across a network of social relationships, personal and professional. Scholars describe this blurring of the boundaries between individual and collective memories as a "connective turn."[18] Within this connected environment, past and present fold into each other as the platform assembles a seemingly endless stream of images, videos, comments, and advertisements. Browsing this "timeline," one is likely to encounter a range of mediated memories: from moments of intimacy and personal significance to events of global importance. Unlike the photo album stored on a shelf, the multimodal, connected form of remembering on social media can be disorienting, embarrassing, enlightening, distressing.

Money, as a form of media, is also a technology of memory. Indeed, scholars across fields and for varied purposes have argued as much. For example, in 1998, Narayana Kocherlakota, an economist and former president of the United States Federal Reserve Bank of Minneapolis, published a paper simply titled "Money Is Memory." In it, he uses game design to show how "money" (defined as a set of tokens) and "memory" (defined as the ability to remember past interactions) both provide the same affordances across various economic environments. In an environment with memory, an "imaginary balance sheet" is maintained for each agent. In an environment with money, those tokens are a physical way of maintaining this balance sheet. Money, then, is a "technological innovation" that simulates memory and allows "societies to implement allocations that would not otherwise be achievable."[19] Having conducted these thought experiments, Kocherlakota argues that the real reason money exists is that it helps to keep track of the past.

The anthropologist Keith Hart points out that the word "money" comes from *Moneta*, a Roman translation of the Greek *Mnemosyne*, the goddess of memory. Money is, for Hart, a "memory bank." It is a form of shared credit, a way of remembering promises of value, projecting them into the future, and sharing them with other members of an economy, a society, or a transactional community. He argues that money is primarily "an instrument of collective memory" and "a way of keeping track of some of the exchanges we each enter into with the rest of humanity."[20] Money, like language, is a memory infrastructure. It is a distributed, invisible record of human exchange.

In both of these views, money's memory bank, unless set into record, remains inchoate, amorphous. The way that money remembers isn't the same way that humans do, necessarily. Rather, money is a technology that enables a kind of external collective memory system. Cash circulates hand to hand. It lives a life not too different from those described by eighteenth-century English "it-narratives," a popular genre of fiction in which inanimate objects, such as currency, told their life story.[21] In Thomas Bridges's 1771 "The Adventures of a Bank-Note," our hero passes from a milliner to a bishop's wife to the bishop to a bookseller to a pastry cook and to a seller of dead dogs. In these stories, money objects want to move. As Liz Bellamy points out, in tales like the autobiographies of the banknote, the shilling, and the rupee, being saved by a miser and kept from circulation is "unnatural" and akin to "imprisonment."[22] Money is made to move, and as it moves, it collects "memories." In this way, money has what the anthropologist Bill Maurer calls "distributed agency": it records "the stories of humanity, mapping relations in time, space, and value, and memorializing" the actions of humans.[23]

For cash and coin, the only real evidence, however, of the memory journey of money is the way that it pools and accrues in certain places—with certain people—and not others. These money objects trace human interactions, but they do not physically bear the traces of their history, their memory. This is part of cash's capacity as an antisurveillance tool. For the sociologist Georg Simmel, cash allowed early moderns to live as strangers, unknown and surveilled, in newly urban environments.[24] Since the 1990s, cypherpunks dreamed of creating "digital cash" that would afford the same privacy online yet still function as a viable money form.[25] For those who are looking for freedom from being remembered, cash remembers just enough.

But not all money technologies remember in the same way. Some are designed to keep track of, as the anthropologist Jane Guyer puts it, "accounts in both the narrative and mathematical senses."[26] In a description of a contemporary Ecuadorian informal family bank, or *caja*, the anthropologist Taylor Nelms illustrates the narrative memorial capacity of money and the records used to track it.[27] The point of the *caja* is to help members of the family get by economically, but it also keeps the family close, obligated to each other. It's an intentional instantiation of Simmel's vision of patrimonial bondage. Members of the family contribute to and draw from the bank, and a trusted member of the family keeps careful account of these transactions. Nelms writes, "Such documentation serves as external memory device; as confirmation and sometimes evidence; as testimony to a transaction realized and sum transferred; and as visible display of one's status, credibility, and trustworthiness."[28] The ledger book is like a family Bible inscribed with births, deaths, and marriages. As the matriarch records, remembers transactions, she creates solidarity among family members; she gathers it from the past and pitches it into the future.

Like the members of the family *caja*, people often seem to be building systems to capture the memories that money makes. They make registry websites like Where's George? to track dollar bills. They try to make physical their "earmarking" of "special monies" by enclosing them in special envelopes or folding them into origami keepsakes.[29] They graffiti cash for political or superstitious reasons or simply to assert their onetime possession of the bill. The technologist Jaron Lanier argues that cash is "too forgetful" a technology to support a fair, digital economy of the future.[30] Instead, he advocates for the development of "economic avatars" that help us remember and be remembered by those with whom we transact. A money that remembers better is, for many people, the "dream" promised by blockchain: a perfect transactional memory, a truly distributed ledger of all money's distributed agency, eternal and transcendent of human incapacity, remembering everything and beholden to no one.[31]

Even when no one is overtly trying to keep account of accounts for sentimental or political purposes, money leaves mementos.

Where's George? is an advertising-supported site that tracks the travels of US currency.

Nelms points out, "Even supposedly anonymous cash leaves traces as it travels: credits and debits scratched into account books; receipts spit out by ATMs or handed over by clerks."[32] These artifacts have a politics. The literary scholar Mary Poovey describes how, in early-modern Europe, the emergence and standardization of double-entry bookkeeping signified that such records should be considered facts and that those who maintain such records should be considered honest and prudent.[33] The reality of business is messy, but the transformation of transactions into account books, the concretization of memory, made it seem more precise, less fallible. The historian Jacob Soll demonstrates how the maintenance—and crucially *publication*—of state accounts led to the French Revolution.[34] Accounting came to imply accountability. Poovey and Soll point out that social relations are configured by how accounting records count as fact and evidence and who maintains and has access to viewing these records.

Venmo may seem strange for its "public displays of transaction."[35] Indeed, as Quinn DuPont and Bill Maurer point out, accounting records themselves were once considered "private and precious."[36] Financial records—like diaries—were confidential affairs, only accessible to male heads of household and their trusted advisers. Indeed, there is a longer history here. Venmo is just the latest in a long line of consumer payment technologies that organize how money remembers.

The communication scholar Lee Humphreys describes the kind of memory work that people do with social media as "media accounting."[37] We have long used a variety of media forms—scrapbooks, diaries, letters—to "account": to offer evidence of our subjective experience of the world for others and for the future. Financial accounting and media accounting have a lot in common. They both involve not only quantifying by keeping track of experience but also, as Humphreys points out, "qualifying" by describing it. The concept of media accounting helps us see the qualification practices that lie beneath the surface of monetary media accounting. The same themes—how records transform memory into "fact," who has access to these records, and how they configure social relations—recur in the history of both kinds of personal accounting.

The payments industry has undergone a series of shifts since the mid-twentieth century. Modern checking disciplined the transactional memory of individuals. Early charge cards transformed this memory keeping into a luxury service. Debit cards automated the connection between institutional and personal accounting. With the Visa/Mastercard network, payment cards more broadly generated a massive amount of transactional data, mostly used for operational purposes. Of late, this data—transactional memory itself—has become an object of speculative interest by Silicon Valley.

The modern checkbook—the kind that is rapidly disappearing but can still be seen, much bemoaned, in grocery-store checkout lines—is a device made up of two complementary parts: a stack of tear-away checks for payment and a book of ledger paper. Their design implies their ideal use case: you write the check, making note of its purpose in the "memo" field, tear it from the book, and dutifully deduct the amount from the ledger. Checks are personal promises fulfilled by institutions. Balancing a checkbook is remembering those promises.

Checkbooks compel account holders to maintain a transactional memory system parallel to but independent of the bank's institutional memory. Maintaining a checkbook's ledger takes work. Account holders are obliged to collect receipts, anticipate fees, and set aside time to perform the necessary calculations. In order to avoid bouncing checks, they must stay one step ahead of the bank, anticipating which checks have not yet cleared. As Bank of America put it in a pamphlet for customers in 1976, a balanced checkbook offers "a built-in review of your daily financial situation."[38]

Technically, of course, checkbooks are personal affairs—individuals are not obliged to keep double-entry surveyable accounts the way publicly traded companies are. Certainly, over the years, many people have opted to rely on their own memory, even intuition, rather than the ledger. In the words of one abstainer, "I just write them and rip them out."[39] The checkbook itself is ultimately beyond the reach of institutional surveillance or control. But while banks could not force check writers also to be checkbook balancers, they could assemble systems that brought personal memory practice in line with that of the institution.

Checks are an old technology—the Smithsonian Money Gallery holds checks from George Washington, produced long before his face appeared on the one-dollar bill—but they became widespread in the United States in the 1950s. The overall number of checking accounts in the United States doubled between 1939 and 1952, rising to forty-seven million.[40] In the same time period, checking became standardized and automated, due to technologies like magnetic ink character recognition (MICR), which standardized routing and account numbers as well as the font and ink used to print them and allowed them to be machine readable, and Bank of America's Electronic Recording Machine, Accounting (ERMA), which automated check processing and helped banks overcome what was becoming a "paper-handling crisis."[41]

Banks compelled check writers to keep up with these new technologies of efficiency. A report circulated by the American Bankers Association in 1961 outlined a "six-step procedure" for balancing a checkbook, emphasizing the responsibility of individual account holders to ensure that their records were correct.[42] A staff writer for the *Los Angeles Times* compared checkbook management to flossing one's teeth: "onerous but necessary for financial health."[43] A correctly balanced checkbook became a symbol of personal responsibility. Personal memory that was fully in sync with authoritative memory became a marker of virtue.

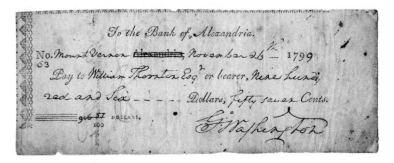

A 1799 check for $906.57 from George Washington.

While banks are required by law to provide account holders access to their records, they may charge a fee for balance inquiries. In 1963, a representative of the First National City Bank in New York complained that customers who "can't or won't" balance their checkbooks were wasting the time of branch employees with "frequent and costly" balance inquiries.[44] The checkbook ledger was also the only real means to dispute the records kept by banks. "The bank statement-checkbook balancing chore should be attended to as soon as possible," chided one writer at the *Chicago Daily Tribune*. "Unless you report errors to the bank, the statement will be considered correct."[45] Impeccable personal record keeping was seen as the only defense against error in the official record.

While checks were a far more ubiquitous noncash payment form, the mid-twentieth century also saw the addition of the charge card to Americans' pockets and pocketbooks. As much as offering a new way to pay, the charge card offered a new way to manage personal transactional memory. The burden of accounting for payment was lifted from elite cardholders. Whereas banks asked checking-account holders to manage a private transactional memory, the providers of charge cards repackaged everyday bookkeeping into a service.

Charge cards, such as the Diners Club card, which debuted in the 1950s, allowed elites to pay for things at restaurants, department stores, and other businesses and then be sent one itemized bill at the end of the month, which they were expected to pay in full.[46] The chore of tracking checks was replaced by the monthly statement. As one contemporary observer put it, the Diners Club statement was "in orderly contrast to the promiscuous scattering of bills."[47] You could bounce a check if you didn't keep careful accounts, but if you held a Diners Club card, you didn't need to remember or account for every transaction; it was assumed that you'd settle the one bill when it came.

Charge cards reorganized audiences for personal transactional memories. Most Diners Club cards were used for business purposes, and Diners Club mailed a list of itemized receipts to the cardholder's office, effectively outsourcing the labor of settling employee travel expenses. This became particularly useful when, in the late 1950s, the IRS raised the standards of documentation for tax-deductible business entertainment expenses. Submitting a stack of well-organized Diners Club statements was the "perfect way to squelch the doubting Thomases at the Bureau of Internal Revenue."[48] The Diners Club statement transformed travel and entertainment into official business expenses. It also made elite businessmen accountable to their managers, and their managers to the IRS.

In addition to disciplining the employee and appeasing the auditor, the record that charge cards provided was a means of surveillance within the family. The typical primary cardholder was a professional man, and he could—by just checking a box on the Diners Club application—have his personal statement along with that of his wife sent to his office rather than to his home, thus providing a mechanism to monitor his wife's spending and obscure his own. The sexism of this information asymmetry contrasted with women's responsibility for the management of home finances. By 1975, the Bank of Ravenswood in Chicago estimated that nearly two-thirds of the checks drawn from joint checking accounts were endorsed by women.[49]

In the 1980s, credit cards—associated with a line of rotating credit that allowed a cardholder to carry a balance—became more common than charge cards. In 1985, a *New York Times* writer described credit cards as "a superb instrument for record keeping" but also warned against the dangers of "impulse buying, excessive buildup of debt and using the credit card as a loan instrument."[50] In advertisements of the day, BankAmericard urged consumers to use their credit card like a store of value, to "think of it as money." But, according to the *New York Times* article, those who instead thought of their card as a record-keeping device were seen as "judicious," and those who used it as a line of credit were described as "junkies."[51]

In the 1990s, the checkbook and the payment card seemed to merge. The "check card" or "enhanced ATM card"—as the debit card was initially branded to avoid a sound-alike association with credit card "debt"—combined the form factor of the payment card with the institutional structure of the checking account.[52] By 1999, debit cards outnumbered credit cards and were described in the *New York Times* as "provid[ing] the records a business person needs."[53] When processed as "online transactions"—online in the sense that they were processed through the card networks immediately, not online in today's "on the internet" sense—debit cards eliminated the delay between writing and clearing a check.

While this development might have freed cardholders from reconciling personal and institutional accounting, it also unsettled existing temporal practices. Many people—either daredevils or simply those trying to make ends meet at the end of the month—wrote checks not fully knowing if there would be sufficient funds in the account to cover them. It was impossible to "kite" a payment with a debit card. With online transactions, the deduction from a debit card payment was made instantly and automatically, thanks to cooperative data networks linking merchants and banks.[54] Instead, the card would simply be declined, regardless of what the cardholder had written in his or her checkbook. For banks, debit transactions were cheaper to process, and the option to automatically decline a payment eliminated the need to manage "bounced" checks.[55]

In practice, not all transactions were processed instantly. Banks therefore maintained the expectation that account holders would manage their own personal ledgers of transactional memory. As late as 2000, conventional wisdom maintained that debit transactions should be recorded in a checkbook, lest one lose track of one's balance and accidentally overdraft.[56] Forgetting to do so could be costly—$35 overdraft fees added up quickly.

If anything, debit cards made personal financial memory keeping more complex. Mixing card and check payments from the same account substantially complicated the work of balancing one's checkbook. In 1991, Kathy M. Kristof, a financial advice columnist for the *Los Angeles Times*, cautioned new debit card holders to be mindful of their swipes. "Because you don't need to pull out your checkbook," she warned, "you might fail to record the fact that you electronically deducted [a] purchase amount from your account."[57] Even the most disciplined checkbook balancers struggled to keep track of the transaction fees levied by banks and merchants. Depending on the merchant, network, and bank, using a debit card could incur fees ranging up to two dollars, a levy that could amount to a substantial, and unpredictable, sum at the end of each month.

In spite of the record-keeping challenge, the adoption of debit cards quickly outpaced credit cards in the United States.[58] As debit card holders wrote fewer and fewer checks, they began to leave their checkbooks at home. Banks began offering "overdraft protection," small lines of credit designed to absorb the cost of an accidental overdraft. This allowed cardholders to save face at the point of sale, but critics held that overdraft protection "tempted" checking-account holders—particularly younger people—into taking on debts with unusually high interest rates.[59] Meanwhile, banks and merchants celebrated a shift toward "bigger" and "freer" payments among debit card holders.[60] "If you drive into a gas station with $20 in your pocket, you put in $10 [worth of gasoline]," suggested one Mastercard representative, "With a debit card, you fill it up."[61] Balancing a checkbook began to seem like a "lost art."[62]

Today, debit cards are still the most widely used noncash payment form, but few people balance their checking account, especially not with a physical ledger, instead monitoring their balances through online banking portals. Checking-account holders aren't expected to maintain their own transactional memory systems; they're expected to trust and track the authoritative record.

With the emergence of the card networks—the rails on which both debit and credit cards run—in the 1970s, there came a shift in transactional memory systems. An important aspect of this shift was scale: the payments industry began to generate a massive amount of transactional data. Another was type: for the most part, this data is used for operational purposes. As David L. Stearns describes, the card network is a system of sending and receiving standardized messages that instruct the flow of funds.[63] It is fundamentally a system of connected record keeping that requires shared metadata standards. It links the transactional memories of cardholders, issuers, acquirers, processors, and merchants together in a shared communicative environment.

Nevertheless, while these various parties in the payment process have long had access to different components of the transactional record, no single actor has been able to witness the whole chain of activity. In this traditional card model, which persists to this day, I can see my statements, and I have access to my memory of purchases, which I can keep account of in various ways. But I don't know much about the transactional lives of others, including those whom I pay and who pay me. I also don't know much about what others—card issuers, merchants—know about me and how information about me circulates.

My card issuer knows a lot about me: account balances, repayment behavior, and anything revealed when I applied for a card. The issuer can see where I shop and when I shop and how much I spend. It can track me over time and make inferences about my transactional life. This is true not just for me but for the issuer's millions of cardholders. A card issuer can't, however, see *what* I buy. It can see that I've spent $150 at Trader Joe's on August 15, but it can't see which products fill my cart. And, of course, any one issuer only gets a partial view of my spending: Chase can't see what I buy with my UVA Credit Union debit card.

Conversely, merchants can see what I buy but, historically, not a whole lot more.[64] Even merchants with relatively simple systems can keep track of item-level data using SKUs, or stock keeping units. Nevertheless, there's a lot that merchants can't see unless I tell them. Merchants don't know very much about me as an individual. They can't see all the things I'm buying at other stores. They can't track any one customer's purchasing behavior over time. Some merchants, like drugstores, have tried to learn more about customers by offering loyalty cards—the little plastic kind you're supposed to put on your key ring and scan at checkout—to get a longitudinal view.

Historically, various actors in the payments industry have attempted to use this data in various ways: risk assessment, card-linked marketing, and other predictive analytics. While, as Josh Lauer points out, credit bureaus were really the first data brokers, this credit-granted function was somewhat siloed from actual transactions.[65] But it took the imagination of social media, an industry driven by the promised value of social data, to animate serious shifts around the potential value of transactional data. The data imperative of Silicon Valley transformed—or at least has the goal of transforming—transactional memories into a source of value.

When payment becomes fully "social media," it will do so in a very specific meaning of the term. Although these new systems promise personalization and emphasize the social nature of payment, they are also "social" in the Silicon Valley sense of the word: like other forms of social media, they are tied to business models predicated on gathering data about users.[66] Indeed, the transition of payment to a form of social media marks a larger but as yet largely unrealized shift in the payments industry: from transactional fees to transactional data. In 2012, *TechCrunch* argued that we were "in the midst of a great revolution in the payments space": it predicted that "payment data is more valuable than payment fees."[67] In order to figure out how to make a shift from transactional fees to transactional records, payment apps will have to do more than figure out how to reconfigure who is able to see what. They also have to figure how to make that data valuable.

The goal of most new payment systems is to create a new set of sieves for collecting data.[68] The "wallet wars," as some people in the industry have dubbed the race to release a successful mobile payment system in the United States, are in many ways a set of conflicts over ownership of and access to transactional data.[69] Mobile payment apps not only collect payment data but link it to all the other streams of personal, social, and locational data passing through the payer's smartphone. An important component of the payment-app data imperative is shuffling who can see what.

The race to produce a widely adopted mobile app is not simply about producing and selling a new technology. Rather, the winner of these "wars" will be in the best position to exploit the much more lucrative interest in transactional data that will result from the mass adoption of new payment practices. The emergent data imperative creates a market for audienceship for the transactional record.

Just as payment generates incidental records of the past, our moment-to-moment activities on connective media systems like Facebook leave behind traces of our social lives. Beyond the photos we upload and comments we post, social media platforms also track the links we click, videos we watch, and even the drafts of comments that we *don't* post.[70] The automatic collection of behavioral data, however momentary or insignificant, is a fundamental component of the logic of social media. This process, termed "datafication" by the theorists José van Dijck and Thomas Poell, is premised on a belief that these bits of digital ephemera will yield value in the aggregate.[71] Indeed, social media platforms expend tremendous resources to record the minute activities of their users in the hope of one day exploiting that data for financial gain.[72]

As Silicon Valley turns its attention to payment, the logics of social media are being applied to the records generated by our everyday financial activity. They structure the memory function of payment in two ways. First, from the perspective of a social media business, the records of payment are an underexploited resource, a new genre of personal data to add to companies' existing portfolios of user surveillance. Second, the social media industry builds multisided platforms, marketplaces where the data generated by one set of stakeholders (us) is sold to another set of stakeholders (advertisers). In the context of social media, payment is yet another mediated social activity that produces data to be aggregated, analyzed, packaged, and sold.

As new "social" payment systems document transactions, they produce a persistent ledger that previously existed as an unarticulated form of transactional memory, personal and collective.

In addition to reifying the sociality of payments as a record, these systems enclose it. Transactions have become transactional data. Previously thought of as a form of "personal data," transactions have become a kind of "social data" that promises to—someday, maybe—be a source of revenue. The memories of our transactional lives are newly materialized, surveyable, and privatized. What should we make of this interest in records of our transactional memories? What can be learned if we turn—as Anna Reading and other social media scholars suggest—to the political economy of our payment memory factories?[73]

Google has perhaps the clearest plan for extracting value from transactional data, but it has struggled to bring a successful payment product to market. Beginning in 2011, Google has offered several iterations of payment service: Android Pay, Google Wallet, Google Pay, Google Pay Send. While the underlying structure of Google's payment product has changed with each new version, the overarching vision remains characteristic of Google's standard model: targeted marketing.[74] Marketers are the new—or at least newly important—viewers of the transactional record. As marketing pundits put it, mobile payment apps represent the "holy grail" of online marketing: the ability to track highly targeted advertising messages through to an actual point of purchase, in real location and time.[75]

Although Google (and its parent company, Alphabet) promise "moonshots"—ambitious, risky projects that just might change the world—it tends to generate revenue in the same way, over and over: advertising. It offers products and services—search, mail, maps, documents, video—for "free" in exchange for data that it can sell to marketers. In 2017, Google's ad revenues amounted to approximately $95 billion and accounted for about 87 percent of the company's total revenue.[76] According to the company's annual reports to the Securities and Exchange Commission, advertising on mobile, the kind most relevant to mobile payments, drove the company's annual revenue up more than $44 billion from 2013 to 2017.[77] Google does not allow direct access to user data; instead, it brokers filtered access to web users. Advertisers bid to have their ads placed in the search engine and on other websites according to the individual user's search history and proprietary Google profile.[78] An industry has grown up around Google's advertising. Third-party companies, many of which are certified "Google Partners," help advertisers interface with Google's products.[79] When Google changes its policies or practices, advertisers and advertising consultants must change their tactics accordingly. Because Google overwhelmingly dominates the way people experience the internet, it is the gatekeeper to how the internet is monetized.

The 2011 launch video for Google Wallet provides an early idealized version of the Google vision of payments.[80] It shows the journey of a group of friends as they buy gifts on the way to another friend's birthday brunch. One man searches—using Google, of course—on his home computer for a gift, and he finds a local shop that has what he wants and is offering, through Google Wallet, a discount coupon. With a click, he sends the coupon to his phone and stops to buy the gift on his way to brunch. One woman, waiting in line while picking up a cup of on-the-go coffee, is delighted to see that she can tap her phone to a poster and, through near-field communication (NFC), automatically sign up for a loyalty program and get her tenth coffee for free. She then uses her phone to search for "Deals Near Me" and is off to find flowers. This is a "transaction-sorted" geography.[81] Tracking and personalization grow legs like an evolving fish and emerge from the internet into public space. In the same way that Google search organizes our interaction with and access to online information, Google Wallet organizes space and our movement through it.

Whatever form the Google way to pay finally takes, it creates a ledger of transactional memory that can be put into conversation with existing personal and social data sets and then used for targeted marketing. Google has gone to great lengths to secure its access to this data, betting that it will be worth more than the costs of collecting it. Whatever form Google's payment product ultimately takes, the transactional data that Google collects through Google Wallet will most likely be organized and made available according to similar principles as the data it collects about other user behavior.

The Google Wallet, as a social payment system, creates a new way of recording and viewing transactional memories, which is offered up to marketers to direct "traffic" through the web and—ideally—the world. It doesn't allow marketers to see these records directly, but they are treated as fact by marketers that hope to reach targeted populations. The results—optimized search results—are experienced as fact by users.

But what does the information that Google sells to advertisers represent? Does Google test the validity of the data caught in its dragnet? The media theorist John Cheney-Lippold argues that the power of surveillance companies rests on their ability to analyze massive stores of trace data to preexisting social categories such as gender, race, and class.[82] Companies like Facebook and Google perform this inferential work continuously and automatically, resulting in streams of metadata about the users who populate their platforms. Marketers bidding for ad space assume that this categorization of users is accurate, that the "algorithmic identities" produced by these systems are meaningfully related to the human beings clicking, tapping, and swiping somewhere out in the world. Yet, with the incomplete picture provided by the platform, there is no guarantee. Payment data—verifiable records of actual transactions—appears to close this gap.

Perhaps because of Google's dominance on the web, the company has faced resistance from nearly all fronts in its efforts to bring a digital wallet to market. It has clashed with device makers and mobile-network operators over territorial control of mobile phone hardware. It has struggled to find models that circumvent paying interchange fees to card issuers without collecting them from acquirers and merchants. Perhaps most importantly, it has failed to find a compelling consumer-use case.

In the 2014 launch presentation for Apple Pay, CEO Tim Cook argued that the time had come to "replace" the wallet with the mobile phone. Many other companies had been trying, but they "started by focusing on creating a business model that was centered around their self-interest, instead of focusing on the user experience." Apple, he argued, was the right company to steward this part of everyday life. As Cook put it, "security is at the core of Apple Pay, but so is privacy."[83] In the payments industry, security—the ability to protect personal information from those who would use it for illegal purposes—has always been paramount. But in the "social" technology industry, privacy—the ability to control the flow of personal information from those who would use it for legal purposes—has been limited. At the intersection of these two industry imaginaries, security is necessary, but privacy is a luxury.

Unlike Google, which is an advertising company, Apple is a maker of luxury devices. In an interview with the *New York Times* following the launch, Tim Cook said, "We're not looking at it through the lens that most people do of wanting to know what you're buying, where you buy it at, how much you're spending and all these kinds of things. We could care less."[84] Apple's official online product-support guide reads, "Apple Pay doesn't collect any transaction information that can be tied back to you. Payment transactions are between you, the merchant, and your bank."[85]

In this way, Apple Pay offers privacy not just from those who are legally seeking to monetize personal data but from those who are seeking to steal it: Apple can't leak what it doesn't have. Apple Pay was released at the same time as Apple Watch, which could be integrated with Apple Pay to make purchases, as well as to collect data about the wearer's physical health. Transactional memory becomes, alongside steps walked and nutritional macros consumed, part of the array of "quantified self" applications. And as the communication scholar Deborah Lupton notes, this kind of "self-tracking," of memory work, "represents the apotheosis of the neoliberal entrepreneurial citizen ideal."[86] Apple positioned itself as a steward of these most intimate and potentially valuable data sets. The record of transactional memories remain, as Quinn DuPont and Bill Maurer have suggested, safe and "in the closet" with Apple.[87]

Cook's appeal to privacy and security outlined a technological arrangement, as much as a business-model promise. Whereas mobile providers had been able to bar Google from accessing the "secure element" on phones that they resell, Apple controls all of the hardware and software that make up its ecosystem. As a result,

Apple has the ability to unilaterally standardize and implement new technological features. Apple Pay uses a technology called "tokenization" to better ensure customers' data protection. Each iPhone or Apple Watch has a specific device-only token—effectively an alias of a card provided to Apple by the issuer—that is stored in a "secure element" on the device itself. No actual account numbers are stored either on the device or on Apple servers. In theory, this means that the only parties with any access to the personal information tied to transactions are the customer and the customer's card issuer. If someone steals this token and tries to use it from another phone, it won't work, because the token is specific to your device and the associated cryptography will tell the issuer that it is not on your device.[88]

In order to achieve this arrangement, Apple had to broker deals with major issuers, including JPMorgan Chase, Bank of America, and Citigroup. Although the details of these deals aren't public, it seems that the issuers will pay Apple from the interchange fees they collect from acquirers, which acquirers collect from merchants.[89] Through this partnership, Apple can access the existing payment infrastructure, which is incredibly complex and has proven intractable, while ensuring that big financial firms will continue to play a role in the system. These large banks may also see promise in Apple's commitment to improving security—for example, the company has been a leader in the adoption of tokenization, a technological arrangement in which the card number is shielded from even the merchant accepting it, something banks themselves have been slow to implement because of associated costs. By meeting some of the payments industry's existing needs, Apple has made itself part of the value chain of actual money, not just transactional data, which is merely the promise of eventual monetization.

Of course, as is the case with American Express and rewards cards like Chase Sapphire Reserve, merchants have proven willing to accept high interchange if it means having access to the "best" customers, and Apple certainly boasts some of the most affluent people in the world as users. As one technology pundit put it, "From the day it slipped out of Steve Jobs' womb and onto credit card bills, the iPhone was a dearly coveted bourgeois object. It was expensive, fancy without ostentation, and semi-affluent white people loved it like their own progeny. It is the phone of actors, models, rappers, academics, and graphic designers living beyond their means. There's never in history been an electronic class beacon so clear as the iPhone."[90] When merchants agree to accept Apple Pay and place the Apple logo by their cash registers, they signal their place in the circuits of the discriminating, high-end consumer. Privacy becomes a question of control over transactional memory. While the wealthy—and, indeed, on a global scale, iPhone users are among the wealthiest and make up only a small percentage of all smartphone users—can pay for control over their privacy by purchasing iPhones, everyone else pays for their transactional services with their privacy.

More recently, in 2019, Apple launched the Apple Card. Although the credit card was issued in partnership with Goldman Sachs, promotion materials described it as "a new kind of credit card. Created by Apple, not a bank."[91] Unlike cards created by banks, Apple implied, "it represents all the things Apple stands for. Like simplicity, transparency, and privacy."[92] In a way, the card was an admission of defeat: if Apple Pay had seen wider adoption in the five years since it was released, there would have been no need to create a new product that included an actual physical card. But the physical card itself—albeit titanium and "Apple designed"—was backgrounded. Indeed, it was described by Mastercard as the first-ever "Digital-First" card.[93] The card primarily "lives on your iPhone," and that, as Apple put it, "makes all kinds of new things possible."[94] Some of these newly possible things included elegant visualizations of transactional memory—interest owed, purchases made. With a tap, unrecognized or unremembered purchases can be pinpointed on a map and in time. The primary value proposition of the card, then, lies in its embeddedness in the trusted exomemory of the already existing Apple ecosystem.[95]

Google and Apple both imagine wallets on the phone—even have images of cards displayed on the phone screens. A wallet is not just a means of payment; it is a portfolio of payments. The mobile wallet is a gateway to collect—or obscure—whatever information passes through it. But the "mobile wallet" might prove akin to the "horseless carriage," a concept that imagines the future only in terms of the past. While Google Wallet and Apple Pay piggyback on existing payment practices, Venmo is quietly altering the every-day rhetoric of payment. Venmo is not a wallet; it is a conversation.

Before the success of Venmo, many people in the payments industry believed that peer-to-peer mobile payments were a losing proposition. Traditionally, the merchant pays to be paid, and in peer-to-peer transactions, there is no merchant. Indeed, Venmo does not charge users any fees to receive money or make payments from debit cards or bank transfers. Nevertheless, Venmo was acquired by Braintree, a payments processor that mostly serves "sharing economy" platforms like Uber and Airbnb, for $26.2 million in 2012, despite not ever making a profit.[96] Braintree itself was acquired by PayPal for $800 million in 2013.[97]

The potential value that Venmo promises to investors and partners is communicative. It is the conversation, the newly fixed-in-record transactional memory. In addition, one of Venmo's most valuable assets at this time might be the way the word "Venmo" has, among its twenty-something users, caught on as a generic verb for sending money, the way "Google it" means "to search" and "Facebook me" means "let's keep in touch."[98] Venmo's value as a company is based on the transformation of everyday social norms around one of the most taboo forms of social inter-action: money between friends.

Much of the think-piece concern over Venmo pertains to these shifting norms. It has been described as the ultimate in social media "overshare" culture.[99] One technology commentator wrote, "It's not bad enough that I have to know that the girl I used to sit next to in social studies just took her 4-year-old to the dentist," referring to a typical social media update. "Now I have to know that one of you paid your roommate for the phone bill??? People, you are just GIVING your privacy away! About sensitive things like money!"[100]

Venmo transactions are public by default. This means that anyone can see your transactions—not just people in your feed or interested friends of friends but anyone who clicks on the global-feed icon in the Venmo app. Many Venmo users make their transactions private—visible to just the person they are paying or getting paid by or visible just to their friends. But many others leave their transactions public, not entirely minding—as Chloe didn't in the story at the beginning of this chapter—if their new guy's ex can learn a little bit about them.

In addition, the global feed may be manipulated by anyone who can write a script to crawl the app's public-facing application programming interface (API). In 2014, two programmers did exactly this and created the site Vicemo, which searches for and publicly posts payments that are tagged by their participants as being related to "drugs, booze, and sex."[101] In a typical Vicemo set of transactions, we learn that "Ryan paid Brandon [for] Walmart meth supplies," that "Michael paid Danielle [for] Gay Jewish strippers," and that "Emily paid Kayla [for] Clean pee for [her] drug test." Vicemo links to the actual transactions on Venmo's website, which links to the rest of each of the participants' public transaction history, so just a little more clicking can reveal that some of that Venmo balance that Emily used to pay Kayla for the drug-free urine came from a "rent" payment from what appears to be her mother.

Of course, some of these comments are probably jokes. Nevertheless, Venmo's terms of service—like all social payment systems—explicitly prohibit use of the service to facilitate certain transactions, illegal or simply morally suspect, including drugs, drug paraphernalia, sexually oriented materials and services, and pornography, or to violate existing restrictions around tobacco or alcohol.[102] Regardless, Vicemo demonstrates that there are thousands of such transactions made every day. As demonstrated in chapter 4, account freezes are unpredictable and dire. Many savvy users make actual illicit transactions private or don't annotate them honestly. While this action prevents the transactions from entering the public record, it does not remove them from Venmo's private transactional memory.

One's future self, exes, exes of soon-to-be exes, and clever programmers trying to make a joke or an art project—these are not the only audiences of Venmo transactions. Venmo has long envisioned its transactions as having the potential to create a "new form of advertising by providing the genuine social interactions brands are so desperate to tap into."[103] Indeed, in 2016, Venmo began allowing merchants to accept payments, brokering access to, as the Venmo website put it, "real friends, real talk." As Venmo explained to potential merchant clients, "Venmo connects friends with friends—the ones they listen to, share with, and trust. Accepting Venmo can bring your brand front and center in these conversations."[104]

The stakes of lowering social taboos around everyday transactions and the potential value in documenting and annotating them are heightened when considered in light of the larger political economy of transactional data analytics in the tech industry. Consider, for example, Palantir, one of the most important, if not widely heard of, data and analytics companies. Palantir is a spinoff of PayPal, which owns Venmo. It is widely described as the most valuable privately held company in Silicon Valley. Palantir, named after the "seeing stone" used by evil wizards in J. R. R. Tolkien's *Lord of the Rings* trilogy, grew out of PayPal's techniques for detecting and thwarting fraudulent activity on eBay, particularly as perpetrated by Russian organized-crime groups.[105] Palantir specializes in the production of predictive analytics using massive, complex sets of data.

Palantir's clients include the Central Intelligence Agency, Department of Homeland Security, National Security Agency, Federal Bureau of Investigation, and Centers for Disease Control; the Marine Corps, Air Force, Special Operations Command, and West Point; the Recovery Accountability and Transparency Board; the National Center for Missing and Exploited Children; Medicaid and Medicare; police departments including the Los Angeles Police Department; the International Consortium of Investigative Journalists; and a number of private companies in the pharmaceutical, legal, and finance sectors.[106] In 2014, Palantir partnered with First Data, one of the oldest and largest global credit card processors, to produce Insightics, a platform that infers demographic and behavioral information about customers from merchants' payment records, which typically do not include such details.[107]

It's not clear, however, if Venmo's transactional record reflects true user behavior. People aren't always literal in their Venmo annotations: they joke about drugs when paying each other for coffee and refrain from mentioning drugs when they actually are paying for them; they label rent and utility payments with tropical-drink emojis to seem to be more interesting; they make private jokes to entertain their payment partner and intrigue anyone else who might be scrolling by.[108] Some transactional memory lies hidden, submerged beneath glib captions. But the social feed makes another truth claim, one that is much less easily obfuscated. As with Facebook, the value of the social data produced by Venmo lies in the "social graph" formed by connections, not just in what is said but to whom it is said.

Although PayPal—and therefore Venmo—and Palantir may not have a data-sharing agreement, the world that Palantir predicts and is best adapted to thrive in is one in which the records of transactional memory produced by mobile payments aren't kept private by rivals like Google or siloed for use by individual mer-chants, as would be the case with Apple Pay. Instead, Palantir would benefit from the Venmo approach, in which money's soci-ality is made public, durable, and accessible to all—friends, future employers, the intelligence community—like most other forms of social media.

Consider, again, WeChat. The Chinese "everything app" is able to constitute the "everything" of many everyday lives.[109] It is also deeply imbricated with the Chinese government. It creates a vec-tor of commercial and state surveillance that is unprecedented in its comprehensiveness. When the payments industry imagines what a "WeChat for the US market" will be, who does it imagine will be party to its records, and on what terms?

For the art project *Public by Default: Venmo Stories of 2017*, Hang Do Thi Duc downloaded all public Venmo transactions of 2017, a total of 207,984,218 transactions.[110] She used this data not to advertise or to build systems to someday catch terrorists and oth-ers who might find themselves targeted by the CIA. Instead, she used it to build portraits of real people living real transactional

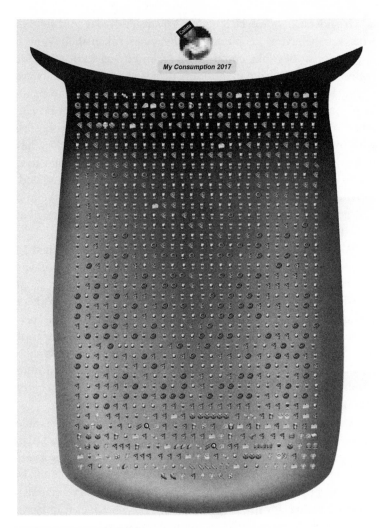

In 2017, the artist Hang Do Thi Duc used Venmo's public API to document the financial lives of five unsuspecting people. One, whom Do Thi Duc calls the "YOLOist," referring to the slang acronym for "you only live once," recorded 965 transactions for sodas, alcoholic drinks, fast food, and sweets in eight months. Do Thi Duc asks, "Do you want an artist (or anybody really) to be able to judge your diet from data they're able to freely download from the Internet?" And she suggests, "If not, change your Venmo privacy settings."

▼ data:
  ▼ 0:
        payment_id: 2166421558
        permalink: "/story/5d24b3c77addfb4bc79f2b5"
        via: ""
        action_links: {}
      ▼ transactions:
        ▼ 0:
          ▼ target:
              username: "MelanieMRamos"
            ▼ picture: "https://venmopics.appspot.com/u/v1/m/bfee2231-d711-449a-
                             be4f-81bc77c79475"
              is_business: false
              name: "Melanie Ramos"
              firstname: "Melanie"
              lastname: "Ramos"
              cancelled: false
              date_created: "2017-04-19T16:15:35"
              external_id: "2196561492705280641"
              id: "20414305"
        story_id: "5d24b3c77addfb4bc79f2b5"
        comments: []
        updated_time: "2019-07-09T15:33:27Z"
        audience: "public"
      ▼ actor:
          username: "Nydi07"
        ▼ picture: "https://venmopics.appspot.com/u/v1/m/c745be51-056b-4c6b-
                           b76c-667007bf09cd"
          is_business: false
          name: "Nydia Martinez"
          firstname: "Nydia"
          lastname: "Martinez"
          cancelled: false
          date_created: "2017-12-12T01:20:15"
          external_id: "2367882704977920418"
          id: "29825683"
        created_time: "2019-07-09T15:33:27Z"
        mentions: []
        message: "🍖 weekend"
        type: "payment"
      ▼ likes:
          count: 0
          data: []

This is the result, rendered in JavaScript Object Notation (JSON), of pinging the Venmo API, as Hang Do Thi Duc did. Can you make sense of it?

lives, forming transactional memories. *Public by Default* is intended to be cautionary. Do Thi Duc reminds us, again and again, how easy it is to change Venmo's privacy settings and even provides a step-by-step guide to doing so.

But the portraits that Do Thi Duc produces are also poignant. There is a subtlety to *Public by Default* that undercuts what could be an overly didactic message. Do Thi Duc presents a list of the surnames most frequently found in her data set, and it feels like America: Smith, Brown, Nguyen, Garcia, Kim, Anderson all sit near the top. There are love stories, of course, both happy and sad. There are friendships. There is an "all-American" young couple trying to make ends meet in the suburbs. There is a Mexican food-cart vendor and his most frequent customer, who labels her payments with the items she purchased—"elote," "chicharrón," and "mango"—and sometimes just with "Gracias."

Each profile concludes with a compelling reason to change settings. These are modern horrors: a stalker who might be able to take a good guess where you will be eating lunch on any given workday, an insurance company that might end your policy on the basis of the nearly one thousand transactions for junk food you made in eight months.

As the account of our accounts becomes crystallized as posts in a social feed—and as machine-readable objects in a data stream—it becomes public to many different audiences. Perhaps the greatest emergent concern, though, is one not just of viewership but of interpretation. Who will make sense of our transactional memories?

6 TRANSACTIONAL PUBLICS

Loyalty and Digital Money

In January 2018, the Starbucks executive chairman, former CEO, and future presidential candidate Howard Schultz made industry news when he used the first-quarter-earnings call with investors to talk not just about the future of Starbucks but about the future of currency.[1] Schultz asked listeners to look back twenty years and to remember the first time they'd heard about the internet. He marveled at how, in the decades since, "the world has been completely transformed and we're all connected in ways that no one could have possibly ever imagined."[2] He then asked them to think about the future and suggested that in the coming twenty years, the next comparable transformative technology would be digital currencies.

Schultz was quite clear that he was not talking about the current big-name cryptocurrency: "I don't believe that Bitcoin is going to be a currency today or in the future."[3] Rather, he anticipated that, soon enough, there would be "one or two" digital currencies, which would be produced by companies like Starbucks.

The idea of a Starbucks digital currency sounds like c-suite science fiction. But a variety of technologists, activists, and entrepreneurs have long imagined futures in which money is digital and issued by something other than governments.[4] These futures have seemed all the nearer at hand in the aftermath of the 2008 global financial crisis, when many people have been eager to try something—anything, perhaps—other than money-as-usual, including cryptocurrencies and community currencies.[5] But the Starbucks vision—digital currency issued and managed by a multinational corporation—was rather distinct from the visions that had animated other currency dreams.

Starbucks—which had made most of its headlines that year for innovations like the limited-edition Instagram-ready Unicorn Frappuccino Blended Crème—might not be the most obvious cradle of a currency revolution. But Schultz made an interesting case. He argued that Starbucks was in a unique position to issue a digital currency for three reasons. First, with close to thirty thousand locations on all continents except Antarctica, it had the global network both to make such a currency useful and also to support it.[6] Every Starbucks is both a merchant that accepts its currency as a form of payment and, potentially, a "branch" of the quasi-institution that would issue, store, and transfer it.

Second, beginning in 2001 with the refillable Starbucks Card, the company not so quietly had been building its fin-tech capacity.[7] The Starbucks mobile payment app was rolled out in 2011.[8] By 2018, industry analysts declared that the "winner" of the race to mainstream mobile payments in the United States was, to everyone's continued surprise, not a technology company or bank but Starbucks.[9]

But more important, perhaps, to Schultz's vision than even global reach or technology was, as he put it, "the strength, the trust, and the confidence in terms of Starbucks as a brand."[10] What made the imagined Starbucks digital currency superior to Bitcoin was the "trust and legitimacy" that, Schultz emphasized over and over, Starbucks garnered from consumers. Customers do seem to trust Starbucks with more than just their morning coffee. One 2016 analysis pointed out that there was $1.2 billion loaded into Starbucks accounts worldwide, which is more than is held in many regional banks and more than in Green Dot, the largest prepaid debit company.[11]

In 2010, the satirical newspaper the *Onion* ran a story with the headline, "U.S. Economy Grinds to Halt as Nation Realizes Money

Just a Symbolic, Mutually Shared Illusion." In the fake news report, people all over the country stop in their tracks as they re-
consider "little green drawings of buildings and dead white men
they once used to measure their adequacy and importance as human beings." Although the article was humorous, it reflected larger
cultural and technical changes that emerged in the wake of the
2008 global financial crisis. As the general public learned about
such arcane financial instruments as credit default swaps and
collateralized debt obligations, money itself had become strange.
And it remains that way. In the context of this chaos and creativ-
ity, some people saw an opportunity to create new kinds of money,
to forge new transactional communities. During the next few
years, artists, activists, engineers, and entrepreneurs produced an
array of new money forms.

In 2008, an individual or group using the pseudonym Satoshi
Nakamoto posted a white paper outlining a digital cash system
called Bitcoin. The system would use a decentralized, peer-to-peer
network to produce and transmit currency tokens, or Bitcoins.
Between 2010 and 2014, Bitcoin took hold of the public imagination as a mysterious form of money, impossibly complex and
outrageously valuable. When a transactional community is intentionally formed, it is usually to overcome existing problems of
value, identity, space, time, politics. Bitcoin was an attempt to
rethink all of these. It was designed to be a kind of "digital gold,"
whose value was backed not by traditional governments but by
markets and cryptographic scarcity, as well as a form of "digital
cash" that was able to move at the global scale of the internet
without the fees or surveillance associated with traditional payment intermediaries.[12] Its developers and users saw it as a kind of
"Magic Internet Money," as Bitcoin users advertised it on the news-
aggregation message board Reddit. The absence of a central au-
thority appealed to computer-savvy libertarians, cryptocurrency
activists or cypherpunks, and cryptoanarchists, many of whom
ran early nodes on the network and promoted a stateless vision
for the future of money.[13]

Despite Bitcoin's mystique, it is based on a few straightforward
principles. Again, the Bitcoin system is a decentralized, peer-to-peer

network for the production and transmission of value tokens, or "electronic cash."[14] Bitcoin functions like cash in the sense that value is transferred directly from payer to payee without first passing through an intermediary such as a bank or social media platform. But unlike cash, every Bitcoin transaction is appended to a public ledger, the blockchain. To protect the identities of payers and payees, each transaction is encrypted. To verify new transactions and keep the ledger up-to-date, Bitcoin depends on a network of cooperating computers. The operators of these computers, in return for their voluntary labor, are occasionally and automatically rewarded with newly generated Bitcoin by the system.

This process of volunteering labor by hosting the blockchain and sometimes receiving Bitcoins in return is called "mining," inspired by the limited supply of precious metals on Earth. The first Bitcoin client was released in 2009, and the first "genesis block" of Bitcoins was mined. To extend the analogy with precious metals, the rate at which new Bitcoins can be mined slows down over time. One day, all of the Bitcoin will have been mined. So while Bitcoin was designed to serve as a form of "digital cash," in practice, it is used more like "digital gold," a speculative commodity. Speculative trading in Bitcoin produced enormous volatility.

Yet many Bitcoin enthusiasts held onto the vision of an alternative currency, free of state intervention: a money form that would outlast the US government.[15] While the first "real-world" Bitcoin payment—ten thousand Bitcoins for two delivered Papa John's pizzas, worth $30 in May 2010, $200,000 (an all-time high) in February 2017, and $7,600 in May 2018—was heralded as proof of the coin's viability in everyday life, relatively few merchants have ever accepted Bitcoin. Those that do, however, subtly signal their belonging to a particular transactional community. Indeed, while many Bitcoin enthusiasts gravitated to the system because it seemed free of the foibles of human cooperation, users habitually refer to themselves, collectively, as "the Bitcoin community."[16] As much as Bitcoin is imagined as a "coin" that is "mined," it is fundamentally defined by the blockchain, a persistent record of Bitcoin's transactional community, past and present.

Bitcoin magazine, 2012.

But Bitcoin was not the only new currency created in the years after the 2008 crisis. Indeed, this same time period saw a spike of interest in alternative currencies.[17] These took a variety of forms, including Time Banks, LETS (local exchange trading systems), and local currencies.[18] Like Bitcoin, these intentional transactional communities were formed to overcome interrelated problems of value, identity, space, time, and politics. Lakotacoin, a cryptocurrency launched in 2014, was intended to create self-determination, political autonomy, and economic prosperity for Oglala Lakota of the Pine Ridge Indian Reservation.[19] While alternative currencies saw a surge of interest in the 2010s, they aren't exactly new. The Ithaca HOURs, currently the oldest and largest local currency, have been around for nearly thirty years and take as their inspiration the 1827 Cincinnati Time Store experiment.[20]

When alternative currencies take a physical form, they are, like any currency, designed to evoke the identities, geographies, and value of the transactional community they draw together. Berkshares, a local currency in western Massachusetts, features images of mountains and the motto "Community, Economy, Ecology, Sustainability." Most of these systems are intended to create a sense of belonging and social cohesion rather than a viable

economic alternative. These currencies attempt to set apart their
localities as transactional communities rooted in shared hopes
for the future, manifest, if only glimpsed, in the present.

In a 2013 essay, the writer and activist Brett Scott captured
the DIY money zeitgeist well.[21] He suggested that the idea that
money is valuable is "just a socially sanctioned pretense, a prag-
matic, covert, wink-wink, let's-not-talk-about-this charade," but
that, slowly but surely, "the fantasy becomes such a deep habit
that no one person can stand up and point out the absurdity of
the situation," and then soon, "it's the dissidents who seem mad,
while the people swapping useful goods for bits of metal, paper
or meaningless electronic data look perfectly sane." He suggested
that we begin "peeling back the façade" of the "Money Matrix" by
tinkering with alternatives: cryptocurrencies, local money like the
Bristol Pound, and even a near-joke currency called Punk Money,
which does the work of money simply by making transferable
promises on Twitter using the hashtag #punkmoney.[22]

The Bristol Pound, launched in 2012, is the largest local alternative currency in the
United Kingdom. According to its website, its goal is to "create a more resilient
and sustainable independent business sector in Bristol and, in turn, a fairer and
more inclusive local economy."

With all of this new money in circulation, it can seem like creating money is easy. The economist Hyman Minsky once remarked, "Everyone can create money. The problem is to get it accepted."[23] Minsky was discussing the importance of central banks, but taken slightly out of context, his point is still relevant: which institutions but for nation-states could create the structures necessary to ensure that a new money is accepted?[24] If money is nothing more than, as visionary Visa founder Dee Hock put it, information socially "guaranteed" to be a valuable, what are the terms of that guarantee?[25] Money may be, as the *Onion* suggested, shared delusion, but it requires structures that produce, maintain, and make usable its value. If, as the theorist James Carey theorizes, our shared reality is "produced, maintained, repaired, and transformed" through communication, what kinds of entities have the capacity—the way nations and other states have and do—to sustain our shared monetary reality?[26]

We may indeed be hurtling toward a future of money plurality, one in which states do not have a monopoly on the means of exchange. Some people, depending on their politics, look with optimism to cryptocurrencies or community currencies, and scholars have worked to understand the implications, good and bad, of these new money forms. But what about the *corporate* currency that Schultz described?

Howard Schultz was not alone in his prediction of a world of multiple, nonstate currencies, some of them, at least, corporate. In a 2017 book about the future of money, the payments industry guru Dave Birch suggests that one hundred years in the future, an array of currencies will be common: "London parking places, Facebook Florins, Nuclear Electricity, and some sort of interest-free loan instrument from the Free State of Wessex."[27]

Starbucks is already issuing something like a private digital currency: its loyalty program, Starbucks Rewards. Members earn "stars" when they make purchases with a registered Starbucks card or mobile app. Starbucks Rewards had, at the beginning of 2019, 16.3 million active members in the United States.[28] These members accounted for nearly 40 percent of Starbucks' US sales.[29]

The coveted Starbucks gold card.

Starbucks Rewards can be earned and spent in the United Kingdom, United States, Canada, Australia, Mexico, Ireland, and Japan.

Stealthily, an array of loyalty programs—frequent-flyer miles, interchange-funded credit card rewards, merchant points—have become an important part of the financial lives of many people. According to the consulting firm McKinsey, three-quarters of households are members of at least one loyalty program, and the average household has eighteen memberships.[30]

Bitcoin gets a lot more attention than loyalty, igniting imaginations (of teens and drug dealers and programmers and venture capitalists and CEOs and scammers) about the potential for digital currency, but more people actually use and care about loyalty than even really know for sure what Bitcoin is. Bitcoin's power comes from its technological mystique and mystification. Loyalty is banal, but that—along with corporate power to scale unilaterally—just might be how it comes to be the mainstream form of digital currency. The headlines may have gone to Bitcoin, but the market turned to loyalty.

Indeed, one prominent mainstream payments attorney said at an event I attended that he thinks that we may soon see "real competition in the money space" between different kinds of currency in everyday life. He was referring not to Bitcoin but to loyalty. In this future, state-issued currency would just be one of the options "competing" to be used. State currency would probably not be fully displaced, but it would be one of many different currencies circulating in coexistence with each other.

Loyalty programs aren't new. One of the earliest versions was the S&H Green Stamps program, which became popular in the 1930s.[31] Customers received small green stamps when they made purchases at participating merchants, such as supermarkets, gas stations, and department stores. Stamps could be redeemed for purchases, often housewares, from Green Stamp stores or its catalog. In the 1980s, airlines began frequent-flyer programs, which were soon yoked to credit cards. In the 1990s, cards were designed with a greater variety of rewards and points systems. Small businesses have long used punch cards and stickers to encourage repeat business, and in recent years, these paper systems have been translated for smartphones.

It might seem like quite a leap for loyalty to go from paying for an occasional latte or even a flight to becoming a full-fledged currency. But many people already talk about loyalty programs as though they issued "real money." Business-school researchers write about how companies can lower the perceived cost of a product by stating it in terms of "combined currency": rewards and dollars.[32] In the payments industry, it is not uncommon to hear loyalty described as just another way to fund a payment, like cash and cards.[33]

In 1999, *Businessweek* reported, "For millions of Americans, frequent-flier miles have become a second currency."[34] In 2002, the *Economist* described frequent-flyer miles as "a new international currency."[35] In 2005, when an estimated fourteen trillion frequent-flyer miles had been issued worldwide, a *Guardian* writer declared, "The gold standard of sterling is long forgotten and now the supremacy of the greenback has been surpassed. The world has a new global currency—airline frequent flyer miles, which have a greater total value than dollars, euros, pounds or yen."[36] More recently, a blogger wrote that she didn't really need Bitcoin because, as she put it, "I already have a cryptocurrency, it's called Sephora Beauty Insider Points."[37]

Schultz was insightful when he emphasized trust in imagining his Starbucks currency. All money derives its value from trust. The US dollar is backed by trust in the market-democratic institutions that manage the nation and its money. Bitcoin is backed by trust in its market value relative to state currency, the cryptographic systems that undergird it, and the community that believes in it.[38] A Starbucks digital currency would be backed by trust in Starbucks as a brand. Transactional communities are networks of shared trust in the communities themselves—their institutions, members, and structures of feeling.

It should come as no surprise, then, that brands like Starbucks would be interested in the business of making money. Brands, the communication scholar Sarah Banet-Weiser argues, form identity and community.[39] This cuts both ways: corporate brands offer identity and community, while religions and political movements use the tools and techniques of branding. Brands are already designed to feel like quasi-nations, and countries engage in nation branding.[40] Currency, insofar as it produces transactional communities, is the ultimate branding tool.

If Starbucks and other companies are getting into the business of making money, what would that mean? The constitutional law scholar Christine Desan describes the issuing of money as a "constitutional undertaking."[41] Desan means this in multiple senses: money is part of the process of constituting a political community, and money is governed by the constitutional rules of that community. Desan defines money in relation to how it is created. Money occurs, she explains, under the following conditions: There is a "stakeholder" who sits at the center of a "community," taking in and distributing "contributions" from members of that community. In return for those contributions, the stakeholder gives members some sort of a receipt showing that they've paid their due to the community. That receipt can then circulate as a standardized token of value authorized by the central stakeholder and by the community itself.

Economists once hypothesized that money emerged from markets: people bartered until they figured out that precious metals like gold and silver were the best commodity to exchange because they were portable, divisible, durable, and, at least in Europe, rare. Instead, Desan argues, along with many anthropologists, sociologists, and historians, money emerged from institutional actors that had the ability to authorize it.[42]

Desan's language of "stakeholder" and "community" and "contributions" is intentionally generic, drawn from and with the potential to be applied to a variety of contexts; but the "stakeholder" is almost always a sovereign ruler, and the "contributions" are usually called "taxes." But not necessarily: Desan writes, "'Private' organizations, cities, commercial collaborators, and other entities can undertake to make money, and many have. As they organize their members, they produce their own politics."[43]

Desan is clear, however, that the form that the "stakeholder" takes—king, church, democratic government, mining company, blockchain, community group, multinational coffee chain—has consequences. Money can be governed as an object of democracy or tyranny. It can be designed to distribute wealth and power in a variety of different ways. In turn, the design of money is constitutive of the community in which that money circulates. A theory of money, then, is a techno-economic imaginary: a theory of the larger social order (or a challenge to it) and a way of materially enacting that theory.[44] At least in the case of state-issued currency, then, transactional communities are also *transactional publics*. In the Enlightenment project, money became the object of market-democratic governance.

The sociologist Georg Simmel argues that money is a "claim upon society": its value is derived from trust in collective systems.[45] But as the sociologist Nigel Dodd points out, "it is far from obvious that the 'society' [Simmel] had in mind when he was describing it was equivalent to a nation-state."[46] If "society" is not a fixed concept, then "money" too can be similarly fluid. This insight is the essence of what motivates Bitcoiners, local-currency activists, and others whom Maurer affectionately refers to as "money nut-ters."[47] Change the currency, change the world.

Dodd is forthright in his 2017 declaration: "The era in which money was defined by the state is coming to an end."[48] Whether Bitcoin, Bristol Pounds, or branded loyalty, many people are imagining—and taking quite seriously!—a coming future in which private money replaces or at least augments state-issued money. Whether crypto, community, or corporate, many of today's dominant visions for the future of money are unlinked from the political and territorial structures of nationhood. Dodd notes that all new currencies are, on some level, "utopian" in that they are part of an unfinished political process and deeply linked to our political imagination.[49]

All of these visions are, on some level, postdemocracy fantasies. The sociologist Manuel Castells has documented a crisis of the institutions of liberal democracy.[50] He shows that, globally, the majority of citizens do not trust established political institutions or governments. The same forces driving the election of populist regimes across the world have driven some people to put their trust in a libertarian global digital currency like Bitcoin or to try to build local networks of resilience through community currencies. For corporations offering branded, for-profit, trust as a service, it is an opportunity.

Indeed, in February 2018, a month after Schultz imagined Starbucks as a potential future issuer of digital currency, Kate Jaspon, the chief financial officer of Starbucks' rival Dunkin' Donuts, also talked to shareholders about digital currency. She described the challenges of navigating a company through extreme uncertainty. She cited Brexit, Donald Trump, and Bitcoin all as evidence of this world in which anything could happen, a world in which all major coffee companies, apparently, have to at least consider their role as currency purveyors.[51] What kind of transactional public could be enacted through these corporate loyalties?

A world of everyday "competition in the money space" seems far-fetched, and state-issued currency is so naturalized that it's hard to imagine any other form of money besides dollars and pounds, yen and euros. But in many places in the world today, dealing with multiple money forms—including things like cell-phone airtime used as currency—is a fact of life.[52] The anthropologist Jane Guyer notes that "very large numbers of ordinary people—the clients, customers, citizens, and workers in the nonincorporated domains of economies and through all of the passing vicissitudes of life— live largely in soft currencies or cash forms of hard currencies."[53]

In addition, money has, historically, more often been both plural and private. The historian Rebecca Spang writes of the French context, "Throughout much of the 1790s (and beyond), however, money's qualities mattered as much as its quantities."[54] Before the advent of universal national currencies in the nineteenth century, the poor in most countries predominantly used private or locally issued low-denomination "petty coin"—that is, if they used cash at all.[55] For the most part, poor people living in small communities simply kept track of their obligations through ledger keeping. In either case, neither system was easily convertible to the kinds of money used by wealthier people, such as notes issued by banks and redeemable for bullion.

This plurality produced what the political scientist Eric Helleiner has described as a "tiered monetary order."[56] People's relationships to those ranked status hierarchies mattered more than any loyalty to a "nation" or broader community of citizens did. Before the late nineteenth century, no country had yet embraced a "one country, one money" principle, which quilted together national imaginaries of membership and market to a geographic terrain.[57] Establishing national currencies was a considerable achievement and a demonstration of the sovereignty of nation-states that required significant effort over decades. It took some time for the Enlightenment project of citizenship to extend to the means of payment.

Prior to that time (and, indeed, even after), all sort of things circulated as currency. In an analysis of everyday money forms in the United States from 1870 to 1930, Viviana Zelizer similarly finds plurality: "food stamps for the poor, supermarket coupons for the ordinary consumer, prison scrip for inmates, therapeutic tokens for the mentally ill, military currency for soldiers, chips

for gamblers, lunch tickets for institutional canteens, gift certificates for celebrations."[58] These money forms were wholly unstan-
dardized: many were counterfeit or fictitious and could be used
to cheat transactional partners or traded at a discount. Being able
to "read" money was one of the many ways in which antebellum
city dwellers had to learn to be defensive and street-smart.[59]

The technologies of money track alongside the technologies
of communication media more broadly. National currency is a
form of *money mass media*. It was designed to enact transactional
communities the size and scope of the nation. It is public infrastructure for use by citizens that could be used for all transactional
purposes. To quote the US dollar bill's autobiography, it is "legal
tender for all debts public and private." State-issued money was a
technology of collective identity that turned "peasants into Frenchmen," creating "citizens" of a liberal transactional public.[60] What
comes after money mass media?

Networked communication technologies are particularly well
suited to many of the things money has been used for—assigning
value, keeping account of it, and transmitting it. In the 1970s, Dee
Hock imagined that with the advent of the credit card network,
money would become nothing more than information and that
banks and governments would be displaced by those who wielded
the technologies that could manage that information. He wrote,
"Inherent in all this might be the genesis of a new form of global
currency."[61]

The democratization of networked communication technologies has led to an attempt to democratize the money form as well.
Since the 1990s, "digital cash" has captured the imaginations of
those who are interested in the potential of cryptography and
related technologies for social and political change. Members of
the Cypherpunks email list, which was formed in 1992, viewed
technology as the key to a future free society, and digital cash was
an essential component of this vision.[62] The group was not homo-
geneous in its political ideologies, however, and two overlapping
but critically different viewpoints emerged. Activists calling themselves "cypherpunks" were deeply concerned with individual
privacy and viewed digital cash as a tool that empowered indi-

viduals to selectively reveal personal financial and transactional information. "Cryptoanarchists," on the other hand, believed that cryptography could be used to reshape society to enable free speech and an anarcho-capitalist market system. To them, digital cash was a means to create a money system untethered to government.

Over the last decades of the twentieth century and the first decades of the twenty-first, there were several attempts to design and implement digital cash systems, drawing from the visions of cypherpunks and cryptoanarchists. These included a 1985 description by the computer scientist David Chaum of an electronic cash system that would "make big brother obsolete"; a fictional cryptographic black market posited by Cypherpunks cofounder Tim May in 1994; an anonymous, distributed electronic cash system called "bmoney," described in 1998 by the computer scientist Wei Dai; and a proposal in the late 1990s and early 2000s by Nick Szabo for "bit gold," a system in which computers would mine for "scarce" digital commodities.[63]

While none of these ideas were brought to fruition, they laid the groundwork for future experiments with systems of digital currency—particularly the 2008 emergence of Bitcoin, as discussed. The geographies and politics of the internet compel the idea of digital cash, and the technology of the internet is good at doing the things money needs to do: transmit value and keep track of it. What technology alone is less good at is guaranteeing and sustaining that value. And, indeed, the technologies of transmission and storing themselves must be sustained and maintained.[64] Nevertheless, the economic anthropologist Keith Hart was prescient of the impact of the internet on currency: "The money form is not standing still."[65]

Because, historically, monetary plurality has been more often the norm than not, it is tempting to think that the future of transactional communities will resemble the past. The media studies scholars Thomas Pettitt and Lars Ole Sauerberg theorize a "Gutenberg parenthesis," the idea that modernity, the period associated with mass media print culture, was an aberration.[66] Digital, network, and social media, the theory goes, have a lot in common with the ephemeral, relational media forms that preceded the

Renaissance. So, too, with social structures like identity, author-
ity, and spatiality. As Pettitt pithily argues, "The future is medieval."[67] Hart has made a similar prediction about money in the
networked, digital age:

> People will voluntarily enter circuits of exchange based on special
> currencies. At the other extreme, we will be able to participate as
> individuals in global markets, using international moneys such as
> the euro, electronic payment systems or even direct barter via the
> internet. It will be a world whose plurality of association, even
> fragmentation, will resemble feudalism more than the Roman
> empire. In such a world, one currency cannot possibly meet all the
> needs of a diversified region's inhabitants. The changing technical
> form of money has exposed the limitations of central banks, re-
> duced now to maintaining a national monopoly whose economic
> inadequacy is exposed on all sides. In response, people have started
> generating their own money, offering individuals a variety of com-
> munity currencies linked by increasingly-sophisticated electronic
> payment systems.[68]

Monetary plurality, then, is not just science fiction. Perhaps it is
also historical reenactment.

And, indeed, *reenactment* may the right term: scholars, activists, and entrepreneurs are looking to the past as they imagine the
future. The internet, as an imaginary, provides a vision of a recent
past layered over a more primordial past, which in turn is used
to pattern both distant and nearer-term futures.

Bitcoin's promoters often compare it to the early days of the
internet, an idealized time marked by potentiality: governments
and their regulators had not yet caught up to technology, big corporations had not yet enclosed and centralized the web, fortunes
were still to be made.[69] The internet was seen as a new frontier, a
blank slate on which to build a society that would correct some
of the errors of modernity, a temporal reset: it was simultaneously
the distant, premodern past and the future.

There is an important comparison to be made between the
utopian techno-economic imaginaries of alternative currencies
and the historical trajectory, present condition, and mythical
recollection of the internet. Early enthusiasts imagined the inter-

net as an unexplored territory to be shaped.[70] From science fiction to congressional subcommittees, the metaphors of the proto-internet—electronic frontier, virtual community, information superhighway, global village—hinted at the political dimensions of these networked futures. In the Bay Area, computing culture combined the self-reliance of the communitarian counterculture of the 1970s with the computerized capitalism of the 1980s, giving rise to a range of collectivist and anarchist visions of the information age.[71]

Like some community currency activists, some computer hobbyists imagined themselves as "homesteaders" staking out new communities of peer learning and artistic expression.[72] Cyber-libertarians, meanwhile, laid the groundwork for Bitcoin funda-mentalism, envisioning cyberspace as not only radically egalitarian but fundamentally ungovernable—"an act of nature" rather than collective action or public policy.[73] Initially, these visions were complementary, producing a shared future populated by millions of people across the globe, exchanging valuable data, peer-to-peer, free of state regulation or oversight.

Visions of the internet as a technology of individual liberty contributed to the speculative investment of the dot-com boom and bust, but the products and services that survived into the twenty-first century had shed their political ethos. Instead of "a civilization of the Mind," we got Facebook.[74] Whereas the archi-tectures of early internet applications like USENET distributed control among a decentralized network of independent nodes, social media systems like Facebook concentrate power and control in a single, private organization.[75] In contrast to the peer-to-peer ideal, social media systems enforce strict hierarchies between platform owners, partners, and users. Facebook controls all of the data that circulates within its walled garden, a system of near-total surveillance with no democratic governance or avenue for redress.[76] Further, Facebook draws information from the rest of the internet and reshapes it to keep users within the platform, resulting in ideological echo chambers produced by algorithms anticipating the kinds of information that you might want to see.[77] In an inversion of the cyber-libertarian vision, then, today's social media platforms retain all of the resistance to regulation and none of the obsession with individual civil liberties.

Loyalty is, at least in this context, the Facebook of money. The techno-social imaginaries of Bitcoin and local currencies both, in different ways, resemble and are directly influenced by those of the early social web. But like today's social media platforms, loyalty is constrained rather than open. It creates new hierarchies. It is fundamentally surveillant. It is resistant to democratic governance, and it offers few opportunities for redress.

The state may indeed be losing its monopoly on money. Bitcoiners and alternative-currency activists are prying its grip loose in our imaginations. But the capacity to bring functioning nonstate money to the mainstream at scale is perhaps only possessed by corporations. The mass money media of state currency will probably be displaced by social money media that acts more like Facebook and that does not aspire to be public or universal, free or fair. As Marx aptly put it, "Men make their own history, but they do not make it as they please."[78]

Loyalty is already money, but only within the transactional communities that it constitutes. Loyalty, as it currently exists, is an example of what Zelizer calls "special monies."[79] Just as state-issued currency is turned into gift cards to make it more appropriate for its role as a present, loyalty programs take money out of general circulation and earmark it for a particular purpose. We pay with dollars—perhaps loaded onto an app—and are given, as change, loyalty. This new money, unlike general-purpose mass money, is constrained in its flows and mode of evaluation. It creates new, similarly constrained transactional communities and hierarchies.

The sociologists Bruce Carruthers and Wendy Espeland describe how money's qualitative meaning is derived from its use, namely, its flow—where that money is going and where it has been; the institution that originally issued it; where it can be used, by whom, and for what.[80] The salient feature of loyalty's flow is constraint.

The value of loyalty is constrained. Points can't be used for all purposes. There are usually fees associated with transferring them to another person, if that's allowed at all. Loyalty can expire if left unused, and its value can disappear entirely if the issuing company goes bankrupt. This produces a shared time horizon of value for those who use loyalty. The value of loyalty is also highly dynamic, determined by the company that issues it, and steered toward particularly transactional purposes. Companies can suddenly change the value of loyalty. This volatility creates a shared set of calculative practices among those who use loyalty.

Like all money, loyalty is a way-finding tool: its place-making function is determined by where it is accepted. Because these communities are niche rather than universal, closed rather than open, loyalty creates invisible walled gardens.

One example comes from frequent-flyer miles, the coin of the realm of what Castells calls the "space of flows," the "habitat" and "spatial organization of the dominant, managerial elite."[81] Frequent-flyer miles are generated in the space of flows—through the flow of business passengers on airplanes from one hub to another and through the flow of money through the card networks. And miles are also *used* in the space of flows. Indeed, in airports such as Newark Liberty International Airport, everything sold in the terminal is denominated in both US dollars and award miles.[82] Airports are becoming places where cash is not accepted as a form of payment. Already, most airlines only accept credit cards for on-board purchases. Frequent-flyer miles are used by frequent flyers—those who live in the space of flows. Money is deterritorialized and then reterritorialized to map a placeless place that is everywhere and nowhere.

But the logics of loyalty are not limited to the "business class." Programs have proliferated for use in a variety of economic niches. These ways to pay also form and reflect transactional communities. Chain truck stops have developed rewards programs to cater to commercial truck drivers. Off highways across North America, truckers can use these rewards like currency. Like other rewards cards issued to employees, trucker rewards are converted through interchange from on-the-job spending into personal tokens. Truckers find that "these cards come in handy when fueling. You can swipe these and earn money while spending your company's."[83]

The territory traced by these rewards follows the contours of the highway system and the North American Free Trade Agreement, mapping another placeless place, a working-class space of flows. Some programs offer access to members-only discounted gas stations, analogous to the first-class lounge to which a business traveler might seek to gain entry through dutiful awards management.

Truck drivers on online forums, such as TruckersReport, Truckers Forum, and TruckStopReport—not to mention, no doubt, in actual truck stops across the continent—share practices for paying with rewards, moving them in and out of state currency as needed. For example, one suggested that an "honest" way to convert rewards to cash is to use them to pay for scale tickets at weigh stations and then get reimbursed for the expense by an employer in state currency.[84]

On one forum, a driver described rewards as "food stamps for truckers."[85] In addition to targeting the preferences of commercial truck drivers, these rewards also exert classed constraints on their economic agency. There have been some attempts by employers to exert ownership of the rewards, for example, pressuring drivers to use them only for work-related expenses or reporting them as fringe benefits on tax forms. Other companies allow drivers to retain rewards and use them as they see fit but have stopped reimbursing drivers for showers and other purchases for which rewards can be easily used.

Truck driver rewards are an important part of how American truck drivers do money. On the forum TruckStopUSA, one driver described how he used rewards to pay for all but $20 of the replacement of an essential part on his truck. Another described how his points have "saved [him] many times" and wrote that he had used points that were about to expire to pay for a credit for a truck-stop shower for another trucker who needed it.[86] Truck driver rewards codify and map this economic subject position and its transactional community.

These new transactional communities create new, constrained hierarchies. First and most obviously, they produce, quite overtly, "status." I attended a wedding not long ago in which the bride, as part of her wedding vows, lovingly described the security that her groom offered. "Life is simply better with you," she said. "I get to be in a better United boarding group with you." Loyalty programs not only produce "rewards"—the transactional token you can buy things with—but also produce class. The marketing professor Xavier Drèze studies people's perceptions of status and uses his research to help companies structure their loyalty programs. He said of his research on tiered status, "If you go back 10 or 15 years, a gold card was really special. Today, if you don't have a platinum card, which confers greater status than gold, you're nobody. The interesting thing is that what has evolved over time is that more and more customers need status. Marketers need to find ways to separate one class of customer from another."[87] The planned economies of corporate loyalty have a status inflation problem.

That status is always differential and relational. The newlyweds may have status in an airport, but they don't have it at a truck stop. Nevertheless, some status is higher than others. Those who are poor in the mainstream economy aren't protected by status in the rewards economy. They may count on their loyalty rewards more—a truck-stop shower is a more fundamental need than an early boarding group. They are also more vulnerable to their loyalty being rendered worthless by the company that issues it.

All of this status is, like everything about loyalty, characterized by restraint. Drèze and his collaborator Joseph C. Nunes characterize rewards as "golden handcuffs" because they lock members into continued patronage even when they are dissatisfied with the service.[88] One blogger wrote, "I long for American every time I sit on a United airplane. And the thought of having to fly United for the next few months of the year in order to reach the top-tier service makes me depressed." But he had a plan for, as he put it, "immigration." He wrote, "Once I hit top tier, I'll get a status match from American so I can be top tier on their network."[89] When you've paid your tax to the sovereign, you want to be able to make your claim on society.

A vision of the sociality of differentiated transactional communities comes from Bitcoin. Many of the Bitcoin aficionados I've interviewed point to the interconnected novels of the science fiction novelist Neal Stephenson. In one of his most popular books,

Diamond Age, the world is no longer divided into territorial nations. Instead, nations have been supplanted by "phyles," or tribes
of people with similar values, ethnicities, religions, or other cultural affinities. These phyles are not bound to any one region or
geographic boundary. Phyles are not states but private organizational entities governed by internal corporate oligarchy. There is
an electronic "Universal Currency"—which many of today's Bitcoin
aficionados see as Bitcoin-like—that can be exchanged between
members of different phyles, but each group has its own money
system, along with its own economic norms. As one leader in the
Bitcoin community told me, "Neal Stephenson is more of a prophet
than a novelist. He had figured it all out."

Can we imagine a post-nation-state world in which we are
imbricated not as citizens of sovereign nations but in private,
transgeographic transactional communities? Maybe not. But we
may be seeing the beginning of deeper stratification of payment
and perhaps the emergence of stratified transactional communities. These niche transactional tokens similarly produce niche
identities that may run in tandem with and inside nationalities.

Just as money has been and may again be plural, so too will
the transactional identities that these monies produce. Rather
than being a member of any one transactional community, we
may find ourselves using multiple monies, running exchanges
within our wallets, oscillating in and out of a variety of transactional identities.[90] The new media literacy scholar James Paul Gee
argues that in the internet era, we will need to develop identities
as "shapeshifting portfolio people," able to wield a toolkit of skill
and practices to adapt to uncertainty.[91] Like our money, we too
may be, as the anthropologist Marilyn Strathern writes, "plural
and composite sites of the relationships that produce them."[92] Our
transactional identities, like our digital wallets, will be portfolios.

Loyalty, like social media, is surveillant. Smartphone technology
is enabling the rise of loyalty programs and enhancing the ways
that businesses benefit from them—for example, by experimenting with features like games, hierarchical status, and intermittent
bonuses to see what drives purchasing behavior.[93] Apps can also

use location data to alert or reward consumers when they are within range of a store or to track store traffic from the most loyal customers. Companies frame requests for data in terms of improving the customer experience—for example, Starbucks asks rewards members to share their favorite drinks and turn on location data in their mobile app, with the ostensible goal of tailoring rewards and making the purchasing experience more efficient. But this valuable data, provided by consumers for the cost of a few free drinks, circulates beyond the control or expectation of the member.[94] It is shared with promotional partners, used to improve marketing and operations, and analyzed to learn how to motivate customers to spend more money.

Brands with robust loyalty programs explicitly view them as data-gathering operations. Brady Brewer, vice president at Starbucks overseeing brand loyalty and the Starbucks card, said in 2010, "We've tried to build a program around recognition—knowing who you are and what you like—and in some ways, that relevance comes from knowing about purchases from data" collected from the loyalty program.[95] A well-designed loyalty program allows a company to build customer "memory," tapping into preferences, profiles, and previous purchases in order to customize an individual's experience with the brand. A survey by Merkle Loyalty of one thousand loyalty-program members found that their top priorities were personalization ("The brand offers relevant rewards and offers"), empathy ("The brand understands me"), and memorable moments ("The brand creates great memories for me").[96] Thanks to loyalty programs, companies can seem as though they are intimately familiar with their loyalty customers—and they are, at least with their data. As the communication scholar Joseph Turow argues, loyalty is "bait" in games that "train people to give up personal data willingly."[97]

So, if state-issued currency turned "peasants into Frenchmen," then loyalty programs, like so much of the information economy, turn Frenchmen into Hervé André-Jezek, who lives at 43 Rue de Sains, Paris, works as an assistant at ASK Agency, is vegan, smokes American Spirits, and last bought condoms on Valentine's Day.[98] (Of course, Hervé, as a citizen of the European Union, would under the General Data Protection Regulation be able to find out the list of six hundred other companies that a payments interme-diary like PayPal shares his data with. Whether Hervé could make sense of any of this is another matter.)[99]

Loyalty may be "food stamps for truckers," and truckers, like those who receive actual welfare, as the surveillance scholars Virginia Eubanks and Nathalie Maréchal have demonstrated, may be at the vanguard of transactional surveillance and control.[100] Indeed, Karen Levy points out that commercial trucking is one of the most surveilled professions.[101] Fleet managers are of particu-lar interest to loyalty credit card issuers because they make deci-sions about contracting for large numbers of trucks.[102] Fleet cards offer managers access to reports on drivers' transactional data, which includes information on fuel type and cost per unit. Because the transactional data includes location, it can be used to estimate costs per mile and miles per gallon. Some programs will capture more data from drivers by prompting them to enter additional information—such as the odometer reading—at the gas pump before being able to make a purchase. In addition to this monitor-ing, fleet managers can use cards to exert direct control over drivers, limiting the amount and location of purchases.

What can consumers do if they are unhappy about the constraints and surveillance that loyalty programs entail? Not much, as it turns out. Unlike state currency, loyalty points have no fixed value and are subject to change as loyalty programs are modified or rebranded. State currency, at least in theory, can be governed by democratic principles. In fact, when the United States was estab-lishing its national currency, there were fierce debates about how that currency should be managed, what kind of national imagina-tion it would foster, and what its flows would be.[103] But how can consumers act as citizens of Starbucks? Loyalty programs are unreliable, unaccountable, and inconsistent, subject to being phased out, rolled into other programs, or changed beyond rec-ognition. When Starwood Preferred Guest (SPG) became Bonvoy, loyalty members could only take to internet forums to puzzle out how to capitalize on their existing points and decide whether it would pay to open any of the newly available credit cards in the Bonvoy line, given restrictions on collecting bonuses.[104]

Perhaps the only recourse that consumers have to push back on unwanted changes to their loyalty programs is social media. When Starbucks made a change to its loyalty programs in 2012, there was, as the *New York Times* put it, "consumer outcry." One thousand people signed an online petition asking Starbucks to restore key features of the program, and members posted "cranky comments" on the company's blog, Facebook page, and other social media.[105] These may seem like overwrought complaints from finicky latte drinkers. But consider the drivers who think of loyalty points as "food stamps for truckers" or those who use Frappuccinos as a meal—for some constituencies, changes to loyalty programs can create genuine economic strain or drastically change members' ability to benefit from the program.

Rewards programs are regulated by a complicated quilt of laws, including those that pertain to sweepstakes, unclaimed property, and gift certificates, and large companies actively engage counsel to ensure limits to their legal liability.[106] US law defines rewards as a "token of legal obligations," like coupons or trading stamps.[107] They represent a contract, a promise on behalf of the issuer, to redeem them for something of value. Ownership of the rewards, however, remains with the issuer, which gives the issuer the ability to control the terms on which the rewards can be redeemed or transferred, to the extent allowed by the original contract.

The obligations created by rewards may be enforceable by criminal penalties, as well as by contract law. For example, in 2014, the California members of the Camel Cash program—a rewards program issued by R. J. Reynolds, makers of Camel cigarettes, won a class-action lawsuit after R. J. Reynolds decided to terminate the program and, in the last issue of the Camel Cash catalog, only offer tobacco products and not the full range of merchandise that members had come to expect.[108] But legally, money or other forms of "negotiable paper," like checks and banknotes, have a higher legal "promissory" burden than rewards do. While the law stepped in to protect members of Camel's loyalty program, it cannot do so every time a loyalty program leaves its members in the lurch.

Despite this relative lack of legal protections, the United States has a long history of using tokens like stamps, scrip, and coupons as substitutes for state-issued currency at times when cash was scarce. In the nineteenth century, American mining and lumber companies commonly issued company scrip to the workers as salary, which could be redeemed only at the "company store," obligating employees to make purchases there, often at high markups.[109] And this isn't ancient history: in 2008, the Supreme Court of Justice in Mexico ruled that Walmart may not pay its workers in vouchers redeemable at Walmart stores.[110] Ultimately, loyalty points have real value to consumers, and when that value is altered, consumers have few options besides complaining to the company.

But loyalty has its pleasures. For "churners"—as people who collaborate to maximize all manner of credit card rewards programs call themselves—there is pleasure in beating the house. The cultural geographers Matthew Zook and Mark Graham describe "airline hacking"—that is, the creative use of airline geographies, credit card churning, and consuming for miles—as "playful mischief" that can be transgressive and even resistant to corporative capitalism while still maintaining and perpetuating hierarchies.[111] But there is pleasure in mischief. And there is pleasure in status. There is pleasure in being recognized, even by automated systems. These are the pleasures of belonging in a transactional community.

"Rewards programs are part of the fiber of the American economy," notes the economist Michael A. Turner. "They are woven through both the warp and the weft. Over time, they have become both pervasive and popular. In fact, it is hard to imagine a scenario in which consumers do not expect rewards programs, including for travel, shopping, grocery, and credit."[112] There seems to be loyalty for everything. Even the marijuana industry is drawing on platforms like springbig, a "holistic loyalty program experience for retailers and consumers," which allows individual cannabis sellers to tailor a loyalty program to their customer base, while collecting customer data to feed back to retailers.[113]

But as loyalty programs become more ubiquitous, regulators are starting to explore whether there should be more oversight. In a 2015 report, the Consumer Financial Protection Bureau (CFPB) noted, "For many consumers, rewards have become central to the decision of which credit cards to acquire and how to use them," and it warned that a lack of transparency about the terms of rewards program makes them difficult to understand.[114] In 2017, in a letter to the CFPB, the American Bankers Association suggested guiding principles for credit card rewards, including greater transparency, ethical considerations for how promotions are structured, and clarity around points forfeiture.[115] However, it is unclear how much, if any, progress will be made toward regulating loyalty programs at the federal level.

Today's loyalty programs tend to adhere to familiar structures. Credit card rewards are funded by interchange fees and can be earned at a range of merchants. Alternatively, companies like Starbucks have created closed-loop, "unitary" systems, where an entire transaction is carried out within an internal economy. Because the currency of the rewards is free food and drinks, the cost of the Starbucks rewards program is offset not by charging interchange but by avoiding it entirely. Furthermore, Starbucks uses the system to collect transactional data from customers, which can be used for targeted marketing and other purposes. A number of other merchants are keen to build closed-looped rewards systems like Starbucks' to avoid paying interchange, capture customer data, and increase customer loyalty.

The models for these new loyalty programs are still emerging. One model, reminiscent of community currencies, explicitly ties loyalty to a particular geography. A second model attempts to remake loyalty as more of a universal payment instrument, widely accepted by retailers and interoperable with other forms of money. This move toward universality, however, is always marked by the constraint characteristic of loyalty.

Some new monies overtly relate to money's capacity to mark space and make place. Place-based loyalty programs, like local currencies, are trying to produce transactional communities tied to local economic geographies. To combat plummeting foot traffic in shopping malls, the mall giants Starwood and Simon have both introduced loyalty programs that track mall-wide spending and reward it with points that can be redeemed at any store in the mall. "We look at this as an opportunity to give our shoppers another reason to come to the mall," Simon's vice president of marketing Ed Vittoria told the *Chicago Tribune*. He added that retail partners "really like the increased traffic they get from this."[116]

Bernal Heights, an affluent San Francisco neighborhood with a long history of community activism, has taken geographic loyalty a step further, creating what has been called the first "digital" community currency. By using a prepaid debit card issued by a local credit union, consumers can earn 5 percent of transactions at participating retailers in the form of Bernal Bucks. The Bucks, printed at home in $10 increments, can be used as cash at those same retailers. By limiting the creation and circulation of rewards to the neighborhood, Bernal Bucks create a form of "fiscal localism," codifying and protecting an existing community and local economy. It makes sense, then, that Bernal Heights is variously described as a "tight-knit community," as "probably the neighborhoodiest neighborhood in San Francisco," and even as "notoriously insular."[117] The politics of Bernal Bucks is, in a way, conservative: preserving what is cherished, excluding and fending off everything else. And the program may not necessarily benefit participating merchants, who have to pay higher interchange when the cards are swiped and then accept the rewards as currency. However, for many people in Bernal Heights, the experience of using the card has a positive psychological effect. As one local blogger wrote, "Honestly, it's like I get a little shot of endorphins every time I use the card to make a purchase, because the physical act of handing my card to a merchant represents the completion of an intentional YIMBY [yes in my back yard] gesture to support local businesses."[118]

Meanwhile, other loyalty programs are positioning themselves as fully developed, universally accepted currencies. Amazon, the online marketplace where one can purchase almost anything, from rolls of toilet paper to a car, now accepts rewards from American Express, Citi, Discover, and Chase as payment for most items. Customers using the site's own Amazon.com Rewards Visa can earn points as they pay. Similarly, companies like PointsPay propose to "free your points" by providing software that allows any merchant, including small businesses, to accept a variety of different rewards as payment. Mastercard is offering issuers the opportunity to use its Pay with Rewards program to apply points to purchases at a variety of participating retailers.[119] The goal is for this "uniformity across different retail sectors" to make loyalty an "adaptable and exchangeable near-currency unit with widespread usage that makes loyalty schemes deeply relevant to consumers' everyday lives."[120]

Multipartner coalition rewards programs are designed to produce confederated loyalty—across different brands for a whole lifestyle—but results have been mixed. The American Express program Plenti once included an impressive array of national brands like Macy's, Rite Aid, Chili's, ExxonMobile, AT&T, and Enterprise. But the program fell apart within three years. Shopping patterns in the United States are highly regional, and the nebulous group of partners that formed Plenti's participating retailers was unlikely to serve as a single consumer's top choices. Without a focal point for the coalition, consumer participation lagged, and eventually brands began pulling out to create their own rewards programs.[121] However, several major coalition rewards programs are operating successfully. If confederated loyalty becomes more popular, it could have the effect of sorting people into holistic market segments based on preferred lifestyle brands.

In the move toward interoperability and universality, some loyalty programs have begun to invoke cryptocurrency and block-chain technologies.[122] Japan's largest retailer, Rakuten, recently announced a loyalty program measured in "Rakuten coin," a corporate cryptocurrency accepted at all Rakuten-affiliated retailers.[123] Starbucks, meanwhile, is also said to be experimenting with a blockchain-based loyalty system, and various social networking sites are said to be working on cryptocurrencies of their own.

There is little evidence, however, that a firm like Starbucks, with its extensive infrastructure for digital payments, or social media platforms like Facebook actually need a blockchain or cryptocurrency to provide digital payments. Rather, as I have argued with the communication scholars Nancy Baym and Andrea Alarcon, blockchain acts as a "convening technology," attracting attention, expertise, and capital.[124] Blockchain offers these firms a mystique of innovation, a feeling of excitement, a whiff of the radical. In this sense, blockchain acts as a Trojan horse, enabling entrenched firms to create closed-loop loyalty systems while appearing to support an open, transparent, peer-to-peer technology.

Rewards may be the Facebook of money. But Facebook may also be the Facebook of money. As I described in the opening of this book, in June 2019, Facebook unveiled its plans for a digital currency called Libra. The announcement was unsurprising as Facebook had been trying to come up with a successful payment service for some time and because, by that point, everyone from Goldman Sachs to turkey farmers was experimenting with blockchain. But Libra, at least as expressed in its white papers and launch materials, was far more ambitious.

Libra is envisioned as a universal, global currency: a one-world money. Whereas private transactional communities—like those enacted by WeChat, Venmo, and loyalty programs—are niche and segmented, Libra aspires to pave over the differences between national currencies and payment systems, to bring all users of money, banked and unbanked, under its auspices. Social media becomes mass media.

Unlike cryptocurrencies like Bitcoin, Libra is not rooted in a libertarian market vision. Whereas cryptocurrency advocates imagined a world without third-party intermediaries and megalithic control systems, Libra embraces them. Whereas state currencies can be subject to democratic governance, Libra is designed to be managed by corporations at the levels of both monetary policy and infrastructure.

If national currency represents liberal democracy, and Bitcoin represents some combination of techno-libertarianism and anarcho-capitalism, then Libra represents Silicon Valley feudalism. Libra is complete with its own round table: its infrastructure and monetary policy is controlled by the Libra Association, which is made up of large corporate entities.[125] This is not a "peer-to-peer" technology; rather, it bestows a peerage.

When Libra was announced, it felt audacious. It also felt inevitable. In Howard Schultz's 2018 vision for a future of private, branded monies, he emphasized trust. If trust is the key to the issuance of currency, then Facebook is an astonishingly unlikely candidate. But money's effectiveness comes not just from trust but from ubiquity. With Facebook's presence on billions of phones worldwide, it has the unique power to coerce users into adopting a new form of currency.

This kind of coercion, rather than trust, is fundamental to some versions of money's origin. The anthropologist David Graeber writes of resource-poor medieval monarchs who could "simply send out royal agents to appropriate things they needed from some hapless townsman or villager, record the value of those things on hazel twigs, and leave the stocks with the victim."[126] These tally sticks were a record of the debt the sovereign owed the subject. The subject could turn around and use the stick for exchange, and once the stick changed hands enough times, it became money, marking a transactional community that accepted the deferred debt of the king as payment. But the shock of the original coerced trade remained. Graeber cites a popular medieval poem that describes the practice. In it, a shepherd laments that all his cattle have been taken and slain by the king, who paid him with "but a stick of tree."[127] What will Facebook leave us with?

Of course, Libra may not be as inevitable as it seemed. Key members have pulled out of the Libra partnership, and the project seems to be crumbling. But in 2019, Facebook had more quietly announced new plans for Facebook Pay, which lacked the audacity of Libra but nevertheless positioned Facebook to fight for dominance in payments, unencumbered by regulatory or public scrutiny. There is power in money's tokens—in currency itself, in the backing and authorizing of it—but there remains power in its rails and ledgers—the communication systems that move money around and collect data on its passage.

7 TRANSACTIONAL FUTURES

Living with New Money

In the 2009 novel *The City and The City*, China Miéville imagines a bizarre landscape simultaneously occupied by two distinct cities: Besźel and Ul Qoma.[1] Although the cities are physically located in the same geographic place, they are experienced as two different places. Set somewhere in eastern Europe, Besźel and Ul Qoma are not marbled but fully superimposed yet invisibly Balkanized. It is left unexplained how and why the two cities came to be cleaved, but the separation is now total. From birth, residents of each city learn to "unsee" the other city and its people. They are disciplined to live their lives in only one city, completely separated from the other city. For residents of Besźel and Ul Qoma, "breaching" the divide between the two places, even accidentally, is a crime worse than murder. Each city has its own distinct character: In Besźel, people drink coffee; in Ul Qoma, tea. In Besźel, a thirty-four-letter alphabet similar to Cyrillic is used; in Ul Qoma, Roman script. And, of course, each city has its own currency. Should you dare to see them both, you would know Besźes or Ul Qomanis by their gait, their affect, and their mode of payment. Money is one of the ways that the border between the two distinct realities is maintained.

The City and The City is a work of fantasy (and also, it's worth noting, a great police procedural!), but it is fantasy that is an exaggeration of mundane life in cities. We are disciplined to unsee the people and places we aren't meant to see. In an essay on the 2012 Olympics, Miéville describes how London is a city with many cities. It's a city of Olympics boosters, protestors, rioters, diasporas, future Brexiters, real estate speculators, wild foxes, feral parakeets, and ghosts. And tourists are "funneled into prescribed walkways," and their "access routes" are "neurotically planned and policed."[2] We all live in cities within cities. Miéville's London is a cacophony of cities, not the low, thrum-like total syncopation of Besźel and Ul Qoma.

But the unseeing of the details of the worlds of others in real life can be quiet as well. Money forms produce and trace the boundaries of these worlds. When I book a room at a Sheraton or other Starwood Preferred Guest—or, rather, Bonvoy—hotel using my Bonvoy credit card or Bonvoy points, I do so through a different phone or web portal than other non-SPG guests do. I am charged different rates. I wait in a different line to check in. I am treated differently by the front-desk clerk. I stay in a room on a designated Bonvoy floor. Sometimes I have access to different breakfasts, different common areas, different Wi-Fi networks. Because of my payment form, my experience is differentiated. The same could be said for truck stops, where most car drivers never notice trucker rewards kiosks. The same could be said for grocery stores, where some customers know to avoid warm rotisserie chicken in favor of chilled rotisserie chicken and then swipe cards that authorize payment for the latter but not the former. These spaces and the transactional communities that lurk within them are not, to use Miéville's terms, "cleaved," but they are "crosshatched."

Beginning in 2017, Chinese visitors to Caesars Entertainment–owned resorts and casinos in Las Vegas were able to forgo cash and cards to make payments through WeChat.[3] They could book a room (and receive a 10 percent discount when doing so) and buy a coffee, a Louis Vuitton handbag, or tickets to a Britney Spears concert, all through WeChat. The only thing they can't do at Caesars through WeChat is gamble.

A so-called "everything app," WeChat is used in China for, well, everything.[4] WeChat users can message friends, connect with new business contacts, post photos and videos, read news articles, play games, order food and car services, pay bills, book doctor's appointments, and apply for visas. They can upload a government ID and use the app in place of a physical ID card. The technology and media analyst Ben Thompson explains, "For all intents and purposes WeChat is your phone, and to a far greater extent in China than anywhere else, your phone is everything. There is nothing in any other country that is comparable: not LINE, not WhatsApp, not Facebook."[5]

"We want to do this for our Chinese customers to make them feel at home," Bruce Bommarito, corporate vice president of international marketing for Caesars Entertainment, told the *Las Vegas Review-Journal*.[6] For Chinese tourists, WeChat *is* home. Indeed, Chinese tourists can now vacation in Las Vegas without ever handling US currency, without ever leaving the transactional community of China (or its pervasive government surveillance and control).

It isn't just Vegas—WeChat Pay is currently accepted in forty-nine countries, and its parent company, Tencent, is aggressively pursuing further expansion.[7] The spread of WeChat as a transactional community doesn't require official partnerships between global corporations. At a Chinese restaurant in Charlottesville, where I live, the owners accept payment using their WeChat account. The restaurant posts menu specials on WeChat "moments" that appeal to Chinese international student tastes, in the vein of the age-old special menu of authentic dishes, written in Chinese. In this small restaurant in central Virginia, steps from Thomas Jefferson's rotunda, money moves from Chinese bank account to Chinese bank account inside WeChat, without ever leaving the Chinese transactional community.

Neal Stephenson's *Diamond Age*, with its "phyles" of shared cultural affinities, each with its own money system and economic norms, is, of course, science fiction. But segmented transactional communities that are aligned with nation-states but not fully overlapping with them, that crosscut geographies in new ways, are already here. The scholar of technology and culture Nathaniel Tkacz argues that payment apps compete on the basis of offering not just payment but, perhaps more importantly, "experience" of the world. He writes that such "experience money" takes up ordinary transactions and "deliberately infuse[s]" them "with a coherent value proposition."[8] If, as Helleiner suggests, state-issued currency created a "common economic language" for citizens of the nation-state, social media money offers a private, cohesively branded experience of economic communication.[9]

It isn't just China, which is all too often used as an Orientalist proxy for techno-dystopian futures. My American students who study abroad frequently talk of paying each other for food, drinks, travel, and living expenses through Venmo. While the purpose of study abroad is usually described as "immersion" in local culture, these students remain largely within the transactional community of their American friends—with money moving from one US bank account to another inside Venmo—no matter where they are in the world.

Venmo allows students to communicate as rapidly with the folks back home as they do with their local friends—literally, one user explained, getting money from their parents and then using it to repay a friend for expenses in Barcelona. That same student explained that it was difficult to include a new Spanish friend into a group trip to Ibiza because all shared expenses were settled through Venmo. The group worked it out by agreeing that the Spanish friend would pay for dinner and drinks in euros to cover her share of the hotel costs—as they put it, she "handled" the euros. As a result, the American students on the trip rarely had to *touch* local currency.

We don't yet know the shape of tomorrow's transactional media nor the terrain of its transactional communities. Those that are emerging are the social media of money: private, surveilled, and rooted in data-driven business models. Some are highly hierarchical and segmented; some are universal and mass. Most require trusting unaccountable corporations with our money and our data, our ability to pay and be paid. Their segmentation means that you could be living in a completely different world than the person sitting next to you. Their plurality could mean that your transactional life is variegated, omnivorous, constantly shifting between different monies, different communities.

Unlike Stephenson's phyles or Miéville's cleaved landscapes—or, indeed, most present-day nation-states—citizenship in future transactional communities will probably not be unitary. Instead, our transactional identities will be multivariate, shifting. We will "handle" many currencies, and our transactional identities will be similarly plural. If money is the "skin of the state," these payment forms create new ways of communicating: touching and not touching, being in bodies, new states, new skins.[10]

ACKNOWLEDGMENTS

ALL books, especially first books, are collective efforts. I am indebted for the mentorship, friendship, care, and criticism of so many. Any contributions this book makes are possible because of them; and, of course, any errors are my own. I fear that one error will be omitting people to whom I feel a great deal of gratitude.

I have been privileged to be among amazing colleagues at the Annenberg School for Communication and Journalism at the University of Southern California, Oxford Internet Institute, Massachusetts Institute of Technology, Microsoft Research New England, Berkman Klein Center for Internet and Society at Harvard University, and University of Virginia.

Manuel Castells offered tremendous intellectual, personal, and material support, including through the Wallis Annenberg Chair in Communication Technology and Society Fellowship and the Balzan Foundation.

Bill Maurer is a chaordic force and a weird sister schoolmarm: I owe him so much.

In addition, I would like to thank the following people who read, commented on a version of, or otherwise guided or supported this work: Taylor Nelms, Dave Stearns, everyone at Glenbrook Partners, Dave Birch, Dan Littman, Josh Lauer, Finn Brunton, Rachel O'Dwyer, Quinn Dupont, Scott Mainwaring, Melissa Wrapp, Jenny Fan, everyone at the UC Irvine Institute for Money, Technology, and Financial Inclusion and the Intel Science and Technology Center for Social Computing, Sarah Myers West, everyone at the USC Research Group on Economic Cultures, Lisa Servon, Liz Moor, Michael Palm, Bernardo Batiz-Lazo, Sarah Jeong, David Birch, Amelia Acker, Morgan Currie, Joan Donovan, Patrick Murck, Jennifer Chayes, Nancy Baym, Mary L. Gray, Tarleton Gillespie, Sharon Gillett, Caroline Jack, Nick Seaver, Butler Lampson, Henry Cohn, Jessa Lingel, Sarah Brayne, Elena Maris, Annette Markham, Paul Dourish, David Hesmondhalgh, Andrea Alarcon, Christopher Persaud, Sarah O'Brien, Siva Vaidyanathan, Camilla Fojas, Liz Ellcessor, Meredith Clark, Laura Portwood Stacer, Kate Larson, Patrick Davidson, Brittany Shook, Megan Vickery, Robert Meister and the Futures of Finance Network, Geert Lovink and everyone at MoneyLab, Mike Ananny, Larry Gross, Sarah Banet-Weiser, Andrew Lakoff, Henry Jenkins, Jonathan Aronson, Vanessa Schwartz, Sharon Hayes, Alison Trope, Tom Goodnight, Francois Bar, Christopher Holmes Smith, Laura Isabel Serna and the dissertation writing group, the UVA writing group crew and all their babies, Susy Garciasalas, Noelia Diaz-Lopez, Reanne Martinez, Barbara Gibbons, generous anonymous reviewers, and many more.

This book really wouldn't have existed without Joseph Calamia, who is a dream editor and also an esoteric Charmander. Thank you as well to Margaret Otzel, Andrew Katz, and everyone at Yale University Press. This book would be a lot less beautiful without Meghan Macera.

Thank you to my friends and family, particularly my mother, Marilyn; and sister, Kayte; the Driscoll family; and my familiar, Cooper. Finally, thank you to Kevin Driscoll, for basically everything.

NOTES

1. THE COMMUNICATION OF MONEY

1. Libra Association Members, "Introduction to Libra."

2. Green and Stavins, "2017 Diary of Consumer Payment Choice."

3. Braudel, *Structures of Everyday Life*, 436.

4. Maurer, "Late to the Party"; Medley, *Highways of Commerce*.

5. See, for example, Kumar, Maktabi, and O'Brien, "2018 Findings from the Diary of Consumer Payment Choice"; Bansal et al., "Global Payments 2018"; KPMG, "Pulse of Fintech 2018."

6. DeYoung and Rice, "How Do Banks Make Money?"; Radecki, "Banks' Payments-Driven Revenues."

7. Star, "Ethnography of Infrastructure"; Edwards, "Infrastructure and Modernity."

8. Light, Burgess, and Duguay, "Walkthrough Method."

9. For an in-depth discussion of various philosophical approaches to money, see Dodd, *Social Life of Money*; Kant, *Philosophy of Law*, 124.

10. Parsons, "On the Concept of Influence," 39.

11. Polanyi, *Primitive, Archaic, and Modern Economics*, 175.

12. But see Liz Moor's fantastic recent article "Money," as well as Sebastian Gießmann's equally fantastic chapter "Toward a Media History of the Credit Card." In addition to communication and media studies, my approach throughout this book is informed by scholars working in the traditions of the social studies of finance (see, for example, MacKenzie, Muniesa, and Siu, *Do Economists Make Markets?*; Preda, *Information, Knowledge, and Economic Life*; Çalışkan and Callon, "Economization, Part 1"; and Çalışkan and Callon, "Economization, Part 2") and cultural economy (see, for example, Pryke and DuGay, *Cultural Economy*; Bennett, McFall, and Pryke, "Editorial"; Hardin, "Politics of Finance").

13. Maurer, "Payment."

14. Carey, *Communication as Culture*, 23.

15. Ibid., 18.

16. Ibid., 13, 16.

17. Peters, *Speaking into the Air*, 119.

18. Lauer, "Money as Mass Communication," 116.

19. Osborne, "Iconography of Nationhood in Canadian Art," 167.

20. Hymans, "Changing Color of Money."

21. Hewitt, *Beauty and the Banknote*, 11.

22. Henkin, *City Reading*; Murthy, "Street Media."

23. Foster, "In God We Trust?," 230.

24. Women On $20s, "Why the $20?"

25. US Department of Treasury, "Treasury Secretary Lew Announces"; Swanson and Ohlheiser, "Harriet Tubman to Appear on $20 Bill."

26. Today Show, ".@RealDonaldTrump speaks out."

27. Rappeport, "Harriet Tubman on the $20?"

28. Manigault, *Unhinged*, 295.

29. Pardes, "Turn Your $20s into Tubmans."

30. Wall, "Harriet Tubman Stamp."

31. MacGregor, "History of the World in 100 Objects."

32. A group related to the Tubman Bill Project assembled the arguments here: Torrone, "Hey Steven Mnuchin."

33. Strassler, "Face of Money," 95.

34. Fiske, *Reading the Popular*.

35. Zelizer, "Social Meaning of Money."

36. Ibid.

37. Ibid., 343.

38. Nelms and Maurer, "Materiality, Symbol and Complexity."

39. Nelms, "Dollarization, Denomination, and Difference."

40. For Carey's own explication of the transmission versus ritual view, see Carey, "Configurations of Culture, History, and Politics."

41. Sterne, "Transportation and Communication," 118.

42. Lievrouw, "Materiality and Media," 50. See also Latour, "Technology Is Society Made Durable," 103.

43. Silverstone, *Why Study the Media?*

44. Marvin, "Reconsidering James Carey," 222.

45. This approach is aligned with what scholars working in science, technology, and society (STS) refer to as "infrastructure studies," which attends to the importance of infrastructures and the classifications and standards that produce and are produced by them (Edwards et al., "Understanding Infrastructure"; Bowker and Star, *Sorting Things Out*; Star, "Ethnography of Infrastructure"). Communication scholars have produced studies of the infrastructures of important communication technologies—see, for example, studies on electricity (Marvin, *When Old*

Technologies Were New), radio (Douglas, *Early Days of Radio Broadcasting*), telephone (Fischer, *America Calling*), internet (Abbate, *Inventing the Internet*), undersea cables (Starosielski, *Undersea Network*), and satellites (Parks, *Cultures in Orbit*).

46. Star, "Ethnography of Infrastructure," 379.
47. Dourish and Bell, "Infrastructure of Experience."
48. Star, "Ethnography of Infrastructure," 389.
49. Edwards, "Infrastructure and Modernity," 191.
50. Dodd, *Social Life of Money*, 272.
51. Bennett, *Vibrant Matter*.
52. See O'Dwyer, "Ether."
53. Russell and Vinsel, "After Innovation, Turn to Maintenance," 2.
54. Carey, *Communication as Culture*, 16; Soderlund, "Communication Scholarship as Ritual."
55. Krämer, *Medium, Messenger, Transmission*, 23; see also Peters, *Speaking into the Air*.
56. Soderlund, "Communication Scholarship as Ritual," 107.
57. Peters, *Speaking into the Air*, 29.
58. Marx, "Private Property and Labor."
59. Krämer, *Medium, Messenger, Transmission*.
60. Zelizer, *Purchase of Intimacy*.
61. Holt, *Lost World of the Golden King*.
62. Helleiner, "National Currencies and National Identities," 1430.
63. Gilbert and Helleiner, *Nation-States and Money*.
64. Gilbert, "Common Cents," 367.
65. Granovetter, "Economic Action and Social Structure."
66. Zelizer, "Circuits of Commerce."
67. McFall, Cochoy, and Deville, "Introduction," 1.
68. Joseph, *Against the Romance of Community*.
69. Krämer, *Medium, Messenger, Transmission*; Peters, *Speaking into the Air*.
70. Gilbert, "Forging a National Currency," 42.
71. See, for example, Papacharissi, "We Have Always Been Social."
72. Livingstone, "From Mass to Social Media?"
73. boyd, "Social Media."
74. Hewitt, *Beauty and the Banknote*, 11.
75. Helleiner, "National Currencies and National Identities," 1414. See also Swartz and Stearns, "Money and Its Technologies"; Maurer, "Payment."
76. Braun, *This Program Is Brought to You By . . .*
77. Facebook, "Send Money to Friends in Messenger."
78. Birch, "Facebook Money Is Overdue."
79. boyd and Ellison, "Social Network Sites."

80. Bary, "Is Venmo the Next Big Social Network?"; Rubin, "Venmo"; Atik, "Public Displays of Transaction."

81. For a discussion of social media techno-panics, see Marwick, "To Catch a Predator?"

82. "Is Venmo Making Us Petty?"; Wolfson, "This Is How Venmo Is Ruining Relationships"; Laneri, "Not App-y about It"; Griswold, "Venmo Scammers Know Something You Don't"; Notopoulos, "Here's Why Venmo Users Should Care"; Andrews, "Why Venmo Is the Absolute Best App."

83. Palleschi, "Friends with Venmo."

84. Henkin, *City Reading*; Carruthers and Babb, "Color of Money."

85. A similar point is made in Swartz and Stearns, "Money and Its Technologies."

86. Zelizer, "Social Meaning of Money," 343.

87. Birch, "Post-functional Cash."

88. Maurer, *How Would You Like to Pay?*, 143.

2. TRANSACTIONAL PASTS

1. Hock, *One from Many*, 97.

2. This chapter covers some of the same ground as the much longer Swartz and Stearns, "Money and Its Technologies."

3. Gilbert, "Forging a National Currency."

4. Anderson, *Imagined Communities*.

5. Peters, *Speaking into the Air*, 119.

6. Hewitt, *Beauty and the Banknote*, 11.

7. Henkin, *City Reading*.

8. Ibid., 146.

9. Simmel, "Metropolis and Mental Life."

10. Helleiner, "National Currencies and National Identities," 1414.

11. Ibid.

12. Mattelart, *Invention of Communication*.

13. John, *Spreading the News*.

14. Grossman, *American Express*, 80.

15. Gilbert, "Forging a National Currency," 42.

16. Fradkin and Holliday, *Stagecoach*, 11.

17. US Postal Service, "United States Postal Service."

18. Wheat and De Long, "California's Bantam Cock," 390.

19. Grossman, *American Express*.

20. For more on the history of the American postal service, see John, *Spreading the News*.

21. Carey, *Communication as Culture*.

22. John, *Network Nation*, 10.

23. Lachter, *Western Union Telegraph Company's Search*.

24. Lachter argues that Western Union never developed sophisticated-enough security—cryptography, identity verification, etc.—or revenue models to make money transfer services possible. Telegraphy, however, did contribute to the practice of modern finance. By spreading the same price information across geographical areas, the telegraph shifted arbitrage from space (buying low in Chicago and selling high in New York) to time (buying low in spring and selling high in summer), creating the commodities market (Carey, *Communication as Culture*, 168). When the telegraph made real-time financial information available outside of formal stock exchanges, speculation was democratized through "bucket shops," shadow markets where ordinary people made trades (Hochfelder, "Where the Common People Could Speculate").

25. Cushing, *Story of Our Post Office*, 207.

26. Grossman, *American Express*.

27. Ibid., 89.

28. Ibid., 94.

29. Cannon, *Clearing-Houses*.

30. Spahr, *Clearing and Collection*; see also Maurer, "Payment."

31. Spahr, *Clearing and Collection*.

32. Quoted in Simmons, *Credit Card Catastrophe*, 89.

33. Evans and Schmalensee, *Paying with Plastic*.

34. R. Mann, *Charging Ahead*.

35. "Traveling? Put It on the Cuff."

36. Grutzner, "Living High without Money."

37. Nocera, *Piece of the Action*.

38. Hyman, *Debtor Nation*; Evans and Schmalensee, *Paying with Plastic*; Stearns, *Electronic Value Exchange*.

39. Evans and Schmalensee, *Paying with Plastic*, 61; Gießmann, "Toward a Media History."

40. Stearns, *Electronic Value Exchange*.

41. Ibid.

42. Hock, *Birth of the Chaordic Age*; Hock, *One from Many*.

43. Rheingold, *Virtual Community*.

44. Barbrook and Cameron, "Californian Ideology."

45. F. Turner, *From Counterculture to Cyberculture*.

46. See Jackson, *PayPal Wars*.

47. Maurer, *How Would You Like to Pay?*

48. Nelms et al., "Social Payments."

49. See Gray and Suri, *Ghost Work*.

50. Mistreanu, "China Is Implementing a Massive Plan."

51. Takahashi, "CryptoKitties."

52. See, for example, from 1972, 1996, and 2019, respectively, Hendrickson, *Cashless Society*; Ice and Demy, *Coming Cashless Society*; Santana, "Is the U.S. on Its Way to Becoming a Cashless Society?"

3. TRANSACTIONAL IDENTITIES

1. Chase, "Chase Reinvents Luxury Credit Card Category."

2. See, for example, TheJokore, "Unboxing the Chase Sapphire Reserve Card"; The Credit Shifu, "Chase Sapphire Reserve Unboxing."

3. Sweet, "Credit Card Sensation."

4. Cowley, "Value-Seekers Warm to a $450 Annual Credit Card Fee."

5. Duhigg, "Amex, Challenged by Chase."

6. NBA, "American Express Jersey Insurance Program."

7. Lauer, *Creditworthy*.

8. Ibid., 35.

9. Consumer Financial Protection Bureau, "Credit Reports and Scores."

10. Nichols, "Data Doubles"; see also Cheney-Lippold, *We Are Data*.

11. See, for example, Cetera, "How to Qualify"; Kelly, "How I Got Approved"; Bostwick, "Insider Q&A"; "Who Gets Approved"; Dornhelm, "US Average FICO Score Hits 700."

12. US Bureau of Labor Statistics, "Usual Weekly Earnings."

13. Espeland and Sauder, "Rankings and Reactivity."

14. Andriotis, "Airport Lounge."

15. See, for example, comments on u/mk712, "Chase Sapphire Reserve."

16. Higgins, "How to Turn Your Renovation into a Vacation."

17. Money, "What Your Date's Credit Card Says."

18. Wilson, "What Your Payment Method Reveals."

19. Geertz, *Interpretation of Cultures*, 6.

20. Wilson, "What Your Payment Method Reveals."

21. Holt, "Who Were the Indo-Greeks?," 14; Holt, *Lost World of the Golden King*.

22. The best resource for understanding all aspects of the payments industry, including issuing, is Benson and Loftesness, *Payments Systems in the U.S.* It is absolutely required reading for anyone interested in the topic.

23. For more on the material and socio-technical arrangements of payment cards, see Deville, "Paying with Plastic"; Gießmann, "Money, Credit, and Digital Payment."

24. Evans and Schmalensee, *Paying with Plastic*, 119

25. Cowley, "Value-Seekers Warm."

26. Evans and Schmalensee, *Paying with Plastic*, 217.

27. The author does not actually have a Chase Sapphire Reserve, though she has considered applying for one—for research purposes.

28. Harrow, "Who Pays for Your Credit Card Rewards?"

29. Schuh, Shy, and Stavins, "Who Gains and Who Loses," 3.

30. For example, compare Turner et al., *Reexamination*; and F. Hayashi, "Do U.S. Consumers Really Benefit."

31. Maurer, "Payment"; see Benson and Loftesness, *Payment Systems in the U.S.*"

32. For more on the history of the credit card, see Mandell, *Credit Card Industry*; Mann, *Charging Ahead*; Stearns, *Electronic Value Exchange*; Evans and Schmalensee, *Paying with Plastic*; Nocera, *Piece of the Action*; Calder, *Financing the American Dream*; Hyman, *Debtor Nation*; Ritzer, *Expressing America*; Wolters, "Carry Your Credit in Your Pocket"; Gießmann, "Toward a Media History."

33. Swartz, "Gendered Transactions," 141.

34. Sutton, "Just Write It on the Tab, Joe."

35. D. Jones, "Credit Card Climb."

36. Grossman, *American Express*

37. Evans and Schmalensee, *Paying with Plastic*.

38. Nocera, *Piece of the Action*.

39. Stearns, *Electronic Value Exchange*.

40. These regulations were steadily eroded over the latter half of the twentieth century, and most interstate banking prohibitions were finally repealed by the Riegle-Neal Interstate Banking and Branching Efficiency Act of 1994.

41. Evans and Schmalensee, *Paying with Plastic*.

42. Stein, "Is There Life after Credit?"

43. Araujo and Kjellberg, "Enacting Novel Agencements," 97; Thurlow and Jaworski, "Alchemy of the Upwardly Mobile."

44. Evans and Schmalensee, *Paying with Plastic*, 213.

45. Stevenson, "Advertising."

46. Chase, "Ink Business Preferred Credit Card."

47. For a comparison to owner-operators in the commercial trucking industry, see Dills, "Play Your Cards Right."

48. Suri and Gray, "Spike in Online Gig Work"; see also Gray and Suri, *Ghost Work*.

49. Katz and Krueger, "Rise and Nature of Alternative Work Arrangements."

50. Dunn, "Debit It!"

51. "Credit Card Users Tighten Up or Drop Out."

52. Servon, *Unbanking of America*, 80.

53. Burhouse et al., "FDIC National Survey."

54. Consumer Financial Protection Bureau, "What Types of Fees."

55. Green Dot, "Green Dot Reloadable Prepaid Debit Cards."

56. Commerce Bank, "Fee Information."

57. Baradaran, *How the Other Half Banks*, 1.

58. Servon, *Unbanking of America*, 80; see also King, "For Prepaid Card Customers."

59. Green Dot, "Our Products."

60. Bluebird, "Bluebird."

61. Servon, *Unbanking of America*.

62. Servon, "Checks."

63. Weinstock et al., "Banking on Prepaid," 15.

64. Lieber, "TV Adviser on Money Offers Card."

65. Lieber, "Suze Orman's Approved Prepaid Debit Cards."

66. Weinstock et al., "Banking on Prepaid."

67. Green Dot, "About NASCAR Prepaid Visa Card."

68. Netspend, "MLB Prepaid Cards."

69. Ellis, "Kardashian Kard Kanceled."

70. Consumer Financial Protection Bureau, "CFPB Finalizes Changes."

71. Ryan, "Green Dot Expands Uber Venture."

72. "Deep Dive."

73. See Santucci, "Secured Credit Card Market."

74. Hardin and Towns, "Plastic Empowerment."

75. Ibid.

76. For a discussion of the history and the potential for postal banking, see Baradaran, *How the Other Half Banks*.

77. Clotteau and Measho, *Global Panorama*, 17.

78. US Postal Service, "Postal Savings System."

79. Postal Banking Act, S. 2755, 115th Cong. (2018), https://web.archive.org/web/20190323202702/https://www.congress.gov/115/bills/s2755/BILLS-115s2755is.pdf.

80. National Postal Museum, "Commemorative Issues"; Goldblatt and Handler, "Toward a New National Iconography"; Greenberg, "Postage and Power"; Brennan, *Stamping American Memory*.

81. F. Hayashi, "Do U.S. Consumers Really Benefit."

82. Federal Reserve System, "Federal Reserve Payments Study."

83. Lipscomb, "Magnises and the Allure of Credit Cards."

4. TRANSACTIONAL POLITICS

1. Alexander, "It Happened to Me."

2. Alexander, Twitter bio.

3. Alexander, "Got this email."

4. WePay, "WePay's Terms of Service as It Relates to Adult Entertainment"; see also WePay, "WePay's Terms of Service as It Relates to Adult"; and Alois, "Update."

5. WePay, "WePay's Terms of Service as It Relates to Adult Entertainment."

6. Girl Daydreams, "Help out @EdenAlexanderXX."

7. WePay, "WePay's Terms of Service as It Relates to Adult Entertainment."

8. K. Fisher, "Eden Alexander Emergency Medical Care Fund."

9. Woyke, "WePay."

10. Paice, "Icing PayPal"; S. Jones, "PayPal Tweaked."

11. Bodnar, "How a Block of Ice Increased One Company's Customers."

12. Alsever, "WePay Is the Anti-PayPal."

13. Dickson, "WePay Withholds Funds."

14. Stryker, "Not Waving" (emphasis in original).

15. Lake and Roux, "Incomplete List"; see also Blue, "PayPal, Square and Big Banking's War."

16. Comment on "WePay suspends medical fundraiser payment."

17. WePay, "WePay's Terms of Service as It Relates to Adult Entertainment."

18. Clerico, "@melissagira @WePay no, we mean the rules."

19. ladiesagainsthumanity, "Douchebro of the Week Award."

20. Star, "Ethnography of Infrastructure"; Edwards, "Infrastructure and Modernity."

21. Meer, "Enemy Known."

22. Zibell and Kendall, "Probe Turns Up Heat."

23. Issa, "Department of Justice's 'Operation Choke Point.'"

24. Benkler, "WikiLeaks and the ProtectIP Act," 156.

25. Poulsen, "PayPal Freezes WikiLeaks Account."

26. Addley and Deans, "WikiLeaks Suspends Publishing."

27. Kreimer, "Censorship by Proxy," 35.

28. Mann, "Autonomous Power of the State"; Castells, *Communication Power*.

29. See, for example, Moyer and Silver-Greenberg, "RushCard Breakdown Affects Thousands"; Y. Hayashi, "Federal Consumer Watchdog"; Gunn, "Is RushCard Really the Problem?"

30. Louis, "@RushCard it's been a whole week."

31. Again, the best resource for understanding all aspects of the payments industry, including acquiring, is Benson and Loftesness, *Payments Systems in the U.S.*

32. For a history and in-depth analysis of the system of standardized messages, see Stearns, *Electronic Value Exchange*.

33. Benson and Loftesness, *Payments Systems in the U.S.*, 99.

34. Starbucks, "Starbucks to Move Payment Processing."

35. Simmel, "Metropolis and Mental Life."

36. See the literature on governmentality, risk, and insurance, for example, Knights and Vurdubakis, "Calculations of Risk"; Simon, "Emergence of a Risk Society"; Barry, Doyle, and Ericson, *Insurance as Governance*.

37. Power, *Riskwork*.

38. Castel, "From Dangerousness to Risk," 281.

39. Ward, "High-Risk Digital World."

40. Saint, "How Pornographers Invented E-Commerce."

41. Fourcade and Healy, "Classification Situations," 564.

42. boyd, *It's Complicated*, 31; see also boyd and Marwick, "Social Privacy."

43. York, ".@WePay's statement is bullshit."

44. York, "@MsMaggieMayhem @melissagira @billclerico @WePay Wow, do they follow."

45. "WePay Launches Veda."

46. O'Malley, "Governmentality and Risk," 17.

47. Gandy, *Panoptic Sort*; Lyon, *Surveillance as Social Sorting*.

48. Lyon, *Surveillance as Social Sorting*, 1.

49. Brayne, "Big Data Surveillance."

50. Fourcade and Healy, "Seeing like a Market," 10.

51. Lunden, "Chase Closes WePay Acquisition."

52. Deville, "Leaky Data"; Deville and van der Velden, "Seeing the Invisible Algorithm."

53. Castel, "From Dangerousness to Risk," 287 (emphasis in original).

54. Zeitlin, "US Sanctions."

55. He, "Automating Machine Learning."

56. Zeitlin, "US Sanctions."

57. O'Reilly, "What Is Web 2.0."

58. In contrast, see Schermer, Custers, and van der Hof, "Crisis of Consent"; and other research in the FAT/ML, a subfield of computer science focused on fairness, accountability, and transparency in machine learning from a technical perspective, for example, Custers and Schermer, "Responsibly Innovating."

59. See Derrida, *Deconstruction and the Possibility of Justice*, 26–28.

60. "WePay Founder Talks Veda's Launch."

61. Lauer, *Creditworthy*.

62. Of course, as work by Josh Lauer and Martha Poon has pointed out, these regulations do little to ensure fairness in credit reporting. Lauer, *Creditworthy*; Poon, "From New Deal Institutions to Capital Markets"; Poon, "Scorecards."

63. See, for example, Kutcher, Nottebohm, and Sprague, "Grow Fast or Die Slow."

64. Knorr-Cetina, "Micro-Social Order," 26.

65. Stryker, "Not Waving."

66. GoFundMe, "Understanding GoFundMe's Policies."

67. Flox, "Adult Content Is Forbidden."

68. Ibid.

69. GoFundMe, "Understanding GoFundMe's Policies."

70. WePay, "WePay's Terms of Service as It Relates to Adult Entertainment."

71. Southern Poverty Law Center, "Cody Rutledge Wilson"; Kestenbaum, "Welcome to Hatreon"; Michel, "White Supremacists' Favorite Fundraising Site."

72. Timberg, "Bitcoin's Boom"; Smith, "Neo-Nazi Wealth."

73. Gillespie, *Custodians of the Internet*.

74. Blue, "Why PayPal's Crackdown."

75. Espeland and Sauder, "Rankings and Reactivity."

76. Penny, "Stand Up for Sex Workers."

77. Popkin, "Why PayPal's Bad Reputation Is Bigger."

78. The case of Eden Alexander is far from the only example. See, for example, missfreudianslit, "UGH PAYONEER"; Stokes, "Soapbox."

79. Meer, "Enemy Known"; M. Bell, "Paypal Regrets Shutting Down Regretsy."

80. Schulberg, "Gab"; Tusikov, "Defunding Hate."

81. sexworkerhelpfuls, "Sex Work Approved Payment Options"; see also Alptraum, "How Sex Workers Get Paid."

82. End Banking for Human Traffickers Act of 2017, S. 952, 115th Cong. (2017), https://web.archive.org/web/20190306023418/https://www.congress.gov/115/bills/s952/BILLS-115s952is.pdf.

83. Hatch, "First Congress Took Sex Workers' Websites."

84. UN Human Rights Council, "Promotion, Protection and Enjoyment."

85. O'Brien, "Understanding Consumer Cash Use."

86. Quoted in Simmons, *Credit Card Catastrophe*, 89.

5. TRANSACTIONAL MEMORIES

1. De Recat, "Common Venmo Charges, Decoded."

2. Gillette, "Cash Is for Losers!"

3. Coffee shops are the primary testing ground for what Scott Mainwaring calls "new payment genres." It seems like every advertisement for new payment systems is set in a coffee shop. Faux coffee shops reign supreme in the exhibition hall at fin-tech conferences. There is, I believe, a substantive reference to Starbucks in every chapter of this book. See Mainwaring, "Dongles."

4. Rachel O'Dwyer makes a related argument in "Cache Society."

5. Guseva and Rona-Tas, "Money Talks," 204.

6. Dodd, *Social Life of Money*, 296; see also Martin, "Mobile Money Platform Surveillance."

7. Gimlet, "Follow the Money."

8. See, for example, Wayne, "Thanks to Venmo"; Dewey, "Why Would Anyone"; Ohikuare, "Venmo Makes Me Feel Bad"; "Millennials Are Getting 'Venmo Anxiety'"; Ihnat, "People Have Gotten Some Really Rude Requests."

9. Levenson, "Why the Venmo Newsfeed Is the Best"; D'Onfro, "Venmo's 'Secret Sauce.'"

10. Cole, "Privacy Researcher."

11. "People Venmo Money."

12. Hearon, "Bachelor's Becca Kufrin"; Kircher, "Somebody Found Sean Spicer's Venmo."

13. LaMagna, "More Social Media Apps"; Bary, "Is Venmo the Next Big Social Network?"

14. Van Dijck and Poell, "Understanding Social Media Logic."

15. Frith, *Smartphones as Locative Media*, 90–91. See also Brown and Hoskins, "Terrorism in the New Memory Ecology."

16. Van Dijck, "Mediated Memories."

17. Van Dijck, "From Shoebox to Performative Agent," 313.

18. Hoskins, "Media, Memory, Metaphor"; Hand, "Persistent Traces."

19. Kocherlakota, "Money Is Memory," 232.

20. Hart, *Money in an Unequal World*, 234.

21. Blackwell, *Secret Life of Things*.

22. Bellamy, "It-Narrators and Circulation," 126. See also Addison, "Adventures of a Shilling"; H. Scott, *Adventures of a Rupee*.

23. Maurer, "Money as Token," 110.

24. Simmel, "Metropolis and Mental Life"; Simmel, *Philosophy of Money*.

25. See Brunton, *Digital Cash*; Swartz, "What Was Bitcoin."

26. Guyer, "Money Is Good to Think," 53.

27. Nelms, "Accounts."

28. Ibid., 43.

29. Zelizer, "Payments and Social Ties"; Maurer, *How Would You Like to Pay?*

30. Lanier, *You Are Not a Gadget*, 284.

31. See Maurer, "Blockchains Are a Diamond's Best Friend"; Swartz, "Blockchain Dreams"; DuPont and Maurer, "Ledgers and Law."

32. Nelms, "Accounts," 49.

33. Poovey, *History of the Modern Fact*.

34. Soll, *Reckoning*.

35. Atik, "Public Displays of Transaction."

36. DuPont and Maurer, "Ledgers and Law."

37. Humphreys, *Qualified Self*, 9–10.

38. Quoted in "How to Balance Your Checkbook."

39. Ibid.

40. McKenney, Copeland, and Mason, *Waves of Change*.

41. Fisher and McKenney, "Development of the ERMA Banking System," 44.

42. Quoted in "6 Step Plan to Balance Checkbook."

43. Vartabedian, "Balance Your Checkbook?"

44. "Bank Imposes Fee."

45. "6 Step Plan to Balance Checkbook."

46. For more on the raced, classed, and gendered socio-technical politics of Diners Club in midcentury America, see Swartz, "Gendered Transactions."

47. Grutzner, "Living High."

48. Tucker, "Credit System Lures 40,000 Eaters-Out."

49. Markoutsas, "More Women Tackle the Family's Checkbooks."

50. Nash, "Credit Cards Best Used Judiciously."

51. Ibid.

52. "What's a Debit Card?"

53. Rosen, "Siren Swipe."

54. Several data networks that were built to link ATM machines and carry debit transactions in the 1980s were interconnected, merged, and acquired by Mastercard and Visa in the 1990s to provide debit card services. See Crenshaw, "Rising Debit Card Use"; Behr, "Most, Honor ATM Networks Agree to Merge."

55. In 1992, the journalist Michael Quint estimated the cost of processing a check at seventy-nine cents and the cost of processing an electronic payment at twenty-five cents; Quint, "Banks' Plea."

56. Heady, "Debit Cards Are Becoming More Important."

57. Kristof, "Beware the Pitfalls."

58. Heady, "Debit Cards Are Becoming More Important."

59. Lloyd, "How Debit Cards Can Burn Holes."

60. Crenshaw, "Rising Debit Card Use."

61. Ibid.

62. Tugend, "Balancing a Checkbook Isn't Calculus."

63. Stearns, *Electronic Value Exchange*.

64. Beyond payment and transactional data, large merchants, as Joe Turow has documented, have become increasingly sophisticated at using what they do have access to—including in-store behavior—to track customers. See Turow, *Aisles Have Eyes*.

65. Lauer, *Creditworthy*.

66. Gehl, *Reverse Engineering Social Media*; van Dijck and Poell, "Understanding Social Media Logic."

67. "Payment Data Is More Valuable."

68. For an exploration of metaphors related to "sieves," see Seaver, "Captivating Algorithms."

69. O'Dwyer, "Money Talks"; see, for example, Pratini, "Who's Winning"; Dangelmaier, "Wallet Wars"; Webster, "Who Won't Win."

70. Gerlitz and Helmond, "Like Economy."

71. Van Dijck and Poell, "Understanding Social Media Logic."

72. Gehl, "Archive and the Processor."

73. Reading, "Seeing Red."

74. See Vaidhyanathan, *Googlization of Everything*.

75. Sterling, "Google Wallet."

76. US Securities and Exchange Commission, "Alphabet Inc. Form 10-K."

77. US Securities and Exchange Commission, "Google Inc. Form 10-K."

78. Google, "About Google Ads."

79. Google, "About Google Partners."

80. See Swartz, "Goodbye, Wallet."

81. Ibid.

82. Cheney-Lippold, *We Are Data*; Cheney-Lippold, "New Algorithmic Identity."

83. See Boden, "Transcript"; Golson, "Live Coverage."

84. Chen and Lohr, "With Apple Pay and Smartwatch."

85. Apple, "Apple Pay Security and Privacy Overview."

86. Lupton, *Quantified Self*, 68. For more on the "quantified self" movement, see Neff and Nafus, *Self-Tracking*.

87. DuPont and Maurer, "Ledgers and Law."

88. EMVCo, "EMV Payment Tokenisation Specification."

89. Dexheimer, "Apple Said to Reap Fees."

90. Biddle, "Android Is Popular."

91. Apple, "Apple Card."

92. Vosburg, "Card for Our Digital Era."

93. Apple, "Apple Card."

94. Ibid.

95. The term "exomemory" comes from the novel *The Quantum Thief*, by Hannu Rajaniemi. I am indebted to Nancy Baym for the recommendation.

96. Wortham, "Braintree."

97. Rao, Perez, and Lunden, "EBay's PayPal Acquires Payments Gateway Braintree."

98. See Cao, "Millennials Say 'Venmo Me.'"

99. See, for example, Palleschi, "Friends with Venmo"; Dewey, "Why Would Anyone"; Walker, "After Snowden"; and Gimlet, "Follow the Money"—all of which include the word "overshare."

100. "Read What Happens."

101. D'Onfro, "Vicemo Lets You See."

102. Venmo, "User Agreement."

103. Robehmed, "Venmo."

104. Venmo, "Purchases."

105. Gorman, "How Team of Geeks Cracked Spy Trade."

106. See Brayne, "Big Data Surveillance"; Burns, "Leaked Palantir Doc."

107. Sidel, "First Data Reports First Quarterly Profit."

108. These behaviors have been documented in my ongoing pilot qualitative research with Venmo users.

109. Mittal, "WeChat."

110. Do Thi Duc, "Public by Default"; Do Thi Duc, "Venmo Stories of 2017."

6. TRANSACTIONAL PUBLICS

1. Faull, "Starbucks' Rewards Scheme"; Lovelace, "Starbucks' Howard Schultz"; Milano, "Starbucks Chairman Is Hot on Blockchain."

2. Starbucks, "Starbucks Corp. (SBUX) Q1 2018 Earnings Call," 22–23.

3. Ibid.

4. Maurer, *Mutual Life*; Brunton, *Digital Cash*.

5. Maurer, "Money Nutters."

6. Statistica, "Number of Starbucks Stores."

7. Starbucks, "Starbucks Company Timeline."

8. Starbucks, "Mobile Payment Debuts Nationally."

9. See, for example, m_watson, "Starbucks' Mobile App"; "Starbucks App Leads Mobile Payment Competitors"; Din, "Four Companies Driving the Bank Tech Discussion"; Tode, "Starbucks Is Worldwide Leader"; Grothaus, "Most Popular Mobile Payments App."

10. Starbucks, "Starbucks Corp. (SBUX) Q1 2018 Earnings Call," 14.

11. Williams and Demos, "Where Money Lives."

12. Maurer, Nelms, and Swartz, "When Perhaps the Real Problem"; Swartz, "Blockchain Dreams."

13. Maurer, Nelms, and Swartz, "When Perhaps the Real Problem"; Brunton, "Keeping the Books"; Golumbia, *Politics of Bitcoin*.

14. See Swartz, "What Was Bitcoin."

15. Brunton, *Digital Cash*; Swartz, "What Was Bitcoin."

16. Maurer, Nelms, and Swartz, "When Perhaps the Real Problem."

17. Gibson-Graham, Cameron, and Healy, *Take Back the Economy*; Fuller, Jonas, and Lee, "Editorial Introduction"; Hlebik, "Analysis of Worldwide Community Economies."

18. North, *Money and Liberation*.

19. Tekobbe and McKnight, "Indigenous Cryptocurrency"; Alcantara and Dick, "Decolonization in a Digital Age."

20. Maurer, *Mutual Life*.

21. Scott, "Riches beyond Belief."

22. See Gothill, "#PunkMoney."

23. Minsky, *Stabilizing an Unstable Economy*, 228.

24. S. Bell, "Hierarchy of Money."

25. Hock, *One from Many*, 95.

26. Carey, *Communication as Culture*, 19.

27. Birch, *Before Babylon*, 228.

28. Starbucks, "Starbucks Reports Q1 Fiscal 2019 Results."

29. Ibid.

30. Segel, Auerbach, and Segev, "Power of Points."

31. Turow, *Aisles Have Eyes*.

32. Drèze and Nunes, "Using Combined-Currency Prices."

33. See, for example, Payments Leader, "Rise of Alternative Payment Types"; Sage, "Rise of the Alternative (Loyalty) Currency."

34. Leonhardt, "Frequent Fliers."

35. "Frequent-Flyer Economics," 62.

36. Clark, "Frequent Flyer Miles Soar."

37. Thériault, "I Already Have a Cryptocurrency."

38. Maurer, Nelms, and Swartz, "When Perhaps the Real Problem"; Swartz, "What Was Bitcoin."

39. Banet-Weiser, *Authentic TM*.

40. Teslik, "Nation Branding Explained."

41. Desan, *Making Money*, 1.

42. See, for example, Graeber, *Debt*; Hart, "Heads or Tails?"; Schmandt-Besserat, *How Writing Came About*; Eagleton and Williams, *Money*; Wray, "Introduction to an Alternative History."

43. Desan, *Making Money*, 7.

44. Brunton, *Digital Cash*; Spang, *Stuff and Money*; Swartz, "What Was Bitcoin."

45. Simmel, *Philosophy of Money*, 176.

46. Dodd, *Social Life of Money*, 9.

47. Maurer, "Money Nutters."

48. Dodd, "Utopian Monies," 234.

49. Ibid.; see also Swartz, "What Was Bitcoin"; Brunton, *Digital Cash*.

50. Castells, *Rupture*.

51. Vlastelica, "Cup of Crypto."

52. Maurer, *How Would You Like to Pay?*

53. Guyer, "Soft Currencies," 2214.

54. Spang, *Stuff and Money*, 172.

55. Cipolla, *Money, Prices, and Civilization*.

56. Helleiner, "National Currencies and National Identities," 1414.

57. Helleiner, *Making of National Money*, 147.

58. Zelizer, *Social Meaning of Money*, 4.

59. Henkin, *City Reading*.

60. Weber, *Peasants into Frenchmen*.

61. Hock, *Birth of the Chaordic Age*, 123.

62. Swartz, "What Was Bitcoin"; Brunton, *Digital Cash*.

63. Chaum, "Security without Identification"; May, "Crypto Anarchy"; Dai, "bmoney"; Szabo, "Bit Gold."

64. Russell and Vinsel, "Innovation Is Overvalued."

65. Hart, *Money in an Unequal World*, 237.

66. Pettitt, "Bracketing the Gutenberg Parenthesis"; Sauerberg, "Gutenberg Parenthesis."

67. Quoted in Starkman, "Future Is Medieval."

68. Hart, "Notes towards an Anthropology of Money."

69. See, for example, De Geer, "Bitcoin Is Where the Internet Was"; Zuckerman, "CNBC Fast Money's Brian Kelly"; Fung, "Marc Andreessen."

70. Mansell, *Imagining the Internet*; Flichy, *Internet Imaginaire*.

71. F. Turner, *From Counterculture to Cyberculture*.

72. Delwiche, "New Left"; Petrick, "Imagining the Personal Computer"; Rankin, *People's History*.

73. Barlow, "Declaration"; Kreiss, "Vision of and for the Networked World."

74. Barlow, "Declaration."

75. Baym, "From Practice to Culture"; Hauben and Hauben, *Netizens*.

76. Vaidhyanathan, *Antisocial Media*.

77. Helmond, "Algorithmization of the Hyperlink"; Pariser, *Filter Bubble*.

78. Marx, *Eighteenth Brumaire of Louis Bonaparte*, 7.

79. Zelizer, "Social Meaning of Money."

80. Carruthers and Espeland, "Money, Meaning, and Morality."

81. Castells, *Rise of the Network Society*, 442.

82. See C. Jones, "Passengers Can Pay with Miles."

83. NickV, "Driver Reward Cards."

84. Hervy, August 22, 2011, comment on NickV, "Driver Reward Cards."

85. Moonpie, April 25, 2014, comment on "Reward Cards."

86. Comment on TruckStopUSA.com.

87. "Lowdown on Customer Loyalty Programs"; see also Drèze and Nunes, "Feeling Superior."

88. Nunes and Drèze, "Your Loyalty Program Is Betraying You."

89. Kepnes, "15 Reasons Why Flying United Airlines Sucks."

90. For more on "oscillation" in and out of economic modalities, see Maurer, *Mutual Life, Limited*, 13.

91. Gee, *Situated Language and Learning*, 91.

92. Strathern, *The Gender of the Gift*, 13.

93. J. Grossmann, "Using Smartphones and Apps."

94. Nissenbaum, *Privacy in Context*.

95. Miller, "Cellphone in New Role."

96. Ferguson, "Persistence of Memory."

97. Turow, *Aisles Have Eyes*, 164.

98. You may recognize Hervé as a character on the French television show *Dix pour cent*.

99. Schneier, "600+ Companies PayPal Shares Your Data With."

100. Eubanks, *Automating Inequality*; Maréchal, "First They Came for the Poor."

101. Levy, "Contexts of Control."

102. "Pros and Cons of Using a Fuel Card."

103. Carruthers and Babb, "Color of Money"; Ritter, *Goldbugs and Greenbacks*.

104. For example, u/perfectviking, "Changes to the Marriott cards."

105. Strom, "Starbucks to Introduce Single-Serve Coffee Maker."

106. Delta, "Legal Issues"; "Legal Problems with Loyalty Programs"; Young, Maher, and Puccio, "Loyalty Programs"; Perkins Coie LLP and Affiliates, "Loyalty Programs."

107. Batten, "Trading Stamps and Coupons."

108. Sateriale v. R. J. Reynolds Tobacco Co., No. 11-55057 (9th Cir. July 13, 2012).

109. Green, *Company Town*.

110. Shaulis, "Mexico Supreme Court Orders Wal-Mart."

111. Zook and Graham, "Hacking Code/Space," 391.

112. M. Turner, "Credit Card Rewards."

113. Pallardy, "Cannabis Loyalty Software Provider Springbig."

114. Consumer Financial Protection Bureau, "Consumer Credit Card Market."

115. O'Neill, "Letter to CFPB."

116. Elejalde-Ruiz, "Woodfield, Orland Square Mall Operator."

117. Romney, "Unified by the Coin of Their Realm"; Sankin, "Bernal Heights Prints Own Currency."

118. Lappin, "Bernal Bucks Card Stars."

119. Mastercard, "Mastercard Pay with Rewards."

120. Johnson, "Are Loyalty Points the New Currency?"

121. Hanifin, "Real Reasons behind the Struggle."

122. Swaminathan, "How Blockchain Can Crack the Holy Grail."

123. Ibid.

124. Baym, Swartz, and Alarcon, "Sonic Publics."

125. According to promotional materials, would-be members of the Libra Association must meet certain criteria, such as having $1 billion market value or greater than $500 million customer balances, reaching greater than twenty million people a year, or being recognized as a top-one-hundred industry leader by an external evaluator such as the Fortune 500. In addition, members are required to commit to a $10 million buy-in as well as provide resources to maintain Libra's technical infrastructure.

126. Graeber, "Tallies," 141.

127. Ibid.

7. TRANSACTIONAL FUTURES

1. Taylor Nelms has also used Miéville's *The City and The City* to describe a world of plural monetary experiences in contemporary Ecuador. See Nelms, "Invisible City."

2. Miéville, "Oh, London."

3. "Caesars Entertainment Launched"; J. Jones, "Vegas Visitors"; Newsdesk, "Caesars Entertainment."

4. Huang, "All the Things You Can—and Can't—Do"; Li, "To Cover China."

5. Thompson, "Apple's China Problem."

6. Prince, "Caesars Launches WeChat Pay."

7. Wu, "Surprising Number of Countries."

8. Tkacz, "Money's New Abstractions."

9. Helleiner, "National Currencies and National Identities," 1414.

10. Foster, "In God We Trust?," 230.

BIBLIOGRAPHY

Abbate, Janet. *Inventing the Internet*. Cambridge, MA: MIT Press, 1999.

Addison, Joseph. "The Adventures of a Shilling." In *Selections from the Writings of Joseph Addison*, edited by Barrett Wendell and Chester Noyes Greenough, 46–50. Boston: Ginn, 1905.

Addley, Esther, and Jason Deans. "WikiLeaks Suspends Publishing to Fight Financial Blockade." *The Guardian*, October 24, 2011. https://web.archive.org/web/20190916030837/https://www.theguardian.com/media/2011/oct/24/wikileaks-suspends-publishing.

Alcantara, Christopher, and Caroline Dick. "Decolonization in a Digital Age: Cryptocurrencies and Indigenous Self-Determination in Canada." *Canadian Journal of Law & Society / La Revue Canadienne Droit et Société* 32, no. 1 (2017): 19–35. https://doi.org/10.1017/cls.2017.1.

Alexander, Eden. "Got this email from @wepay saying they CANCELLED my medical fundraiser bc ill use the money for porn. LITERALLY." Twitter (@EdenAlexanderXX), May 17, 2014. https://web.archive.org/web/20141202091512/https://twitter.com/EdenAlexanderXX/status/467706769578270720.

———. "It Happened to Me: I Am Eden Alexander, the Porn Star Whose Medical Fundraiser Was Confiscated Because of My Profession." xoJane, May 27, 2014. https://web.archive.org/web/20170904074837/http://www.xojane.com/it-happened-to-me/eden-alexander-wepay-giveforward.

———. Twitter bio. Twitter (@EdenAlexanderXX). Accessed August 25, 2015.

Alois, J. D. "Update: Crowdfunding Site Shuts Down Porn Stars Medical Crowdfunding Campaign." Crowdfund Insider, May 17, 2014. https://web.archive.org/web/20190303211947/https://www.crowd fundinsider.com/2014/05/38854-crowdfunding-site-shuts-porn-stars-medical-crowdfunding-campaign/.

Alptraum, Lux. "How Sex Workers Get Paid." Vice Motherboard, January 29, 2016. https://web.archive.org/web/20190222221411/https://motherboard.vice.com/en_us/article/nz7b4k/how-sex-workers-get-paid.

Alsever, Jennifer. "WePay Is the Anti-PayPal." CNN Money, October 12, 2010. https://web.archive.org/web/20190303151543/https://money.cnn.com/2010/10/12/technology/wepay/index.htm.

Anderson, Benedict. *Imagined Communities: Reflections on the Origin and Spread of Nationalism*. London: Verso, 1983.

Andrews, Taylor. "Why Venmo Is the Absolute Best App for Creep-Stalking Your Ex." *Cosmopolitan*, November 15, 2018. https://web.archive.org/web/20190202051807/https://www.cosmopolitan.com/sex-love/a25136353/venmo-stalking/.

Andriotis, AnnaMaria. "The Airport Lounge, Once a Refuge, Is a Total Zoo." *Wall Street Journal*, April 30, 2018.

Apple. "Apple Card." March 2019. https://web.archive.org/web/20190428190623/https://www.apple.com/apple-card/.

———. "Apple Pay Security and Privacy Overview." Apple Support. Accessed March 31, 2019. https://web.archive.org/web/20190331020243/https://support.apple.com/en-us/HT203027.

Araujo, Luis, and Hans Kjellberg. "Enacting Novel Agencements: The Case of Frequent Flyer Schemes in the US Airline Industry (1981–1991)." *Consumption Markets & Culture* 19, no. 1 (2016): 92–110. https://doi.org/10.1080/10253866.2015.1096095.

Atik, Chiara. "Public Displays of Transaction: How Venmo Became the Ultimate Social Network for Voyeurs and Gossips." *Medium* (blog), July 20, 2014. https://web.archive.org/web/20141015140017/https://medium.com/matter/public-displays-of-transaction-cede14426328.

Banet-Weiser, Sarah. *Authentic TM: Politics and Ambivalence in a Brand Culture*. New York: NYU Press, 2012.

"Bank Imposes Fee for Money Query." *New York Times*, June 8, 1963.

Bansal, Sukriti, Phillip Bruno, Olivier Denecker, Madhav Goparaju, and Marc Niederkorn. "Global Payments 2018: A Dynamic Industry Continues to Break New Ground." McKinsey & Company, October 2018.

Baradaran, Mehrsa. *How the Other Half Banks: Exclusion, Exploitation, and the Threat to Democracy*. Cambridge, MA: Harvard University Press, 2015.

Barbrook, Richard, and Andy Cameron. "The Californian Ideology." *Science as Culture* 6, no. 1 (1996): 44–72. https://doi.org/10.1080/09505439609526455.

Barlow, John Perry. "A Declaration of the Independence of Cyberspace." Electronic Frontier Foundation, February 8, 1996. https://web.archive.org/web/20190429004228/https://www.eff.org/cyberspace-independence.

Barry, Dean, Aaron Doyle, and Diana Ericson. *Insurance as Governance*. Toronto: University of Toronto Press, 2003.

Bary, Emily. "Is Venmo the Next Big Social Network?" *Barron's*, March 9, 2017. https://web.archive.org/web/20190331012425/https://www.barrons.com/articles/is-venmo-the-next-big-social-network-1489085179.

Bátiz-Lazo, Bernardo, Thomas Haigh, and David L. Stearns. "How the Future Shaped the Past: The Case of the Cashless Society." *Enterprise & Society* 15, no. 1 (2014): 103–31. https://doi.org/10.1093/es/kht024.

Batten, Donna, ed. "Trading Stamps and Coupons." In *Gale Encyclopedia of American Law*, 3rd ed., vol. 10, 80–81. Detroit, MI: Gale, 2010.

Baym, Nancy. "From Practice to Culture on Usenet." *Sociological Review* 42, no. 1_suppl (1994): 29–52. https://doi.org/10.1111/j.1467-954X.1994.tb03408.x.

Baym, Nancy, Lana Swartz, and Andrea Alarcon. "Sonic Publics | Convening Technologies: Blockchain and the Music Industry." *International Journal of Communication* 13 (2019): 402–21. https://ijoc.org/index.php/ijoc/article/view/8590.

Behr, Peter. "Most, Honor ATM Networks Agree to Merge." *Washington Post*, March 3, 1996.

Bell, Melissa. "Paypal Regrets Shutting Down Regretsy." *Washington Post*, December 6, 2011.

Bell, Stephanie. "The Hierarchy of Money." Working paper, Jerome Levy Economics Institute, April 1998. http://web.archive.org/web/20190428204804/http://www.levy.org/pubs/wp231.pdf.

Bellamy, Liz. "It-Narrators and Circulation: Defining a Subgenre." In *The Secret Life of Things: Animals, Objects, and It-Narratives in Eighteenth-Century England*, edited by Mark Blackwell, 117–33. Lewisburg, PA: Bucknell University Press, 2007.

Benkler, Yochai. "WikiLeaks and the ProtectIP Act: A New Public-Private Threat to the Internet Commons." *Daedalus* 140, no. 4 (2011): 154–64. https://doi.org/10.1162/DAED_a_00121.

Bennett, Jane. *Vibrant Matter: A Political Ecology of Things*. Durham, NC: Duke University Press, 2010.

Bennett, Tony, Liz McFall, and Mike Pryke. "Editorial." *Journal of Cultural Economy* 1, no. 1 (2008): 1–7. doi:10.1080/17530350801913551.

Benson, Carol Coye, and Scott Loftesness. *Payments Systems in the U.S.: A Guide for the Payments Professional*. Menlo Park, CA: Glenbrook Partners, 2013.

Biddle, Sam. "Android Is Popular Because It's Cheap, Not Because It's Good." Gizmodo, January 22, 2013. https://web.archive.org/web/20190604164723/https://gizmodo.com/android-is-popular-because-its-cheap-not-because-its-g-5977625.

Birch, David. *Before Babylon, Beyond Bitcoin: From Money that We Understand to Money That Understands Us*. London: London Publishing Partnership, 2017.

———. "Facebook Money Is Overdue." *Tomorrow's Transactions* (blog), April 16, 2014. https://web.archive.org/web/20190927150848/https://www.chyp.com/facebook-money-is-overdue/.

———. "Post-functional Cash." *Tomorrow's Transactions* (blog), April 15, 2014. https://web.archive.org/web/20190925214639/https://www.chyp.com/post-functional-cash/.

Blackwell, Mark, ed. *The Secret Life of Things: Animals, Objects, and It-Narratives in Eighteenth-Century England*. Lewisburg, PA: Bucknell University Press, 2007.

Blue, Violet. "PayPal, Square and Big Banking's War on the Sex Industry." Engadget, December 2, 2015. https://web.archive.org/web/20190303213302/https://www.engadget.com/2015/12/02/paypal-square-and-big-bankings-war-on-the-sex-industry/.

————. "Why PayPal's Crackdown on ASMR Creators Should Worry You." Engadget, September 14, 2018. https://web.archive.org/web/20190303171919/https://www.engadget.com/2018/09/14/paypal-ban-asmr-sound-art-therapy/.

Bluebird. "Bluebird." Accessed September 12, 2019. https://web.archive.org/web/20180802190038/https://www.bluebird.com/.

Boden, Rian. "Transcript: Apple CEO Tim Cook and SVP Eddy Cue Introduce Apple Pay Mobile Payments and NFC." *NFCW* (blog), September 9, 2014. https://web.archive.org/web/20190916035159/https://www.nfcw.com/2014/09/09/331431/transcript-apple-ceo-tim-cook-svp-eddy-cue-introduce-apple-pay-mobile-payments-nfc/.

Bodnar, Kipp. "How a Block of Ice Increased One Company's Customers by 225%." *HubSpot* (blog), October 20, 2016. https://web.archive.org/web/20190414195919/https://blog.hubspot.com/blog/tabid/6307/bid/7007/How-A-Block-of-Ice-Increased-One-Company-s-Customers-By-225.aspx.

Bostwick, Laura. "Insider Q&A: 25 Questions about Chase Sapphire Reserve." Finance Buzz, November 15, 2016. https://web.archive.org/web/20190307231152/https://financebuzz.com/chase-sapphire-reserve-insider-questions-and-answers.

Bowker, Geoffrey C., and Susan Leigh Star. *Sorting Things Out: Classification and Its Consequences*. Cambridge, MA: MIT Press, 1999.

boyd, danah. *It's Complicated: The Social Lives of Networked Teens*. New Haven, CT: Yale University Press, 2014.

————. "Social Media: A Phenomenon to Be Analyzed." *Social Media + Society* 1, no. 1 (2015). https://doi.org/10.1177/2056305115580148.

boyd, danah, and Nicole B. Ellison. "Social Network Sites: Definition, History, and Scholarship." *Journal of Computer-Mediated Communication* 13, no. 1 (2007): 210–30. https://doi.org/10.1111/j.1083-6101.2007.00393.x.

boyd, danah, and Alice E. Marwick. "Social Privacy in Networked Publics: Teens' Attitudes, Practices, and Strategies." Paper presented at "A Decade in Internet Time: Symposium on the Dynamics of the Internet and Society," Oxford Internet Institute, September 2011. https://ssrn.com/abstract=1925128.

Braudel, Fernand. *The Structures of Everyday Life: Civilization and Capitalism, 15th–18th Century*. Vol. 1. New York: HarperCollins, 1985.

Braun, Josh. *This Program Is Brought to You By . . .: Distributing Television News Online*. New Haven, CT: Yale University Press, 2015.

Brayne, Sarah. "Big Data Surveillance: The Case of Policing." *American Sociological Review* 82, no. 5 (2017): 977–1008. https://doi.org/10.1177/0003122417725865.

Brennan, Sheila. *Stamping American Memory: Collectors, Citizens, and the Post*. Ann Arbor: University of Michigan Press, 2018. https://doi.org/10.3998/mpub.9847183.

Brown, Steven D., and Andrew Hoskins. "Terrorism in the New Memory Ecology: Mediating and Remembering the 2005 London Bombings." *Behavioral Sciences of Terrorism and Political Aggression* 2, no. 2 (2010): 87–107. https://doi.org/10.1080/19434471003597399.

Brunton, Finn. *Digital Cash: The Unknown History of the Anarchists, Utopians, and Technologists Who Created Cryptocurrency*. Princeton, NJ: Princeton University Press, 2019.

———. "Keeping the Books: Inside the Blockchain." *Limn* 6 (March 2016). http://finnb.net/w/bitcoin-limn.pdf.

Burhouse, Susan, Karyen Chu, Keith Ernst, Ryan Goodstein, Alicia Lloro, Gregory Lyons, Joyce Northwood, et al. "FDIC National Survey of Unbanked and Underbanked Households." Federal Deposit Insurance Corporation, 2015. https://web.archive.org/web/20190323210411/https://www.fdic.gov/householdsurvey/2015/2015report.pdf.

Burns, Matt. "Leaked Palantir Doc Reveals Uses, Specific Functions and Key Clients." *TechCrunch* (blog), January 11, 2015. https://web.archive.org/web/20150714034434/http://techcrunch.com/2015/01/11/leaked-palantir-doc-reveals-uses-specific-functions-and-key-clients/.

"Caesars Entertainment Launches the First WeChat Digital Payment Program in Las Vegas." *Las Vegas Blog*, August 9, 2017. https://web.archive.org/web/20190702153417/http://blog.caesars.com/las-vegas/news/wechat-digital-payment-las-vegas/.

Calder, Lendol G. *Financing the American Dream: A Cultural History of Consumer Credit*. Princeton, NJ: Princeton University Press, 2009.

Çalışkan, Koray, and Michel Callon. "Economization, Part 1: Shifting Attention from the Economy towards Processes of Economization." *Economy and Society* 38, no. 3 (2009): 369–98. doi:10.1080/03085140903020580.

———. "Economization, Part 2: A Research Programme for the Study of Markets." *Economy and Society* 39, no. 1 (2010): 1–32. doi:10.1080/03085140903424519.

Cannon, James G. *Clearing-Houses: Their History, Methods and Administration*. London: Smith, Elder, 1900.

Cao, Jing. "Millennials Say 'Venmo Me' to Fuel Mobile-Payment Surge." *Bloomberg*, August 18, 2014.

Carey, James W. *Communication as Culture: Essays on Media and Society*. New York: Routledge, 2008.

———. "Configurations of Culture, History, and Politics." In *Thinking with James Carey: Essays on Communications, Transportation, History*, edited by Jeremy Packer and Craig Robertson, 199–226. New York: Peter Lang, 2006.

Carruthers, Bruce G., and Sarah Babb. "The Color of Money and the Nature of Value: Greenbacks and Gold in Postbellum America." *American Journal of Sociology* 101, no. 6 (1996): 1556–91. https://doi.org/10.1086/230867.

Carruthers, Bruce G., and Wendy Espeland. "Money, Meaning, and Morality." *American Behavioral Scientist* 41 (August 1998): 1384–1408. https://doi.org/10.1177/0002764298041010003.

Castel, Robert. "From Dangerousness to Risk." In *The Foucault Effect: Studies in Governmentality*, edited by Graham Burchell, Colin Gordon, and Peter Miller, 281–98. Chicago: University of Chicago Press, 1991.

Castells, Manuel. *Communication Power*. Oxford: Oxford University Press, 2009.

———. *The Rise of the Network Society*. Cambridge, MA: Blackwell, 1996.

———. *Rupture: The Crisis of Liberal Democracy*. 2nd ed. Cambridge, UK: Polity, 2019.

Cetera, Mike. "How to Qualify for a Premium Rewards Credit Card." *Yahoo! Finance*, September 11, 2017. https://web.archive.org/web/20190330212342/https://finance.yahoo.com/news/qualify-premium-rewards-credit-card-100000417.html.

Chase. "Chase Reinvents Luxury Credit Card Category with Sapphire Reserve, Launching Today." August 23, 2016. https://web.archive.org/web/20190322211626/https://media.chase.com/news/chase-reinvents-luxury-credit-card-sapphire-reserve.

————. "Ink Business Preferred Credit Card." Accessed April 14, 2019. https://web.archive.org/web/20190414170640/https://creditcards. chase.com/a1/InkBusinessPreferred/8tk.

Chaum, David. "Security without Identification: Transaction Systems to Make Big Brother Obsolete." *Communications of the ACM* 28, no. 10 (1985): 1030–44. doi:10.1145/4372.4373.

Chen, Brian X., and Steve Lohr. "With Apple Pay and Smartwatch, a Privacy Challenge." *New York Times*, September 10, 2014. https:// web.archive.org/web/20190821231620/https://www.nytimes. com/2014/09/11/technology/with-new-apple-products-a-privacy-challenge.html.

Cheney-Lippold, John. "A New Algorithmic Identity: Soft Biopolitics and the Modulation of Control." *Theory, Culture & Society* 28, no. 6 (2011): 164–81. https://doi.org/10.1177/0263276411424420.

————. *We Are Data: Algorithms and the Making of Our Digital Selves*. New York: NYU Press, 2017.

Cipolla, Carlo M. *Money, Prices, and Civilization in the Mediterranean World: Fifth to Seventeenth Century*. Princeton, NJ: Princeton University Press, 1956.

Clark, Andrew. "Frequent Flyer Miles Soar above Sterling." *The Guardian*, January 8, 2005. https://web.archive.org/web/20180831105944/ https://www.theguardian.com/money/2005/jan/08/business.theair lineindustry.

Clerico, Bill. "@melissagira @WePay correct, we are required to monitor customer websites and social media. Bc we have to, not bc we want to." Twitter (@billclerico), May 17, 2014. https://web.archive.org/ save/https://twitter.com/billclerico/status/467803836594126848.

Clotteau, Nils, and Bsrat Measho. *Global Panorama on Postal Financial Inclusion 2016*. Berne, Switzerland: Universal Postal Union, 2016. https://web.archive.org/web/20190323204413/http://www.upu.int/ uploads/tx_sbdownloader/globalPanoramaOnPostalFinancialInclu sion2016En.pdf.

Cole, Samantha. "A Privacy Researcher Uncovered a Year's Worth of Breakups and Drug Deals Using Venmo's Public Data." Vice Motherboard, July 17, 2018. https://web.archive.org/web/20190330230408/ https://motherboard.vice.com/en_us/article/j5n8wk/public-by-default-venmo-privacy-settings.

Commerce Bank. "Fee Information." Accessed August 11, 2018. https:// web.archive.org/web/20180801231111/https://www.visaprepaid processing.com/CommerceBank/MySpendingCard/Program/Fee.

Consumer Financial Protection Bureau. "CFPB Finalizes Changes to Prepaid Accounts Rule." January 25, 2018. https://web.archive.org/ web/20180801234945/https://www.consumerfinance.gov/about-us/ newsroom/cfpb-finalizes-changes-prepaid-accounts-rule/.

———. "The Consumer Credit Card Market." December 2015. https://web. archive.org/web/20190430034920/https://files.consumerfinance. gov/f/201512_cfpb_report-the-consumer-credit-card-market.pdf.

———. "Credit Reports and Scores." Accessed August 11, 2018. https:// web.archive.org/web/20190401234426/https://www.consumer finance.gov/ask-cfpb/category-credit-reporting/what-affects-credit-scores/.

———. "What Types of Fees Do Prepaid Cards Typically Charge?" November 28, 2016. https://web.archive.org/web/20170706074653/https:// www.consumerfinance.gov/ask-cfpb/what-types-of-fees-do-prepaid-cards-typically-charge-en-2053/.

Cowley, Stacy. "Value-Seekers Warm to a $450 Annual Credit Card Fee." *New York Times*, September 12, 2016. https://web.archive.org/ web/20190808223904/https://www.nytimes.com/2016/09/13/ business/dealbook/credit-card-rewards-chase-sapphire-reserve-annual-fees.html.

"Credit Card Users Tighten Up or Drop Out." *The Guardian*, April 2, 1994.

Crenshaw, Albert. "Rising Debit Card Use Heralds Change in Spending Habits." *Washington Post*, September 18, 1991.

Cushing, Marshall Henry. *The Story of Our Post Office: The Greatest Government Department in All Its Phases*. Boston: A. M. Thayer, 1893.

Custers, Bart H. M., and Bart W. Schermer. "Responsibly Innovating Data Mining and Profiling Tools: A New Approach to Discrimination Sensitive and Privacy Sensitive Attributes." In *Responsible Innovation 1*, edited by Jeroen van den Hoven, Neelke Doorn, Tsjalling Swierstra, Bert-Jaap Koops, and Henny Romijn, 335–50. Dordrecht: Springer Netherlands, 2014. https://doi.org/10.1007/978-94-017-8956-1_19.

Dai, Wei. "bmoney." Wei Dai's website, 1998. https://web.archive.org/ web/20190302042856/http://www.weidai.com/bmoney.txt.

Dangelmaier, Ralph. "Wallet Wars: The Fight to Dominate Payments Is Just Beginning." Venture Beat, April 18, 2015. https://web.archive. org/web/20170713102545/https://venturebeat.com/2015/04/18/ wallet-wars-the-fight-to-dominate-payments-is-just-beginning/.

"Deep Dive: Why Employers Are Turning to Payroll Cards." PYMNTS. com, July 16, 2018. https://www.pymnts.com/disbursements/2018/ deep-dive-payroll-cards-ingo-money/.

De Geer, Christoffer. "Bitcoin Is Where the Internet Was in 1995." The Street, October 28, 2015. https://web.archive.org/web/20160430083622/ http://www.thestreet.com/story/13338984/1/bitcoin-is-where-the-internet-was-in-1995.html.

Delta, George. "Legal Issues That Affect Awards Programs (2017 Primer)." Incentive Research Foundation, January 25, 2018. https://web. archive.org/web/20181001031826/http://theirf.org/research/legal-issues-that-affect-awards-programs-2017-primer/2379/.

Delwiche, Aaron. "The New Left and the Computer Underground: Recovering Political Antecedents of Participatory Culture." In *The Participatory Cultures Handbook*, edited by Aaron Delwiche and Jennifer Jacobs, 10–21. New York: Routledge, 2013. https://trove.nla. gov.au/version/174571509.

de Recat, Olivia. "Common Venmo Charges, Decoded." *New Yorker*, September 25, 2017. https://www.newyorker.com/humor/daily-shouts/ common-venmo-charges-decoded.

Derrida, Jacques, *Deconstruction and the Possibility of Justice*. New York: Routledge, 1992.

Desan, Christine. *Making Money: Coin, Currency, and the Coming of Capitalism*. Oxford: Oxford University Press, 2014.

Deville, Joe. "Leaky Data: How Wonga Makes Lending Decisions— Charisma—Consumer Market Studies." Charisma, May 20, 2013. https://web.archive.org/web/20190414201517/http://www. charisma-network.net/finance/leaky-data-how-wonga-makes-lending-decisions/.

———. "Paying with Plastic: The Enduring Presence of the Credit Card." In *Accumulation: The Material Politics of Plastic*, edited by Jennifer Gabrys, Gay Hawkins, and Mike Michael, 87–104. New York: Routledge, 2013. https://www.academia.edu/3549613/Paying_with_plastic_The_ enduring_presence_of_the_credit_card.

Deville, Joe, and Lonneke van der Velden. "Seeing the Invisible Algorithm: The Practical Politics of Tracking the Credit Trackers." In *Algorithmic Life*, edited by Louise Amoore and Volha Piotukh, 87–106. London: Routledge, 2015.

Dewey, Caitlin. "Why Would Anyone in Her Right Mind Use Venmo?" *Washington Post*, February 26, 2015.

Dexheimer, Elizabeth. "Apple Said to Reap Fees from Banks in New Payment System." Bloomberg, November 10, 2014.

DeYoung, Robert, and Tara Rice. "How Do Banks Make Money? The Fallacies of Fee Income." *Economic Perspectives* 28, no. 4 (2004): 34–51.

Dickson, E. J. "WePay Withholds Funds from Ailing Sex Worker Eden Alexander." Daily Dot, May 18, 2014. https://web.archive.org/web/20190303151450/https://www.dailydot.com/irl/eden-alexander-wepay-cam-girl/.

Dills, Todd. "Play Your Cards Right." Overdrive, January 4, 2011. https://web.archive.org/web/20131205023816/https://www.overdriveonline.com/play-your-cards-right-5/.

Din, Suleman. "Four Companies Driving the Bank Tech Discussion, with Only One a FAANG." American Banker, June 8, 2018. https://web.archive.org/web/20190428213720/https://www.americanbanker.com/news/four-companies-driving-the-bank-tech-discussion-with-only-one-a-faang.

Dodd, Nigel. *The Social Life of Money*. Princeton, NJ: Princeton University Press, 2014.

———. "Utopian Monies: Complementary Currencies, Bitcoin, and the Social Life of Money." In *Money Talks: Explaining How Money Really Works*, edited by Nina Bandelj, Frederick F. Wherry, and Viviana A. Rotman Zelizer, 230–48. Princeton, NJ: Princeton University Press, 2017.

D'Onfro, Jillian. "Venmo's 'Secret Sauce' Keeps Users Checking the App Even When They're Not Making Payments." Business Insider, December 9, 2015. https://web.archive.org/web/20190330230051/https://www.businessinsider.com/venmo-social-feed-is-its-secret-sauce-2015-12.

———. "Vicemo Lets You See Who Is Buying Drugs and Sex on Venmo." Business Insider, February 23, 2015. https://web.archive.org/

web/20181022033006/https://www.businessinsider.com/vicemo-lets-you-see-who-is-buying-drugs-and-sex-on-venmo-2015-2.

Dornhelm, Ethan. "US Average FICO Score Hits 700." *FICO Blog*, September 24, 2018. https://web.archive.org/web/20190322213955/ https://www.fico.com/blogs/risk-compliance/us-average-fico-score-hits-700-a-milestone-for-consumers/.

Do Thi Duc, Hang. "Public by Default." *22.8miles* (blog), 2018. https:// web.archive.org/web/20190401132905/https://22-8miles.com/ public-by-default/.

———. "Venmo Stories of 2017." *Public by Default*, 2018. https://public bydefault.fyi.

Douglas, George H. *The Early Days of Radio Broadcasting*. Jefferson, NC: McFarland, 1987.

Dourish, Paul, and Genevieve Bell. "The Infrastructure of Experience and the Experience of Infrastructure: Meaning and Structure in Everyday Encounters with Space." *Environment and Planning B: Planning and Design* 34, no. 3 (2007): 414–30. https://doi.org/10.1068/b32035t.

Drèze, Xavier, and Joseph Nunes. "Feeling Superior: The Impact of Loyalty Program Structure on Consumers' Perceptions of Status." *Journal of Consumer Research* 35, no. 6 (2009): 890–905. https://doi. org/10.1086/593946.

———. "Using Combined-Currency Prices to Lower Consumers' Perceived Cost." *Journal of Marketing Research* 59 (February 2004): 59–72.

Duhigg, Charles. "Amex, Challenged by Chase, Is Losing the Snob War." *New York Times*, April 14, 2017.

Dunn, William. "Debit It! New Breed of Cards an Alternative to Cash, Checks, Credit." *Chicago Tribune*, November 18, 1993.

DuPont, Quinn, and Bill Maurer. "Ledgers and Law in the Blockchain." *King's Review*, June 23, 2015. https://web.archive.org/ web/20181027202946/http://kingsreview.co.uk/articles/ledgers-and-law-in-the-blockchain/.

Eagleton, Catherine, and Jonathan Williams, eds. *Money: A History*. 2nd ed. London: British Museum Press, 2007.

Edwards, Paul. "Infrastructure and Modernity: Scales of Force, Time, and Social Organization in the History of Sociotechnical Systems." In *Modernity and Technology*, edited by Thomas J. Misa, Phillip Brey, and Andrew Feenberg, 185–225. Cambridge, MA: MIT Press, 2003.

Edwards, Paul, Steven J. Jackson, Geoffrey C. Bowker, and Cory Knobel. "Understanding Infrastructure: History, Heuristics, and Cyberinfrastructure Policy." *First Monday* 12, no. 6 (2007). https://doi.org/10.5210/fm.v12i6.1904.

Elejalde-Ruiz, Alexia. "Woodfield, Orland Square Mall Operator Simon Launches Loyalty Program." *Chicago Tribune*, September 8, 2014.

Ellis, Blake. "Kardashian Kard Kanceled by 'Fun-Loving' Sisters." CNN Money, November 30, 2010. https://web.archive.org/web/20181030133640/https://money.cnn.com/2010/11/29/pf/kardashian_kard_terminate/index.htm.

EMVCo. "EMV Payment Tokenisation Specification." Technical Framework, Version 2.1, 2019.

Espeland, Wendy Nelson, and Michael Sauder. "Rankings and Reactivity: How Public Measures Recreate Social Worlds." *American Journal of Sociology* 113, no. 1 (2007): 1–40. https://doi.org/10.1086/517897.

Eubanks, Virginia. *Automating Inequality: How High-Tech Tools Profile, Police, and Punish the Poor*. New York: St. Martin's, 2018.

Evans, David S., and Richard Schmalensee. "The Industrial Organization of Markets with Two-Sided Platforms." Working paper, National Bureau of Economic Research, September 2005. https://doi.org/10.3386/w11603.

———. *Paying with Plastic: The Digital Revolution in Buying and Borrowing*. Cambridge, MA: MIT Press, 1999.

Facebook. "Send Money to Friends in Messenger." March 17, 2015. https://web.archive.org/web/20190927150240/https://newsroom.fb.com/news/2015/03/send-money-to-friends-in-messenger/.

Faull, Jennifer. "Starbucks' Rewards Scheme Is Part of Its Much Bigger Vision for a Blockchain-Backed Digital Currency." The Drum, January 31, 2018. https://web.archive.org/web/20190428200641/https://www.thedrum.com/news/2018/01/31/starbucks-rewards-scheme-part-its-much-bigger-vision-blockchain-backed-digital.

Federal Reserve System. "The Federal Reserve Payments Study: 2017 Annual Supplement." December 2017. https://www.federalreserve.gov/newsevents/pressreleases/files/2017-payment-systems-study-annual-supplement-20171221.pdf.

Ferguson, Allison Cripps. "The Persistence of Memory: How Hotel Brands Can Activate Loyalty Data to Create Great Experiences." Merkle

Loyalty Solutions, July 24, 2017. https://web.archive.org/web/20180824121049/http://500friends.com/resources/The-Persistence-of-Memory.

Fischer, Claude S. *America Calling: A Social History of the Telephone to 1940.* Berkeley: University of California Press, 1992.

Fisher, Amy Weaver, and James L. McKenney. "The Development of the ERMA Banking System: Lessons from History." *IEEE Annals of the History of Computing* 15, no. 1 (1993): 44–57. https://doi.org/10.1109/85.194091.

Fisher, Kitty (organizer). "Eden Alexander Emergency Medical Care Fund." Tilt, June 13, 2014. https://web.archive.org/web/20150316001953/https://www.tilt.com/campaigns/eden-alexander-emergency-medical-care-fund/description.

Fiske, John. *Reading the Popular.* Boston: Unwin Hyman, 1989.

Flichy, Patrice. *The Internet Imaginaire.* Cambridge, MA: MIT Press, 2007.

Flox, A. V. "Adult Content Is Forbidden, but Fatal Racism Is Okay." Slantist, August 21, 2014. https://web.archive.org/web/20190303165956/http://slantist.com/wepay-no-porn-yes-racists/.

Foster, Robert J. "In God We Trust? The Legitimacy of Melanesian Currencies." In *Money and Modernity: State and Local Currencies in Melanesia,* edited by David Akin and Joel Robbins, 214–31. Pittsburgh: University of Pittsburgh Press, 1999.

Fourcade, Marion, and Kieran Healy. "Classification Situations: Life-Chances in the Neoliberal Era." *Accounting, Organizations and Society* 38, no. 8 (2013): 559–72. https://doi.org/10.1016/j.aos.2013.11.002.

———. "Seeing like a Market." *Socio-Economic Review* 15, no. 1 (2017): 9–29. https://doi.org/10.1093/ser/mww033.

Fradkin, Philip L., and J. S Holliday. *Stagecoach: Wells Fargo and the American West.* New York: Simon and Schuster, 2003.

"Frequent-Flyer Economics." *Economist,* May 4, 2002.

Frith, Jordan. *Smartphones as Locative Media.* Cambridge, UK: Polity, 2015.

Frommer, Dan. "The Complete Guide to Apple Pay." Quartz, October 20, 2014. http://web.archive.org/web/20190331020836/https://qz.com/284068/the-complete-guide-to-apple-pay/.

Fuller, Duncan, Andrew E. G. Jonas, and Roger Lee. "Editorial Introduction." In *Interrogating Alterity: Alternative Economic and Political*

Spaces, edited by Duncan Fuller, Andrew E. G. Jonas, and Roger Lee, xxii–xxviii. Farnham, UK: Ashgate, 2010.

Fung, Brian. "Marc Andreessen: In 20 Years, We'll Talk about Bitcoin like We Talk about the Internet Today." *Washington Post*, May 21, 2014.

Gandy, Oscar H. *The Panoptic Sort: A Political Economy of Personal Information*. Boulder, CO: Westview, 1993.

Gee, James Paul. *Situated Language and Learning: A Critique of Traditional Schooling*. New York: Routledge, 2004.

Geertz, Clifford. *The Interpretation of Cultures: Selected Essays*. New York: Basic Books, 1973.

Gehl, Robert W. "The Archive and the Processor: The Internal Logic of Web 2.0." *New Media & Society* 13, no. 8 (2011): 1228–44. https://doi.org/10.1177/1461444811401735.

———. *Reverse Engineering Social Media: Software, Culture, and Political Economy in New Media Capitalism*. Philadelphia: Temple University Press, 2014.

Gerlitz, Carolin, and Anne Helmond. "The Like Economy: Social Buttons and the Data-Intensive Web." *New Media & Society* 15, no. 8 (2013): 1348–65. https://doi.org/10.1177/1461444812472322.

Gibson-Graham, J. K., Jenny Cameron, and Stephen Healy. *Take Back the Economy: An Ethical Guide for Transforming Our Communities*. Minneapolis: University of Minnesota Press, 2013.

Gießmann, Sebastian. "Money, Credit, and Digital Payment 1971/2014: From the Credit Card to Apple Pay." *Administration & Society* 50, no. 9 (2018): 1259–79. https://doi.org/10.1177/0095399718794169.

———. "Toward a Media History of the Credit Card." In *Neighborhood Technologies*, edited by Tobias Harks and Sebastian Vehlken, 165–83. Zurich: Diaphanes, 2015.

Gilbert, Emily. "Common Cents: Situating Money in Time and Space." *Economy and Society* 34, no. 3 (2005): 356–87. https://doi.org/10.1080/03085140500111832.

———. "Forging a National Currency." In *Nation-States and Money: The Past, Present and Future of National Currencies*, edited by Emily Gilbert and Eric Helleiner, 25–46. New York: Routledge, 1999.

Gilbert, Emily, and Eric Helleiner, eds. *Nation-States and Money: The Past, Present and Future of National Currencies*. New York: Routledge, 1999.

Gillespie, Tarleton. *Custodians of the Internet: Platforms, Content Moderation, and the Hidden Decisions That Shape Social Media*. New Haven, CT: Yale University Press, 2018.

Gillette, Felix. "Cash Is for Losers! How the Mobile App Venmo Became a Verb. Among Millennials, Anyway." Bloomberg, November 21, 2014. http://web.archive.org/web/20190715165049/https://www.bloomberg.com/news/articles/2014-11-20/mobile-payment-startup-venmo-is-killing-cash.

Gimlet. "Follow the Money." *Reply All* (podcast), December 10, 2014. https://web.archive.org/web/20190401131436/https://www.gimlet-media.com/reply-all/4-follow-the-money.

Girl Daydreams. "Help out @EdenAlexanderXX https://www.giveforward.com/fundraiser/hvm4/eden-alexander-s-medical-care-fund . . . $20 free picset from us $50 free solo emailed to you $100 free membership to Sinfulsolos!!" Twitter (@GirlDaydreams), May 15, 2014. https://web.archive.org/web/20190302010630/https:/twitter.com/GirlDaydreams/status/467115806388518913.

GoFundMe. "Understanding GoFundMe's Policies." September 2, 2014. https://web.archive.org/web/20140905022727/http://www.gofundme.com/2014/09/02/understanding-gofundmes-policies/.

Goldblatt, Laura, and Richard Handler. "Toward a New National Iconography: Native Americans on United States Postage Stamps, 1863–1922." *Winterthur Portfolio* 51, no. 1 (2017): 55–79. https://doi.org/10.1086/693992.

Golson, Jordan. "Live Coverage of Apple's September 2014 IPhone and IWatch Event." MacRumors, September 9, 2014. http://web.archive.org/web/20190630004438/https://www.macrumors.com/2014/09/09/iphone-6-iwatch-event-live/.

Golumbia, David. *The Politics of Bitcoin: Software as Right-Wing Extremism*. Minneapolis: University of Minnesota Press, 2016.

Google. "About Google Ads." Google Ads Help. Accessed March 31, 2019. https://web.archive.org/web/20190331015414/https://support.google.com/google-ads/answer/6349091?visit_id=636895938963110114-3161205183&hl=en&rd=1.

———. "About Google Partners." Google Ads Help. Accessed March 31, 2019. https://web.archive.org/web/20190331015557/https://support.google.com/google-ads/answer/9029203?hl=en&visit_id=636895938963110114-3161205183&rd=3.

Gorman, Siobhan. "How Team of Geeks Cracked Spy Trade." *Wall Street Journal*, September 4, 2009.

Gothill, Eli. "#PunkMoney." Conference presentation at MoneyLab, March 22, 2014. https://vimeo.com/90734577.

Graeber, David. *Debt: The First 5,000 Years*. Brooklyn, NY: Melville House, 2011.

———. "Tallies." In *Paid: Tales of Dongles, Checks, and Other Money Stuff*, edited by Bill Maurer and Lana Swartz, 133–44. Cambridge, MA: MIT Press, 2017.

Granovetter, Mark. "Economic Action and Social Structure: The Problem of Embeddedness." *American Journal of Sociology* 91, no. 3 (1985): 481–510. https://doi.org/10.1086/228311.

Gray, Mary L., and Siddharth Suri. *Ghost Work: How to Stop Silicon Valley from Building a New Global Underclass*. Boston: Eamon Dolan/Houghton Mifflin Harcourt, 2019.

Green, Hardy. *The Company Town: The Industrial Edens and Satanic Mills That Shaped the American Economy*. New York: Basic Books, 2010.

Greenberg, Ivan. "Postage and Power: U.S. Nationalism and the 1970s 'Bicentennial' and 'Americana' Stamp Series." *Journal of Social History* 49, no. 1 (2015): 53–76. https://doi.org/10.1093/jsh/shv045.

Green Dot. "About NASCAR Prepaid Visa Card." Accessed August 2, 2018. https://web.archive.org/web/20180802193359/https://secure.green dot.com/racing/about-our-products.

———. "Green Dot Reloadable Prepaid Debit Cards." Accessed August 1, 2018. https://web.archive.org/web/20180801222721/https://www. greendot.com/help/getting-started/fees-and-limits/green-dot-reload able-prepaid-debit-cards/.

———. "Our Products." Accessed September 15, 2019. https://web.archive. org/web/20190915202158/https://www.greendot.com/for-people/ our-products.

Greene, Claire, and Joanna Stavins. "2017 Diary of Consumer Payment Choice." Federal Reserve Bank of Atlanta, May 2018.

Griswold, Alison. "Venmo Scammers Know Something You Don't." Slate, September 15, 2015. https://web.archive.org/web/20190421130330/ https://slate.com/business/2015/09/venmo-scam-and-fraud-why-its-easy-to-get-ripped-off-through-the-mobile-payments-app.html.

Grossman, Peter Z. *American Express: The Unofficial History of the People Who Built the Great Financial Empire*. New York: Crown, 1987.

Grossmann, John. "Using Smartphones and Apps to Enhance Loyalty Programs." *New York Times*, January 28, 2015.

Grothaus, Michael. "The Most Popular Mobile Payments App Is . . . Starbucks?" Fast Company, May 22, 2018. https://web.archive.org/web/20190428203300/https://www.fastcompany.com/40575953/the-most-popular-mobile-payments-app-isstarbucks.

Grutzner, Charles. "Living High without Money: All the Traveler Needs Is a Thing Called the Credit Card." *New York Times*, December 2, 1956.

Gunn, Dwyer. "Is RushCard Really the Problem?" *Pacific Standard*, October 26, 2015. https://web.archive.org/web/20181205204855/https://psmag.com/economics/the-rise-and-potential-fall-of-rushcard.

Guseva, Alya, and Akos Rona-Tas. "Money Talks, Plastic Money Tattles: The New Sociability of Money." In *Money Talks: Explaining How Money Really Works*, edited by Nina Bandelj, Frederick F. Wherry, and Viviana A. Rotman Zelizer, 201–214. Princeton, NJ: Princeton University Press, 2017.

Guyer, Jane. "Money Is Good to Think: From 'Wants of the Mind' to Conversation, Stories and Accounts." In *Money in a Human Economy*, edited by Keith Hart, 43–60. New York: Berghahn Books, 2017.

———. "Soft Currencies, Cash Economies, New Monies: Past and Present." *PNAS* 109, no. 7 (2012): 2214–21.

Haimann, Alexander T., Roger Brody, and National Postal Museum. "Commemorative Issues." Arago, December 12, 2008. https://web.archive.org/web/20190323191750/https://arago.si.edu/category_2045880.html.

Hand, Martin. "Persistent Traces, Potential Memories: Smartphones and the Negotiation of Visual, Locative, and Textual Data in Personal Life." *Convergence: The International Journal of Research into New Media Technologies* 22, no. 3 (2016): 269–86. https://doi.org/10.1177/1354856514546094.

Hanifin, Bill. "The Real Reasons behind the Struggle at Plenti." Wise Marketer, January 25, 2018. https://web.archive.org/web/20180602061635/http://www.thewisemarketer.com/channels/coalition-loyalty-marketing/real-reasons-behind-struggle-plenti/.

Hardin, Carolyn. "The Politics of Finance: Cultural Economy, Cultural Studies and the Road Ahead." *Journal of Cultural Economy* 10, no. 4 (2017): 325–38. doi:10.1080/17530350.2017.1297249.

Hardin, Carolyn, and Armond Towns. "Plastic Empowerment: Financial Literacy and Black Economic Irrationality." *American Quarterly* 71, no. 4 (2019).

Harrow, Robert. "Who Pays for Your Credit Card Rewards? (It May Be You)." *Forbes*, February 11, 2016. https://www.forbes.com/sites/robertharrow/2016/02/11/whos-paying-for-your-credit-card-rewards/.

Hart, Keith. "Heads or Tails? Two Sides of the Coin." *Man* 21, no. 4 (1986): 637. https://doi.org/10.2307/2802901.

———, ed. *Money in a Human Economy*. New York: Berghahn Books, 2017.

———. *Money in an Unequal World: Keith Hart and His Memory Bank*. New York: Textere, 2001.

———. "Notes towards an Anthropology of Money." *Kritikos: An International and Interdisciplinary Journal of Postmodern Cultural Sound, Text and Image* 2 (June 2005).

Hatch, Jenavieve. "First Congress Took Sex Workers' Websites. Now It's Coming for Their Bank Accounts." Huffington Post, May 28, 2018. https://web.archive.org/web/20190303173230/https://www.huffingtonpost.com/entry/human-trafficking-banking-bill-sex-workers_us_5b045577e4b0740c25e5efd1.

Hauben, Michael, and Ronda Hauben. *Netizens: On the History and Impact of Usenet and the Internet*. Los Alamitos, CA: IEEE Computer Society Press, 1997.

Hayashi, Fumiko. "Do U.S. Consumers Really Benefit from Payment Card Rewards?" *Economic Review*, first quarter (2009): 37–63.

Hayashi, Yuka. "Federal Consumer Watchdog Investigating Russell Simmons' RushCard." *Wall Street Journal*, October 23, 2015.

He, Jun. "Automating Machine Learning for Platform Fraud Detection." *WePay Blog*, July 23, 2015. https://web.archive.org/web/20190303165238/https://blog.wepay.com/2015/07/23/automating-machine-learning-for-platform-fraud-detection/.

Heady, Robert. "Debit Cards Are Becoming More Important than Credit Cards." *Network Journal* 7, no. 10 (2000).

Hearon, Sarah. "The Bachelor's Becca Kufrin Receives Hundreds of Payments on Venmo." *US Weekly*, March 6, 2018. https://web.archive.org/web/20190331011657/https://www.usmagazine.com/

entertainment/news/the-bachelors-becca-kufrin-receives-hundreds-of-payments-on-venmo/.

Helleiner, Eric. *The Making of National Money: Territorial Currencies in Historical Perspective*. Ithaca, NY: Cornell University Press, 2002.

———. "National Currencies and National Identities." *American Behavioral Scientist* 41, no. 10 (1998): 1409–36. https://doi.org/10.1177/0 002764298041010004.

———. "One Money, One People? Political Identity and the Euro." Working paper, Trent International Political Economy Centre, 2002.

Helmond, Anne. "The Algorithmization of the Hyperlink." *Computational Culture* 3 (November 2013). https://web.archive.org/web/20190223191502/http://computationalculture.net/the-algorithmization-of-the-hyperlink/.

Hendrickson, Robert A. *The Cashless Society*. New York: Dodd, Mead, 1972.

Henkin, David M. *City Reading: Written Words and Public Spaces in Antebellum New York*. New York: Columbia University Press, 1998.

Hewitt, Virginia. *Beauty and the Banknote: Images of Women on Paper Money*. London: British Museum Press, 1994.

Higgins, Michelle. "How to Turn Your Renovation into a Vacation." *New York Times*, March 20, 2018.

Hlebik, Sviatlana. "Analysis of Worldwide Community Economies for Sustainable Local Development." In *Another Economy Is Possible: Culture and Economy in a Time of Crisis*, edited by Manuel Castells, 55–81. Malden, MA: Polity, 2017.

Hochfelder, David. "'Where the Common People Could Speculate': The Ticker, Bucket Shops, and the Origins of Popular Participation in Financial Markets, 1880–1920." *Journal of American History* 93, no. 2 (2006): 335–58.

Hock, Dee. *Birth of the Chaordic Age*. San Francisco: Berrett-Koehler, 1999.

———. *One from Many: VISA and the Rise of the Chaordic Organization*. San Francisco: Berrett-Koehler, 2005.

Holt, Frank L. *Lost World of the Golden King: In Search of Ancient Afghanistan*. Berkeley: University of California Press, 2012.

———. "Who Were the Indo-Greeks?" Keynote address, International Conference on Greek Studies: An Asian Perspective, February 25, 2014, New Delhi, India.

Hoskins, Andrew. "Media, Memory, Metaphor: Remembering and the Connective Turn." *Parallax* 17, no. 4 (2011): 19–31. https://doi.org/10.1080/13534645.2011.605573.

"How Does Venmo Make Money?" Quora, 2014. https://www.quora.com/How-does-Venmo-make-money.

"How to Balance Your Checkbook." *Sun Reporter*, March 20, 1976.

Huang, Zheping. "All the Things You Can—and Can't—Do with Your We-Chat Account in China." Quartz, December 28, 2017. https://web.archive.org/web/20180326222352/https://qz.com/1167024/all-the-things-you-can-and-cant-do-with-your-wechat-account-in-china/.

Humphreys, Lee. *The Qualified Self: Social Media and the Accounting of Everyday Life.* Cambridge, MA: MIT Press, 2018.

Hyman, Louis. *Debtor Nation: The History of America in Red Ink.* Princeton, NJ: Princeton University Press, 2011.

Hymans, Jacques E. C. "The Changing Color of Money: European Currency Iconography and Collective Identity." *European Journal of International Relations* 10, no. 1 (2004): 5–31. https://doi.org/10.1177/1354066104040567.

Ice, Thomas, and Timothy J. Demy. *The Coming Cashless Society.* Eugene, OR: Harvest House, 1996.

Ihnat, Gwen. "People Have Gotten Some Really Rude Requests on Venmo." The Takeout, May 31, 2018. http://web.archive.org/web/20190330224106/https://thetakeout.com/people-have-gotten-some-really-rude-requests-on-venmo-1826460026.

Issa, Darrell. "The Department of Justice's 'Operation Choke Point': Illegally Choking Off Legitimate Businesses?" Staff report, US House of Representatives Committee on Oversight and Government Reform, May 29, 2014.

"Is Venmo Making Us Petty?" Marketplace, July 28, 2017. https://web.archive.org/web/20181024191053/https://www.marketplace.org/2017/07/26/life/venmo-making-us-petty.

Jackson, Eric M. *The PayPal Wars: Battles with eBay, the Media, the Mafia, and the Rest of Planet Earth.* New York: WND Books, 2006.

John, Richard R. *Network Nation: Inventing American Telecommunications.* Cambridge, MA: Harvard University Press, 2015.

———. *Spreading the News: The American Postal System from Franklin to Morse.* Cambridge, MA: Harvard University Press, 1998.

Johnson, David. "Are Loyalty Points the New Currency?" FIS Global, June 29, 2017. https://www.fisglobal.com/insights/payments-leader/is-loyalty-the-new-currency/.

Jones, Charisse. "Passengers Can Pay with Miles at Newark Airport." *USA Today*, November 17, 2014.

Jones, Dave. "Credit Card Climb." *Wall Street Journal*, February 21, 1958.

Jones, Jay. "Vegas Visitors Can Now Use Their Electronic Wallet to Pay Hotel Bills or Buy Show Tickets, but Not for Gambling." *Los Angeles Times*, August 21, 2017.

Jones, Steven. "PayPal Tweaked at Its Own Conference for Freezing Funds." *San Francisco Bay Guardian*, October 26, 2010. https://web.archive.org/web/20190302025633/http://sfbgarchive.48hills.org/sfbgarchive/2010/10/26/paypal-tweaked-its-own-conference-freezing-funds/.

Joseph, Miranda. *Against the Romance of Community*. Minneapolis: University of Minnesota Press, 2002.

Kant, Immanuel. *The Philosophy of Law: An Exposition of the Fundamental Principles of Jurisprudence as the Science of Right*. Translated by William Hastie. Edinburgh: Clark, 1887.

Katz, Lawrence F., and Alan B. Krueger. "The Rise and Nature of Alternative Work Arrangements in the United States, 1995–2015." Working paper, National Bureau of Economic Research, September 2016. https://doi.org/10.3386/w22667.

Kelly, Brian. "How I Got Approved for the Chase Sapphire Reserve." *The Points Guy* (blog), September 15, 2016. http://web.archive.org/web/20180619162416/https://thepointsguy.com/2016/09/how-i-got-the-chase-sapphire-reserve/.

Kepnes, Matt. "16 Reasons Why Flying United Airlines Sucks." *Nomadic Matt* (blog), August 5, 2019. https://web.archive.org/web/20190824162119/https://www.nomadicmatt.com/travel-blogs/15-reasons-why-flying-united-airlines-sucks/.

Kestenbaum, Sam. "Welcome to Hatreon, Where Neo-Nazis Go to Crowdfund." The Forward, August 4, 2017. https://web.archive.org/web/20190303171139/https://forward.com/fast-forward/379100/welcome-to-hatreon-where-neo-nazis-go-to-crowdfund/.

King, Thaddeus. "For Prepaid Card Customers, Overdraft Is the Problem—Not the Solution." Pew Charitable Trust, August 25, 2016.

https://web.archive.org/web/20190323205952/https://www.
pewtrusts.org/en/about/news-room/opinion/2016/08/25/for-prepaid-
card-customers-overdraft-is-the-problem-not-the-solution.

Kircher, Madison M. "Somebody Found Sean Spicer's Venmo and Now
People Are Asking Him for Money." Intelligencer, February 6, 2017.
https://web.archive.org/web/20190331011932/http://nymag.com/
intelligencer/2017/02/sean-spicer-is-on-venmo-and-people-are-
asking-him-for-money.html.

Knights, David, and Theo Vurdubakis. "Calculations of Risk: Towards an
Understanding of Insurance as a Moral and Political Technology."
Accounting, Organizations and Society 18, no. 7 (1993): 729–64.
https://doi.org/10.1016/0361-3682(93)90050-G.

Knorr-Cetina, Karin. "The Micro-Social Order: Towards a Reconception."
In *Actions and Structure: Research Methods and Social Theory*, edited
by Nigel Fielding, 21–53. London: Sage, 1988.

Kocherlakota, Narayana R. "Money Is Memory." *Journal of Economic
Theory* 81, no. 2 (1998): 232–51. https://doi.org/10.1006/jeth.
1997.2357.

KPMG. "The Pulse of Fintech 2018." July 31, 2018.

Krämer, Sybille. *Medium, Messenger, Transmission: An Approach to Media
Philosophy*. Amsterdam: Amsterdam University Press, 2015.

Kreimer, Seth F. "Censorship by Proxy: The First Amendment, Internet
Intermediaries, and the Problem of the Weakest Link." *University
of Pennsylvania Law Review* 155, no. 1 (2006): 11–101. https://doi.
org/10.2307/40041302.

Kreiss, Daniel. "A Vision of and for the Networked World: John Perry
Barlow's *A Declaration of the Independence of Cyberspace* at Twenty."
In *Media Independence: Working with Freedom or Working for Free?*,
edited by James Bennett and Niki Strange, 117–38. London: Routledge, 2014.

Kristof, Kathy. "Beware the Pitfalls of Using a 'Debit Card.'" *Los Angeles
Times*, July 5, 1991.

Kumar, Raynil, Tayeba Maktabi, and Shaun O'Brien. "2018 Findings from
the Diary of Consumer Payment Choice." Cash Product Office,
Federal Reserve System, November 1, 2018.

Kutcher, Eric, Olivia Nottebohm, and Kara Sprague. "Grow Fast or Die
Slow." McKinsey & Company, April 2014. https://web.archive.org/

web/20190212125126/https://www.mckinsey.com/industries/high-tech/our-insights/grow-fast-or-die-slow.

Lachter, Joshua Elias. *The Western Union Telegraph Company's Search for Reinvention, 1930–1980*. Cambridge, MA: Harvard University Press, 2009.

ladiesagainsthumanity. "The Douchebro of the Week Award (Let's Make That a Real Thing, Mmk?) Goes to the Fuckers at WePay, an Online Fundraising Site That Recently Canceled The." Tumblr, May 18, 2014. https://web.archive.org/web/20181214092407/http://ladies againsthumanity.tumblr.com/post/86124530602/the-douchebro-of-the-week-award-lets-make-that-a.

Lake, Ashley, and Liara Roux. "Incomplete List of Legal Discrimination against Sex Workers," Google Doc, August 1, 2018. https://docs.google.com/document/d/1c1nqawo1QuiVlpA3bhS8xyDxzDDlR q6BoogAoc91OmU/edit#.

LaMagna, Maria. "More Social Media Apps Have Become Payment Apps—Even Skype." MarketWatch, August 2, 2017. https://web.archive.org/web/20190331012216/https://www.marketwatch.com/story/why-companies-want-you-to-pay-for-stuff-everywhere-even-skype-2017-08-02.

Laneri, Raquel. "Not App-y about It: Paranoid Millennials Now Suffering 'Venmo Anxiety.'" *New York Post*, June 24, 2018.

Lanier, Jaron. *You Are Not a Gadget: A Manifesto*. New York: Vintage, 2011.

Lappin, Todd. "The Bernal Bucks Card Stars in Today's Wall Street Journal." *Bernalwood* (blog), October 6, 2011. http://web.archive.org/web/20190513222621/https://bernalwood.com/2011/10/06/the-bernal-bucks-card-stars-in-todays-wall-street-journal/.

Latour, Bruno. "Technology Is Society Made Durable." In *A Sociology of Monsters: Essays on Power, Technology, and Domination*, edited by John Law, 103–31. New York: Routledge, 1991.

Lauer, Josh. *Creditworthy: A History of Consumer Surveillance and Financial Identity in America*. New York: Columbia University Press, 2017.

———. "Money as Mass Communication: U.S. Paper Currency and the Iconography of Nationalism." *Communication Review* 11, no. 2 (2008): 109–32. https://doi.org/10.1080/10714420802068359.

"Legal Problems with Loyalty Programs." *Hilfer Law* (blog), December 7, 2018. https://web.archive.org/web/20190622211942/https://kbhilferlaw.com/legal-problems-loyalty-programs/.

Leonhardt, David. "Frequent Fliers: Make Sure You Don't Get Clipped." *Businessweek*, January 18, 1999.

Levenson, Eric. "Why the Venmo Newsfeed Is the Best Social Network Nobody's Talking About." *Atlantic*, April 29, 2014. https://web. archive.org/web/20190330224422/https://www.theatlantic.com/ entertainment/archive/2014/04/why-the-venmo-newsfeed-is-the-best-social-network-nobodys-talking-about/361342/.

Levy, Karen E. C. "The Contexts of Control: Information, Power, and Truck-Driving Work." *Information Society* 31, no. 2 (2015): 160–74. https://doi.org/10.1080/01972243.2015.998105.

Libra Association Members. "How to Become a Founding Member." Libra, June 18, 2019. https://libra.org/en-US/becoming-founding-member/.

———. "An Introduction to Libra." Libra. Accessed September 15, 2019. https://libra.org/en-US/white-paper/.

Lieber, Ron. "Suze Orman's Approved Prepaid Debit Cards Are Quietly Discontinued." *New York Times*, June 16, 2014.

———. "TV Adviser on Money Offers Card." *New York Times*, January 9, 2012.

Lievrouw, Leah A. "Materiality and Media in Communication and Technology Studies: An Unfinished Project." In *Media Technologies: Essays on Communication, Materiality, and Society*, edited by Tarleton Gillespie, Pablo J. Boczkowski, and Kirsten A. Foot, 21–52. Cambridge, MA: MIT Press, 2014.

Light, Ben, Jean Burgess, and Stefanie Duguay. "The Walkthrough Method: An Approach to the Study of Apps." *New Media & Society* 20, no. 3 (2018): 881–900. https://doi.org/10.1177/1461444816675438.

Lipscomb, Sam. "Magnises and the Allure of Credit Cards as Status Symbols." *The Points Guy* (blog), February 9, 2019. https://web.archive. org/web/20190414172352/https://thepointsguy.com/news/magnises-credit-cards-status-symbols/.

Livingstone, Sonia. "From Mass to Social Media? Advancing Accounts of Social Change." *Social Media + Society* 1, no. 1 (2015). https://doi. org/10.1177/2056305115578875.

Li Yuan. "To Cover China, There's No Substitute for WeChat." *New York Times*, January 9, 2019.

Lloyd, Nancy. "How Debit Cards Can Burn Holes in Student Pockets." *New York Times*, September 3, 2000.

Louis, Brittany. "@RushCard it's been a whole week without money, it's hard out here. Single mother no help. I work hard for my money and now I can't get it#t11[??180]." Twitter (@Induetime_loyal), October 19, 2015. https://web.archive.org/web/20190303161016/ https://twitter.com/Induetime_loyal/status/656124624221175808.

Lovelace, Berkeley, Jr. "Starbucks' Howard Schultz: A 'Trusted' Digital Currency Is Coming, but It Won't Be Bitcoin." CNBC, January 26, 2018. https://web.archive.org/web/20190401201628/https://www. cnbc.com/2018/01/26/starbucks-schultz-a-digital-currency-is-coming-but-wont-be-bitcoin.html.

"Lowdown on Customer Loyalty Programs, The: Which Are the Most Effective and Why." *Knowledge@Wharton*, September 6, 2006. https://web.archive.org/web/20150510114707/http://knowledge. wharton.upenn.edu/article/the-lowdown-on-customer-loyalty-programs-which-are-the-most-effective-and-why/.

Lunden, Ingrid. "Chase Closes WePay Acquisition, a Deal Valued Up to $400M." *TechCrunch* (blog), December 4, 2017. https://web.archive. org/web/20171204164359/https://techcrunch.com/2017/12/04/chase-closes-wepay-acquisition-a-deal-valued-up-to-400m/.

Lupton, Deborah. *The Quantified Self: A Sociology of Self-Tracking*. Cambridge, UK: Polity, 2016.

Lyon, David. *Surveillance as Social Sorting: Privacy, Risk, and Digital Discrimination*. New York: Routledge, 2002.

MacGregor, Neil. "A History of the World in 100 Objects: 1. Mummy of Hornedjitef." British Museum. Accessed May 22, 2019. https://web. archive.org/web/20190522174551/https://www.britishmuseum.org/ explore/a_history_of_the_world/objects.aspx?byCulture&_ ga=2.151781690.2001717674.1554673184-308070257.1554673184.

MacKenzie, Donald, Fabien Muniesa, and Lucia Siu, eds. *Do Economists Make Markets? On the Performativity of Economics*. Princeton, NJ: Princeton University Press, 2007.

Mainwaring, Scott. "Dongles." In *Paid: Tales of Dongles, Checks, and Other Money Stuff*, edited by Bill Maurer and Lana Swartz, 1–12. Cambridge, MA: MIT Press, 2017.

Mandell, Lewis. *The Credit Card Industry: A History*. Boston: Twayne, 1990.

Manigault, Omarosa N. *Unhinged: An Insider's Account of the Trump White House*. New York: Gallery Books, 2018.

Mann, Michael. "The Autonomous Power of the State: Its Origins, Mechanisms and Results." *European Journal of Sociology* 25, no. 2 (1984): 185. https://doi.org/10.1017/S0003975600004239.

Mann, Ronald J. *Charging Ahead: The Growth and Regulation of Payment Card Markets*. Cambridge: Cambridge University Press, 2006.

Mansell, Robin. *Imagining the Internet: Communication, Innovation, and Governance*. Oxford: Oxford University Press, 2012.

Maréchal, Nathalie. "First They Came for the Poor: Surveillance of Welfare Recipients as an Uncontested Practice." *Media and Communication* 3, no. 3 (2015): 56–67. https://doi.org/10.17645/mac.v3i3.268.

Markoutsas, Elaine. "More Women Tackle the Family's Checkbooks and Balances: Wives Learn It Pays to Be Wizard of Finances." *Chicago Tribune*, March 22, 1975.

Martin, Aaron. "Mobile Money Platform Surveillance." *Surveillance & Society* 17, nos. 1–2 (2019): 213–22. https://doi.org/10.24908/ss.v17i1/2.12924.

Marvin, Carolyn. "Reconsidering James Carey: How Many Rituals Does It Take to Make an Artifact?" *American Journalism* 7, no. 4 (1990): 216–26. https://doi.org/10.1080/08821127.1990.10731302.

———. *When Old Technologies Were New: Thinking about Electric Communication in the Late Nineteenth Century*. New York: Oxford University Press, 1988.

Marwick, Alice E. "To Catch a Predator? The MySpace Moral Panic." *First Monday* 13, no. 6 (2008). https://doi.org/10.5210/fm.v13i6.2152.

Marx, Karl. *The Eighteenth Brumaire of Louis Bonaparte*. London: Electric Book, 2000.

———. "Private Property and Labor." Translated by Gregor Benton. In *Early Writings*, 341–44. London: Penguin, 1992.

Mastercard. "Mastercard Pay with Rewards." Accessed April 28, 2019. https://web.archive.org/web/20190428220800/https://www.mastercard.ca/en-ca/issuers/products-and-solutions/grow-manage-your-business/loyalty-solutions/pay-with-rewards.html.

Mattelart, Armand. *The Invention of Communication*. Minneapolis: University of Minnesota Press, 1996.

Maurer, Bill. "Blockchains Are a Diamond's Best Friend: Zelizer for the Bitcoin Moment." In *Money Talks: Explaining How Money Really Works*, edited by Nina Bandelj, Frederick F. Wherry, and Viviana

A. Rotman Zelizer, 215–29. Princeton, NJ: Princeton University Press, 2017.

———. *How Would You Like to Pay? How Technology Is Changing the Future of Money*. Durham, NC: Duke University Press, 2015.

———. "Late to the Party: Debt and Data." *Social Anthropology* 20, no. 4 (2012): 474–81. https://doi.org/10.1111/j.1469-8676.2012.00219.x.

———. "Money as Token and Money as Record in Distributed Accounts." In *Distributed Agency*, edited by N. J. Enfield and Paul Kockelman, 109–16. Oxford: Oxford University Press, 2017.

———. "Money Nutters." *Economic Sociology: The European Electronic Newsletter* 12, no. 3 (2011): 5–12.

———. *Mutual Life, Limited: Islamic Banking, Alternative Currencies, Lateral Reason*. Princeton, NJ: Princeton University Press, 2005.

———. "Payment: Forms and Functions of Value Transfer in Contemporary Society." *Cambridge Journal of Anthropology* 30, no. 2 (2012): 15–35. https://doi.org/10.3167/ca.2012.300202.

Maurer, Bill, Taylor C. Nelms, and Lana Swartz. "'When Perhaps the Real Problem Is Money Itself!': The Practical Materiality of Bitcoin." *Social Semiotics* 23, no. 2 (2013): 261–77. https://doi.org/10.1080/1 0350330.2013.777594.

May, Tim. "Crypto Anarchy and Virtual Communities." December, 1994. Available at https://web.archive.org/web/20190719123042/http:// groups.csail.mit.edu/mac/classes/6.805/articles/crypto/cypher punks/may-virtual-comm.html.

McFall, Elizabeth, Franck Cochoy, and Joe Deville. "Introduction: Markets and the Arts of Attachment." In *Markets and the Arts of Attachment*, edited by Franck Cochoy, Elizabeth McFall, and Joe Deville, 10–21. London: Routledge, 2017.

McKenney, James L., Duncan G. Copeland, and Richard O. Mason. *Waves of Change: Business Evolution through Information Technology*. Boston: Harvard Business School Press, 1995.

Medley, Bill. *Highways of Commerce: Central Banking and the U.S. Payments System*. Kansas City, MO: Public Affairs Department of the Federal Reserve Bank of Kansas City, 2014. https://www.kansascityfed. org/publications/aboutthefed/highwaysofcommerce.

Meer, Alec. "Enemy Known: Xenonauts vs Paypal." Rock Paper Shotgun, October 9, 2011. https://web.archive.org/web/20190303160149/

https://www.rockpapershotgun.com/2011/10/09/enemy-known-xenonauts-vs-paypal/.

Michel, Casey. "White Supremacists' Favorite Fundraising Site May Be Imploding." Think Progress, March 13, 2018. https://web.archive.org/web/20190303171318/https://thinkprogress.org/white-supremacist-fundraiser-dead-bdee08eeb5a6/.

Miéville, China. *The City and The City*. New York: Random House, 2010.

———. "Oh, London, You Drama Queen." *New York Times*, March 1, 2012.

Milano, Annaliese. "Starbucks Chairman Is Hot on Blockchain, Cold on Bitcoin." Coindesk, February 27, 2018. https://web.archive.org/web/20180315062405/https://www.coindesk.com/starbucks-chairman-hot-blockchain-cold-bitcoin/.

"Millennials Are Getting 'Venmo Anxiety.'" Yahoo! Finance, June 25, 2018. https://finance.yahoo.com/video/millennials-getting-venmo-anxiety-171753958.html.

Miller, Claire Cain. "Cellphone in New Role: Loyalty Card." *New York Times*, May 31, 2010.

Minsky, Hyman P. *Stabilizing an Unstable Economy*. New Haven, CT: Yale University Press, 1986.

missfreudianslit. "UGH PAYONEER IS GONNA MAKE ME SPIT GLASS." Tumblr, 2014. https://web.archive.org/web/20140811165120/http://missfreudianslit.tumblr.com/post/72699647615/ugh-payoneer-is-gonna-make-me-spit-glass-i-am.

Mistreanu, Simina. "China Is Implementing a Massive Plan to Rank Its Citizens, and Many of Them Want In." *Foreign Policy*, April 3, 2018. https://web.archive.org/web/20190920181024/https://foreignpolicy.com/2018/04/03/life-inside-chinas-social-credit-laboratory/.

Mittal, Mohit. "WeChat—The One App That Rules Them All." Harvard Business School Digital Initiative, August 25, 2017. https://web.archive.org/web/20190928182609/https://digital.hbs.edu/innovation-disruption/wechat%E2%80%8A-%E2%80%8Athe-one-app-rules/.

Money, J. "What Your Date's Credit Card Says about His Personality (and His Bank Account)." *Budgets Are Sexy* (blog), April 24, 2015. https://web.archive.org/web/20190915193701/https://www.budgetsaresexy.com/what-your-dates-credit-card-says-about-his-personality-and-his-bank-account/.

Moor, Liz. "Money: Communicative Functions of Payment and Price." *Consumption Markets & Culture* 21, no. 6 (2018): 574–81. https://doi.org/10.1080/10253866.2017.1359953.

Moyer, Liz, and Jessica Silver-Greenberg. "RushCard Breakdown Affects Thousands of Prepaid Debit Card Users." *New York Times*, October 20, 2015.

Murthy, Rekha. "Street Media: Ambient Messages in an Urban Space." Master's thesis, Massachusetts Institute of Technology, 2005.

m_watson. "Starbucks' Mobile App: A Winner in Bridging the Retail/Digital Divide." Digital Innovation and Transformation, January 31, 2018. https://web.archive.org/web/20190428202050/https://digit.hbs.org/submission/starbucks-mobile-app-a-winner-in-bridging-the-retail-digital-divide/.

Nash, Nathaniel. "Credit Cards Best Used Judiciously." *New York Times*, September 29, 1985.

NBA. "American Express Jersey Insurance Program." NBA Store. Accessed March 22, 2019. https://web.archive.org/web/20180916103750/https://store.nba.com/jersey-assurance/x-143713+z-91829756-2442190644.

Neff, Gina, and Dawn Nafus. *Self-Tracking*. Cambridge, MA: MIT Press, 2016.

Nelms, Taylor C. "Accounts." In *Paid: Tales of Dongles, Checks, and Other Money Stuff*, edited by Bill Maurer and Lana Swartz, 41–52. Cambridge, MA: MIT Press, 2017.

———. "Dollarization, Denomination, and Difference: Rounding Up in Quito, Ecuador." Unpublished manuscript, 2017. Available at http://www.taylornelms.net/money-finance-technology.

———. "Invisible City: A Speculative Guide." Society for Cultural Anthropology, December 18, 2018. https://web.archive.org/web/20190313213507/https://culanth.org/fieldsights/invisible-city-a-speculative-guide.

Nelms, Taylor C., and Bill Maurer. "Materiality, Symbol and Complexity in the Anthropology of Money." In *The Psychological Science of Money*, edited by Erik Bijleveld and Henk Aarts, 37–70. New York: Springer, 2014. https://doi.org/10.1007/978-1-4939-0959-9_3.

Nelms, Taylor C., Bill Maurer, Lana Swartz, and Scott Mainwaring. "Social Payments: Innovation, Trust, Bitcoin, and the Sharing Economy." *Theory, Culture & Society* 35, no. 3 (2018): 13–33. https://doi. org/10.1177/0263276417746466.

Netspend. "MLB Prepaid Cards." Accessed September 15, 2019. https:// web.archive.org/web/20180802193027/https://www.netspend.com/ prepaid-debit/features/mlb/?aid=mlb_corp&siteid=MLBTile.

"New Logo and Stagecoach for Wells Fargo: The Cart before the Horse." Brand New, January 30, 2019. https://web.archive.org/web/ 20190622175415/https://www.underconsideration.com/brandnew/ archives/new_logo_and_stagecoach_for_wells_fargo.php.

Newsdesk. "Caesars Entertainment Launches WeChat Digital Payment Program." Travel Agent Central, August 9, 2017. https://web.archive. org/web/20190917190119/https://www.travelagentcentral.com/des tinations/caesars-entertainment-launches-wechat-digital-payment-program.

Nichols, Joshua. "Data Doubles: Surveillance of Subjects without Substance." *CTheory*, February 17, 2004, 2–17.

NickV. "Driver Reward Cards." LifeAsATrucker.com. Accessed June 11, 2018. http://web.archive.org/web/20180619165644/http://www. lifeasatrucker.com/driver-reward-cards.html.

Nissenbaum, Helen Fay. *Privacy in Context: Technology, Policy, and the Integrity of Social Life*. Stanford: Stanford Law Books, 2010.

Nocera, Joseph. *A Piece of the Action: How the Middle Class Joined the Money Class*. New York: Simon and Schuster, 1994.

North, Peter. *Money and Liberation: The Micropolitics of Alternative Currency Movements*. Minneapolis: University of Minnesota Press, 2007.

Notopoulos, Katie. "Here's Why Venmo Users Should Care If Sean Spicer Is Being Trolled." Buzzfeed News, February 7, 2017. https://web. archive.org/web/20180726001450/https://www.buzzfeednews.com/ article/katienotopoulos/heres-why-venmo-users-should-care-if-sean-spicer-is-being-tr.

Nunes, Joseph, and Xavier Drèze. "Your Loyalty Program Is Betraying You." *Harvard Business Review*, April 2006. https://web.archive.org/ web/20180427101222/https://hbr.org/2006/04/your-loyalty-program-is-betraying-you.

O'Brien, Shaun. "Understanding Consumer Cash Use: Preliminary Findings from the 2016 Diary of Consumer Payment Choice." Federal Reserve Bank of San Francisco, November 28, 2017. https://web.

archive.org/web/20190303173704/https://www.frbsf.org/cash/pub
lications/fed-notes/2017/november/understanding-consumer-cash-
use-preliminary-findings-2016-diary-of-consumer-payment-choice/.

O'Dwyer, Rachel. "Cache Society: Transactional Records, Electronic
Money, and Cultural Resistance." *Journal of Cultural Economy* 12,
no. 2 (2019): 133–53. https://doi.org/10.1080/17530350.2018.15452
43.

———. "Ether." In *Paid: Tales of Dongles, Checks, and Other Money
Stuff*, edited by Bill Maurer and Lana Swartz, 237–48. Cambridge,
MA: MIT Press, 2017.

———. "Money Talks: The Enclosure of Mobile Payments." In *MoneyLab
Reader: An Intervention in Digital Economy*, edited by Geert Lovink,
Nathaniel Tkacz, and Patricia De Vries, 230–44. Amsterdam: Insti-
tute of Network Cultures, 2015.

Ohikuare, Judith. "Venmo Makes Me Feel Bad about All the Plans I Don't
Have." Refinery29, March 20, 2018. http://web.archive.org/
web/20190330222629/https://www.refinery29.com/en-us/how-
venmo-inspires-feelings-of-fomo.

O'Malley, Pat. "Governmentality and Risk." In *Social Theories of Risk and
Uncertainty*, edited by Jens Zinn, 52–75. Oxford, UK: Blackwell,
2009.

———. *Risk, Uncertainty, and Government*. London: Glasshouse, 2004.

O'Neill, Virginia. "Letter to CFPB on Card Rewards Program." American
Bankers Association, November 14, 2017. https://www.aba.com/-/
media/documents/comment-letter/cl-creditcard-rewards20171114.
pdf.

O'Reilly. "What Is Web 2.0." September 30, 2005. https://web.archive.org/
web/20190303165438/https://www.oreilly.com/pub/a/web2/archive/
what-is-web-20.html.

Osborne, Brian. "The Iconography of Nationhood in Canadian Art." In
The Iconography of Landscape, edited by Denis Cosgrove and Stephen
Daniels, 162–78. Cambridge: Cambridge University Press, 1992.

Paice, Kyle. "Icing PayPal: How We Did It." *WePay Blog*, October 28, 2010.
http://web.archive.org/web/20120106171720/http://blog.wepay.
com/2010/10/28/icing-paypal-how-we-did-it/.

Pallardy, Carrie. "Cannabis Loyalty Software Provider Springbig Hits
685% Year-Over-Year Growth and Reaches 1.9 Million Consumers."

New Cannabis Ventures, October 19, 2018. https://web.archive.org/
web/20181022002850/https://www.newcannabisventures.com/
cannabis-loyalty-software-provider-springbig-hits-685-year-over-
year-growth-and-reaches-1-9-million-consumers/.

Palleschi, Amanda. "Friends with Venmo." The Billfold, February 23,
2015. https://web.archive.org/web/20190401130529/https://www.
thebillfold.com/2015/02/friends-with-venmo/.

Papacharissi, Zizi. "We Have Always Been Social." *Social Media + Society*
1, no. 1 (2015). https://doi.org/10.1177/2056305115581185.

Pardes, Arielle. "Turn Your $20s into Tubmans with This DIY 3-D Printed
Stamp." *Wired*, October 12, 2017. https://web.archive.org/web/
20190301185307/https://www.wired.com/story/stamp-puts-harriet-
tubmans-face-on-a-20-dollar-bill/.

Pariser, Eli. *The Filter Bubble: What the Internet Is Hiding from You*.
New York: Penguin, 2011.

Parks, Lisa. *Cultures in Orbit: Satellites and the Televisual*. Durham, NC:
Duke University Press, 2005.

Parsons, Talcott. "On the Concept of Influence." *Public Opinion Quarterly*
27, no. 1 (1963): 37–62. https://doi.org/10.1086/267148.

"Payment Data Is More Valuable than Payment Fees." *TechCrunch* (blog),
August 18, 2012. https://web.archive.org/web/20120819175815/
http://techcrunch.com/2012/08/18/payment-data-is-more-valuable-
than-payment-fees/.

Payments Leader. "The Rise of Alternative Payment Types Series Part 2:
Rewards Currency." FIS, August 7, 2014. https://web.archive.org/
web/20161023071612/http://www.paymentsleader.com/rewards-
currency/.

Penny, Laurie. "Stand Up for Sex Workers: Eden Alexander, WePay and
Whorephobia." Laurie Penny Dot Com, May 18, 2014. https://web.
archive.org/web/20190303172133/http://laurie-penny.com/stand-
up-for-sex-workers-eden-alexander-wepay-and-whorephobia/.

"People Venmo Money to Their Friends Just to Say 'Hi.'" *Money*, August
10, 2017. https://web.archive.org/web/20190330231041/http://
money.com/money/4893457/people-venmo-money-to-their-friends-
just-to-say-hi/.

Perkins Coie LLP and Affiliates. "Loyalty Programs: Legal Issues." January 2008. https://web.archive.org/web/20190622212635/https://www.

perkinscoie.com/images/content/1/3/v2/13994/efs-10-12-perkins-coie-loyalty-program-whitepaper.pdf.

Peters, John Durham. *Speaking into the Air: A History of the Idea of Communication*. Chicago: University of Chicago Press, 1999.

Petrick, Elizabeth. "Imagining the Personal Computer: Conceptualizations of the Homebrew Computer Club 1975–1977." *IEEE Annals of the History of Computing* 39, no. 4 (2017): 27–39. https://doi.org/10.1109/MAHC.2018.1221045.

Pettitt, Thomas. "Bracketing the Gutenberg Parenthesis." *Explorations in Media Ecology* 11, no. 2 (2012): 95–114. https://doi.org/10.1386/eme.11.2.95_1.

Polanyi, Karl. *Primitive, Archaic, and Modern Economics: Essays of Karl Polanyi*. Edited by George Dalton. Garden City, NY: Anchor Books, 1968.

Poon, Martha. "From New Deal Institutions to Capital Markets: Commercial Consumer Risk Scores and the Making of Subprime Mortgage Finance." CSI Working Papers Series, Centre de Sociologie de l'Innovation (CSI), Mines ParisTech, January 2009. https://EconPapers.repec.org/RePEc:emn:wpaper:014.

———. "Scorecards as Devices for Consumer Credit: The Case of Fair, Isaac & Company Incorporated." *Sociological Review* 55, no. 2 (2007): 284–306. https://doi.org/10.1111/j.1467-954X.2007.00740.x.

Poovey, Mary. *A History of the Modern Fact: Problems of Knowledge in the Sciences of Wealth and Society*. Chicago: University of Chicago Press, 1998.

Popkin, Helen. "Why PayPal's Bad Reputation Is Bigger than Regretsy." Today, December 7, 2011. https://web.archive.org/web/20190915162107/https://www.today.com/money/why-paypals-bad-reputation-bigger-regretsy-118696.

Poulsen, Kelvin. "PayPal Freezes WikiLeaks Account." *Wired*, December 4, 2010. https://web.archive.org/web/20140430233822/http://www.wired.com/2010/12/paypal-wikileaks/.

Power, Michael, ed. *Riskwork: Essays on the Organizational Life of Risk Management*. Oxford: Oxford University Press, 2016.

Pratini, Napala. "Who's Winning the Digital Wallet Wars." Fin, November 22, 2016. https://web.archive.org/web/20190331013728/https://fin.plaid.com/articles/whos-winning-the-digital-wallet-wars.

Preda, Alex. *Information, Knowledge, and Economic Life: An Introduction to the Sociology of Markets*. Oxford: Oxford University Press, 2009.

Prince, Todd. "Caesars Launches WeChat Pay for Chinese Visitors." *Las Vegas Review-Journal*, August 9, 2017.

"Pros and Cons of Using a Fuel Card vs. a Corporate Card for Fleet Fuel Expenses." *Automotive Fleet*, May 1, 2011. http://web.archive.org/web/20180619174324/https://www.automotive-fleet.com/147364/pros-and-cons-of-using-a-fuel-card-vs-a-corporate-card-for-fleet-fuel-expenses.

Pryke, Michael, and Paul DuGay. *Cultural Economy: Cultural Analysis and Commercial Life*. London: Sage, 2002.

Quint, Michael. "Banks' Plea: Drop That Checkbook; Will High Postage Help Wean People Away from Checks?" *New York Times*, March 7, 1992.

Radecki, Lawrence. "Banks' Payments-Driven Revenues." *Economic Policy Review* (Federal Reserve Bank of New York) 4, no. 2 (1999): 53–70.

Rajaniemi, Hannu. *The Quantum Thief*. London: Gollancz, 2010.

Rankin, Joy Lisi. *A People's History of Computing in the United States*. Cambridge, MA: Harvard University Press, 2018.

Rao, Leena, Sarah Perez, and Ingrid Lunden. "EBay's PayPal Acquires Payments Gateway Braintree For $800M In Cash." *TechCrunch* (blog), September 26, 2013. https://web.archive.org/web/20140811173430/http://techcrunch.com/2013/09/26/paypal-acquires-payments-gateway-braintree-for-800m-in-cash/.

Rappeport, Alan. "Harriet Tubman on the $20? Trump's Treasury Dept. Won't Commit." *New York Times*, June 8, 2018.

Read, Simon. "Is PayPal Right to Freeze Customers' Accounts?" *The Independent*, September 24, 2011. https://web.archive.org/web/20190303164539/https://www.independent.co.uk/money/spend-save/simon-read-is-paypal-right-to-freeze-customers-accounts-2360058.html.

Reading, Anna. "Seeing Red: A Political Economy of Digital Memory." *Media, Culture & Society* 36, no. 6 (2014): 748–60. https://doi.org/10.1177/0163443714532980.

"Read What Happens When a Bunch of Over-30s Find Out How Millennials Handle Their Money." Quartz, October 7, 2014. https://web.

archive.org/web/20141007191658/http://qz.com/277509/read-what-happens-when-a-bunch-of-over-30s-find-out-how-millennials-handle-their-money/.

"Reward Cards." Truckers Forum message board, April 25, 2014. http://web.archive.org/web/20180619170135/https://www.truckersforum.net/threads/reward-cards.80213/.

Rheingold, Howard. *The Virtual Community: Homesteading on the Electronic Frontier*. Reading, MA: Addison-Wesley, 1993.

Ritter, Gretchen. *Goldbugs and Greenbacks: The Antimonopoly Tradition and the Politics of Finance in America, 1865–1896*. Cambridge: Cambridge University Press, 1999.

Ritzer, George. *Expressing America: A Critique of the Global Credit Card Society*. Thousand Oaks, CA: Sage, 1995. https://doi.org/10.4135/9781452243115.

Robehmed, Natalie. "Venmo: The Future of Payments for You and Your Company." *Forbes*, July 2, 2013. https://web.archive.org/web/20130705233634/http://www.forbes.com/sites/natalie robehmed/2013/07/02/venmo-the-future-of-payments-for-you-and-your-company.

Romney, Lee. "Unified by the Coin of Their Realm." *Los Angeles Times*, February 6, 2012.

Rosen, Jan. "The Siren Swipe of the Debit Card." *New York Times*, October 31, 1999.

Rubin, Ben Fox. "Venmo: The Secret, Hip Social Network You've Never Heard Of." CNET, March 11, 2017. https://web.archive.org/web/20180825143424/https://www.cnet.com/news/venmo-paypal-wacky-social-mo-pay-the-rent-get-likes-and-jokes/.

Russell, Andrew, and Lee Vinsel. "After Innovation, Turn to Maintenance." *Technology and Culture* 59, no. 1 (2018): 1–25.

Ryan, Phillip. "Green Dot Expands Uber Venture for Instant Pay to Drivers." Bank Innovation, May 5, 2016. https://web.archive.org/web/20190323190454/https://bankinnovation.net/2016/05/green-dot-expands-instant-pay-functionality-for-uber-drivers/.

Sage, Mark. "The Rise of the Alternative (Loyalty) Currency." Customer Think, October 5, 2014. https://web.archive.org/web/20190428205816/http://customerthink.com/the-rise-of-the-alternative-loyalty-currency/.

Saint, Nick. "How Pornographers Invented E-Commerce." Business Insider, August 6, 2010. https://web.archive.org/web/20190303161854/ https://www.businessinsider.com/the-producer-of-middle-men-talks-to-us-about-how-pornographers-invented-e-commerce-2010-8.

Sankin, Aaron. "Bernal Heights Prints Own Currency." *HuffPost* (blog), July 13, 2011. https://www.huffpost.com/entry/bernal-heights-issues-own-currency_n_897835.

Santana, Shelle. "Is the U.S. on Its Way to Becoming a Cashless Society?" *Harvard Business Review*, July 23, 2019. https://web.archive.org/ save/https://hbr.org/2019/07/is-the-u-s-on-its-way-to-becoming-a-cashless-society.

Santucci, Larry. "The Secured Credit Card Market." Discussion paper, Federal Reserve Bank of Philadelphia, November 2016. https://doi. org/10.21799/frbp.dp.2016.nov.

Sauerberg, Lars Ole. "The Gutenberg Parenthesis—Print, Book and Cognition." *Orbis Litterarum* 64, no. 2 (2009): 79–80. https://doi. org/10.1111/j.1600-0730.2009.00962.x.

Schermer, Bart Willem, Bart Custers, and Simone van der Hof. "The Crisis of Consent: How Stronger Legal Protection May Lead to Weaker Consent in Data Protection." *Ethics & Information Technology* 16, no. 2 (2014): 171–82. https://doi.org/10.1007/s10676-014-9343-8.

Schmandt-Besserat, Denise. *How Writing Came About*. Austin: University of Texas Press, 1996.

Schneier, Bruce. "The 600+ Companies PayPal Shares Your Data With." *Schneier on Security* (blog), March 14, 2018. https://web.archive. org/web/20190417071051/https://www.schneier.com/blog/ archives/2018/03/the_600_compani.html.

Schuh, Scott D., Oz Shy, and Joanna Stavins. "Who Gains and Who Loses from Credit Card Payments? Theory and Calibrations." FRB of Boston Public Policy Discussion Paper No. 10–3, August 31, 2010. https://doi.org/10.2139/ssrn.1652260.

Schulberg, Jessica. "Gab, Neo-Nazis' Favorite Social Media Platform, Frozen by Payment Processor for . . . Porn." Huffington Post, October 3, 2018. https://web.archive.org/web/20190328165314/https:// www.huffpost.com/entry/gab-stripe-pornography-andrew-torba_n_5bb52e0be4b028e1fe3a3ac2.

Scott, Brett. "Riches beyond Belief." Aeon, August 28, 2013. https://aeon. co/essays/so-you-want-to-invent-your-own-currency.

Scott, Helenus. *The Adventures of a Rupee: Wherein Are Interspersed Various Anecdotes Asiatic and European*. London: J. Murray, 1782.

Seaver, Nick. "Captivating Algorithms: Recommender Systems as Traps." *Journal of Material Culture* 24, no. 4 (2019): 421–36. https://doi. org/10.1177/1359183518820366.

Segel, Liz Hilton, Phil Auerbach, and Ido Segev. "The Power of Points: Strategies for Making Loyalty Programs Work." McKinsey & Company, June 2013. https://web.archive.org/web/20190108135244/ https://www.mckinsey.com/business-functions/marketing-and-sales/ our-insights/the-power-of-points-strategies-for-making-loyalty-programs-work.

Servon, Lisa J. "Checks." In *Paid: Tales of Dongles, Checks, and Other Money Stuff*, edited by Bill Maurer and Lana Swartz, 13–18. Cambridge, MA: MIT Press, 2017.

———. *The Unbanking of America: How the New Middle Class Survives*. Boston: Houghton Mifflin Harcourt, 2017.

sexworkerhelpfuls. "Sex Work Approved Payment Options." Tumblr, March 12, 2015. https://web.archive.org/web/20140622104403/ http://sexworkerhelpfuls.tumblr.com/post/81030602902/sex-work-approved-payment-options.

Shaulis, Joe. "Mexico Supreme Court Orders Wal-Mart to Stop Paying Workers in Store Vouchers." Jurist, September 5, 2008. https://web. archive.org/web/20190428215722/https://www.jurist.org/ news/2008/09/mexico-supreme-court-orders-wal-mart-to/.

Sidel, Robin. "First Data Reports First Quarterly Profit in More than Seven Years." *Wall Street Journal*, February 10, 2015.

Silverstone, Roger. *Why Study the Media?* London: Sage, 1999. https://doi. org/10.4135/9781446219461.

Simmel, Georg. "The Metropolis and Mental Life." In *The Sociology of Georg Simmel*, translated by Kurt H. Wolff, 409–24. New York: Free Press, 1950.

———. *The Philosophy of Money*. Edited by David Frisby. Translated by Tom Bottomore and David Frisby. 3rd ed. London: Routledge, 2004.

Simmons, Matty. *The Credit Card Catastrophe: The 20th Century Phenomenon That Changed the World*. New York: Barricade Books, 1995.

Simon, Jonathan. "The Emergence of a Risk Society: Insurance, Law and the State." *Socialist Review*, no. 97 (1987): 61–89.

"6 Step Plan to Balance Checkbook." *Chicago Daily Tribune*, September 26, 1961.

Smith, Jack. "Neo-Nazi Wealth Is Rapidly Growing. Why? Bitcoin." Mic, December 1, 2017. https://web.archive.org/web/20180103205323/ https://mic.com/articles/186438/neo-nazi-wealth-is-rapidly-growing-why-bitcoin#.gQ1wYxKKC.

Soderlund, Gretchen. "Communication Scholarship as Ritual: An Examination of James Carey's Cultural Model of Communication." In *Thinking with James Carey: Essays on Communications, Transportation, History,* edited by Jeremy Packer and Craig Robertson, 101–16. New York: Peter Lang, 2006.

Soll, Jacob. *The Reckoning: Financial Accountability and the Rise and Fall of Nations.* New York: Basic Books, 2014.

Southern Poverty Law Center. "Cody Rutledge Wilson." Accessed March 3, 2019. https://web.archive.org/web/20190303170224/https://www.splcenter.org/fighting-hate/extremist-files/individual/cody-rutledge-wilson.

Spahr, Walter E. *The Clearing and Collection of Checks.* New York: Bankers, 1926.

Spang, Rebecca. *Stuff and Money in the Time of the French Revolution.* Cambridge, MA: Harvard University Press, 2017.

Star, Susan Leigh. "The Ethnography of Infrastructure." *American Behavioral Scientist* 43, no. 3 (1999): 377–91. https://doi.org/10.1177/00027649921955326.

Starbucks. "Mobile Payment Debuts Nationally at Starbucks." Starbucks Stories, January 19, 2011. https://stories.starbucks.com/stories/2011/mobile-payment-debuts-nationally-at-starbucks/.

———. "Starbucks Company Timeline." Accessed April 14, 2019. https://web.archive.org/web/20190414202620/https://www.starbucks.com/about-us/company-information/starbucks-company-timeline.

———. "Starbucks Corp. (SBUX) Q1 2018 Earnings Call (Corrected Transcript)." FactSet CallStreet, LLC, January 25, 2018. https://investor.starbucks.com/events-and-presentations/current-and-past-events/event-details/2018/Q1-Fiscal-2018-Starbucks-Earnings-Conference-Call-tentative/default.aspx.

———. "Starbucks Reports Q1 Fiscal 2019 Results." Financial release, December 30, 2018. https://web.archive.org/web/20190430023547/https://s22.q4cdn.com/869488222/files/doc_financials/quarterly/2019/q1/Q1-FY19-Earnings-Release-FINAL.pdf.

———. "Starbucks Reports Record Q2 Fiscal 2018 Results." Starbucks Stories, April 26, 2018. https://stories.starbucks.com/press/2018/starbucks-q2-fy18-earnings/.

———. "Starbucks to Move Payment Processing to JPMorgan Chase & Co." Starbucks Stories, October 22, 2015. https://stories.starbucks.com/stories/2015/starbucks-moves-payment-processing-to-jpmorgan-chase/.

"Starbucks App Leads Mobile Payment Competitors." eMarketer, May 22, 2018. https://web.archive.org/web/20190428202503/https://newsroom.emarketer.com/newsroom/index.php/starbucks-app-leads-mobile-payment-competitors/.

Starkman, Dean. "'The Future Is Medieval.'" *Columbia Journalism Review*, June 7, 2013. https://web.archive.org/web/20170312122500/http://archives.cjr.org/the_audit/the_future_is_medieval.php.

Starosielski, Nicole. *The Undersea Network*. Durham, NC: Duke University Press, 2015.

Statistica. "Number of Starbucks Stores Worldwide 2018." 2019.

Stearns, David L. *Electronic Value Exchange: Origins of the VISA Electronic Payment System*. New York: Springer, 2011.

Stein, Jeannine. "Is There Life after Credit? . . .: Yes, but It Requires Adjusting to a Very Different Set of Rules." *Los Angeles Times*, October 12, 1987.

Stephenson, Neal. *The Diamond Age; or, A Young Lady's Illustrated Primer*. New York: Bantam Doubleday Dell, 1995.

Sterling, Greg. "Google Wallet + Offers + Check-Ins = Closed Loop." Screenwerk, May 26, 2011. https://web.archive.org/web/20110531023207/http://www.screenwerk.com/2011/05/26/google-wallet-offers-check-ins-closed-loop.

Sterne, Jonathan. "Transportation and Communication: Together as You've Always Wanted Them." In *Thinking with James Carey: Essays on Communications, Transportation, History*, edited by Jeremy Packer and Craig Robertson, 117–36. New York: Peter Lang, 2006.

Stevenson, Richard. "Advertising: Visa Aims at American Express." *New York Times*, February 10, 1988.

Stokes, Wendy. "The Soapbox: How PayPal & WePay Discriminate against the Adult Industry." The Frisky, September 23, 2018. https://web.archive.org/web/20190114224430/https://thefrisky.com/the-soapbox-how-paypal-wepay-discriminate-against-the-adult-industry/.

Strassler, Karen. "The Face of Money: Currency, Crisis, and Remediation in Post-Suharto Indonesia." *Cultural Anthropology* 24, no. 1 (2009): 68–103. https://doi.org/10.1111/j.1548-1360.2009.00027.x.

Strathern, Marilyn. *The Gender of the Gift*. Berkeley: University of California Press, 1988.

Strom, Stephanie. "Starbucks to Introduce Single-Serve Coffee Maker." *New York Times*, September 20, 2012.

Stryker, Kitty. "Not Waving, but Drowning: How WePay Failed Eden Alexander." *Purr Versatity* (blog), May 17, 2014. https://web.archive.org/web/20140521231315/http://kittystryker.com:80/2014/05/not-waving-but-drowning-how-wepay-failed-eden-alexander/.

Suri, Siddharth, and Mary Gray. "Spike in Online Gig Work: Flash in the Pan or Future of Employment?" Social Media Collective, November 17, 2016. https://web.archive.org/web/20190414171111/https://socialmediacollective.org/2016/11/17/spike-in-online-gig-work-flash-in-the-pan-or-future-of-employment/.

Sutton, Horace. "Just Write It on the Tab, Joe." *Washington Post and Times Herald*, September 21, 1958.

Swaminathan, Ketharaman. "How Blockchain Can Crack the Holy Grail of Loyalty Programs." *Finextra* (blog), June 5, 2018. https://web.archive.org/web/20190301120508/https://www.finextra.com/blogposting/15430/how-blockchain-can-crack-the-holy-grail-of-loyalty-programs.

Swanson, Ana, and Abby Ohlheiser. "Harriet Tubman to Appear on $20 Bill, While Alexander Hamilton Remains on $10 Bill." *Washington Post*, April 20, 2016.

Swartz, Lana. "Blockchain Dreams: Imagining Techno-Economic Alternatives After Bitcoin." In *Another Economy Is Possible: Culture and Economy in a Time of Crisis*, edited by Manuel Castells, 82–105. Malden, MA: Polity, 2017.

———. "Gendered Transactions: Identity and Payment at Midcentury." *Women's Studies Quarterly* 42, nos. 1–2 (2014): 137–53. https://doi.org/10.1353/wsq.2014.0029.

———. "'Goodbye, Wallet'!: Toward a Transactional Geography of Mobile Payment." *Media Fields Journal* 6 (2013). https://web.archive.org/

web/20170508081223/http://mediafieldsjournal.squarespace.com/
goodbye-wallet/2013/9/23/goodbye-wallet-towards-a-transactional-
geography-of-mobile-p.html.

———. "What Was Bitcoin, What Will It Be? The Techno-Economic
Imaginaries of a New Money Technology." *Cultural Studies* 32, no. 4
(2018): 623–50. https://doi.org/10.1080/09502386.2017.1416420.

Swartz, Lana, and David Stearns. "Money and Its Technologies in
the Modern Era." In *History of Money: The Modern Era*, edited by
Taylor C. Nelms and David Peterson. London: Bloomsbury,
2019.

Sweet, Ken. "Credit Card Sensation: The Hottest New Plastic Is Metal."
Associated Press, September 8, 2016. https://web.archive.org/
web/20180106230039/https://apnews.com/053f4eac5eb74c50a561
79f389645205.

Szabo, Nick. "Bit Gold." *Unenumerated* (blog), December 27, 2008. https://
web.archive.org/web/20180409234621/https://unenumerated.
blogspot.com/2005/12/bit-gold.html.

Takahashi, Dean. "CryptoKitties Blockchain Sensation Raises $12 Mil-
lion." *VentureBeat*, March 20, 2018. https://web.archive.org/web/
20190628005704/https://venturebeat.com/2018/03/20/cryptokitties-
blockchain-sensation-raises-12-million.

Tekobbe, Cindy, and John Carter McKnight. "Indigenous Cryptocurrency:
Affective Capitalism and Rhetorics of Sovereignty." *First Monday*
21, no. 10 (2016). https://doi.org/10.5210/fm.v21i10.6955.

Teslik, Lee Hudson. "Nation Branding Explained." Council on Foreign
Relations, November 9, 2007. https://web.archive.org/web/
20180301131334/https://www.cfr.org/backgrounder/nation-branding-
explained.

The Credit Shifu. "Chase Sapphire Reserve Unboxing." YouTube, October
3, 2016. https://www.youtube.com/watch?v=ELeADf6TgCY.

TheJokore. "Unboxing the Chase Sapphire Reserve Card—The 100,000
Point Card!" YouTube, August 29, 2016. https://www.youtube.com/
watch?v=X5eH8YnFcTY.

Thériault, Anne. "I Already Have a Cryptocurrency: It's Called Sephora
Beauty Insider Points." Flare, February 26, 2018. https://web.
archive.org/web/20190428210741/https://www.flare.com/news/
intersecting-histories-of-women-finances-and-alternative-currencies/.

Thompson, Ben. "Apple's China Problem." *Stratechery* (blog), May 3, 2017. https://web.archive.org/web/20190702163831/https://stratechery.com/2017/apples-china-problem/.

Thurlow, Crispin, and Adam Jaworski. "The Alchemy of the Upwardly Mobile: Symbolic Capital and the Stylization of Elites in Frequent-Flyer Programmes." *Discourse & Society* 17, no. 1 (2006): 99–135. https://doi.org/10.1177/0957926506058066.

Timberg, Craig. "Bitcoin's Boom Is a Boon for Extremist Groups." *Washington Post*, December 26, 2017.

Tkacz, Nathaniel. "Money's New Abstractions: Apple Pay and the Economy of Experience." *Distinktion: Journal of Social Theory*, September 26, 2019, 1–20. doi:10.1080/1600910X.2019.1653348.

Today Show. ".@RealDonaldTrump speaks out about putting Harriet Tubman on the $20 bill #TrumpTODAY." Twitter (@TODAYshow), April 21, 2016. https://web.archive.org/web/20190526124614/https:/twitter.com/TODAYshow/status/723126482906714114.

Tode, Chantal. "Starbucks Is Worldwide Leader in Mobile Payment Transactions: Exec." Retail Dive, January 31, 2012. https://web.archive.org/web/20190428202926/https://www.retaildive.com/ex/mobilecommercedaily/starbucks-exec-says-retailer-is-worldwide-leader-in-mobile-payment-transactions-dollars.

Torrone, Phillip. "Hey Steven Mnuchin, Making Harriet Tubman $20s Seems Totally OK @ustreasury @stevenmnuchin1." *Adafruit* (blog), October 15, 2017. https://web.archive.org/web/20181213064501/https://blog.adafruit.com/2017/10/15/hey-steven-mnuchin-making-harriet-tubman-20s-seems-totally-ok-ustreasury-stevenmnuchin1/.

"Traveling? Put It on the Cuff: A New, All-Purpose Credit Card Lets You Do Just That." *Changing Times: The Kiplinger Magazine*, February 1952.

TruckStopUSA.com. Accessed April 1, 2015. http://truckstopusa.com/archive/index.php/t-31491.html.

Tucker, Carl. "Credit System Lures 40,000 Eaters-Out in 1st Year of Operation: Diners' Club Has Big Attraction: Ready Made Expense List to Show Tax Collector." *Wall Street Journal*, March 28, 1951.

Tugend, Alina. "Balancing a Checkbook Isn't Calculus. It's Harder." *New York Times*, June 24, 2006.

Turner, Fred. *From Counterculture to Cyberculture: Stewart Brand, the Whole Earth Network, and the Rise of Digital Utopianism*. Chicago: University of Chicago Press, 2008.

Turner, Michael. "Credit Card Rewards: Context, History, and Value; A White Paper on Credit Card Rewards." Durham, NC: PERC, August 2012. https://web.archive.org/web/20190430034516/http://www.perc.net/wp-content/uploads/2013/12/WP-2-Layout.pdf.

Turner, Michael, Patrick Walker, Sukanya Chaudhuri, Joseph Duncan, Robin Varghese, and Walter Kitchenman. *A Reexamination of Who Gains and Who Loses from Credit Card Payments*. Durham, NC: Policy and Economic Research Council, 2013.

Turow, Joseph. *The Aisles Have Eyes: How Retailers Track Your Shopping, Strip Your Privacy, and Define Your Power*. New Haven, CT: Yale University Press, 2017.

Tusikov, Natasha. "Defunding Hate: PayPal's Regulation of Hate Groups." *Surveillance & Society* 17, nos. 1–2 (2019): 46–53. https://doi.org/10.24908/ss.v17i1/2.12908.

u/mk712. "Chase Sapphire Reserve—The Morning After." Reddit, August 23, 2016. https://www.reddit.com/r/churning/comments/4za31p/chase_sapphire_reserve_the_morning_after/.

UN Human Rights Council. "The Promotion, Protection and Enjoyment of Human Rights on the Internet." Resolution, United Nations General Assembly, June 27, 2016. https://doi.org/10.1163/2210-7975_HRD-9970-2016149.

u/perfectviking. "Changes to the Marriott cards once Bonvoy rolls out." Reddit, January 23, 2019. https://www.reddit.com/r/churning/comments/aj0cei/changes_to_the_marriott_cards_once_bonvoy_rolls/.

US Bureau of Labor Statistics. "Usual Weekly Earnings of Wage and Salary Works of Fourth Quarter 2018." New release. January 17, 2019.

US Department of Treasury. "Treasury Secretary Lew Announces Front of New $20 to Feature Harriet Tubman, Lays Out Plans for New $20, $10 and $5." Press release. April 20, 2016. https://web.archive.org/web/20190513085841/https://www.treasury.gov/press-center/press-releases/Pages/jl0436.aspx.

"U.S. Economy Grinds to Halt as Nation Realizes Money Just a Symbolic, Mutually Shared Illusion." *The Onion*, February 16, 2010. https://web.archive.org/web/20180205202843/https://www.theonion.com/

u-s-economy-grinds-to-halt-as-nation-realizes-money-ju-1819571322.

US Postal Service. "Postal Savings System." July 2008. https://web.archive.org/web/20190323204251/https://about.usps.com/who-we-are/postal-history/postal-savings-system.pdf.

———. "The United States Postal Service: An American History, 1775–2006." 2007. https://web.archive.org/web/20190915162240/https://about.usps.com/publications/pub100.pdf.

US Securities and Exchange Commission. "Alphabet Inc. Form 10-K for the Fiscal Year Ended December 31, 2017." Annual report. https://web.archive.org/web/20190410005149/https://www.sec.gov/Archives/edgar/data/1652044/000165204418000007/goog10-kq42017.htm.

———. "Google Inc. Form 10-K for the Fiscal Year Ended December 31, 2015." Annual report. https://web.archive.org/web/20190915162544/https://www.sec.gov/Archives/edgar/data/1288776/000128877615000008/goog2014123110-k.htm.

Vaidhyanathan, Siva. *Antisocial Media: How Facebook Disconnects US and Undermines Democracy*. New York: Oxford University Press, 2018.

———. *The Googlization of Everything: And Why We Should Worry*. Berkeley: University of California Press, 2011.

van Dijck, José. "From Shoebox to Performative Agent: The Computer as Personal Memory Machine." *New Media & Society* 7, no. 3 (2005): 311–32. https://doi.org/10.1177/1461444805050765.

———. "Mediated Memories: Personal Cultural Memory as Object of Cultural Analysis." *Continuum* 18, no. 2 (2004): 261–77. https://doi.org/10.1080/1030431042000215040.

van Dijck, José, and Thomas Poell. "Understanding Social Media Logic." *Media and Communication* 1, no. 1 (2013): 2–14. https://doi.org/10.17645/mac.v1i1.70.

Vartabedian, Ralph. "Balance Your Checkbook? Why? Some Call It a Waste of Time, but the Experts Say You Ignore It at Your Peril." *Los Angeles Times*, November 12, 1991.

Venmo. "Purchases." Accessed July 9, 2018. https://web.archive.org/web/20180709150906/https://venmo.com/business.

———. "User Agreement." Accessed August 31, 2018. https://web.archive.org/web/20180831041350/https://venmo.com/legal/us-user-agreement/.

Vlastelica, Ryan. "A Cup of Crypto: Starbucks and Dunkin' Both Discussed Bitcoin in Their Analyst Days." MarketWatch, February 14, 2018. https://web.archive.org/web/20190215044451/https://www.market watch.com/story/a-cup-of-crypto-starbucks-and-dunkin-both-discussed-bitcoin-in-their-analyst-days-2018-02-13.

Vosburg, Craig. "A Card for Our Digital Era." *BeyondTheTransaction* (blog), Mastercard, March 25, 2019. https://web.archive.org/ web/20190401025131/https://newsroom.mastercard.com/2019/ 03/25/a-card-for-our-digital-era/.

Walker, Rob. "After Snowden and the Age of the Overshare, Startups and Citizens Find the Value of Privacy." Yahoo! Finance, February 5, 2014. https://web.archive.org/web/20181007205034/https://finance. yahoo.com/news/in-the-age-of-snowden-and-online-oversharing-privacy-75621205340.html.

Wall, Dano. "Harriet Tubman Stamp" Awesome Foundation, September 2018. https://web.archive.org/web/20190915181221/https://www. awesomefoundation.org/en/projects/107274-harriet-tubman-stamp.

Ward, Terrence. "The High-Risk Digital World of Occult Sales and Psychic Services." Wild Hunt, March 22, 2017. https://web.archive.org/ web/20190303161444/https://wildhunt.org/2017/03/the-high-risk-digital-world-of-occult-sales-and-psychic-services.html.

Wayne, Teddy. "Thanks to Venmo, We Now All Know How Cheap Our Friends Are." *New York Times*, July 21, 2017.

Weber, Eugen. *Peasants into Frenchmen: The Modernization of Rural France, 1870–1914*. Stanford, CA: Stanford University Press, 2007.

Webster, Karen. "Who Won't Win the Mobile Wallet 'Wars' and Why." PYMNTS.com, April 27, 2015. https://web.archive.org/web/ 20150518155711/http://www.pymnts.com/news/2015/who-wont-win-the-mobile-wallet-wars-and-why/.

Weinstock, Susan, Andrew Blevins, Joy Hackenbracht, Thaddeus King, and Rachel Siegel. "Banking on Prepaid." Pew Charitable Trusts, June 2015.

WePay. "WePay's Terms of Service as It Relates to Adult Entertainment." *WePay Blog*, May 17, 2014. https://web.archive.org/web/ 20140519154936/http://blog.wepay.com/post/86048891401/wepays-terms-of-service-as-it-relates-to-adult.

"WePay Founder Talks Veda's Launch, Future." PYMNTS.com, May 9, 2013. http://web.archive.org/web/20190414203432/https://www.pymnts.com/news/2013/wepay-founder-talks-veda-s-launch-future/.

"WePay Launches Veda Social Risk Engine." The Paypers, May 9, 2013. https://web.archive.org/web/20190303163724/https://www.thepaypers.com/digital-identity-security-online-fraud/wepay-launches-veda-social-risk-engine/751089-26.

"WePay suspends medical fundraiser payment to adult model/cam girl Eden Alexander." Reddit, May 17, 2014. https://www.reddit.com/r/SRSDiscussion/comments/25t59g/wepay_suspends_medical_fundraiser_payment_to/chko1gw/.

"What's a Debit Card?" *Washington Post*, July 23, 1997.

Wheat, Carl I., and Charles E. De Long. "'California's Bantam Cock': The Journals of Charles E. De Long, 1854–1863 (Continued)." *California History* 9, no. 4 (1930): 345–97. https://doi.org/10.2307/25178100.

"Who Gets Approved for the Chase Sapphire Reserve?" *AskSebby* (blog), January 4, 2017. http://web.archive.org/web/20180619162808/https://blog.asksebby.com/who-gets-approved-for-the-chase-sapphire-reserve-89ea9c6a1a?gi=c9add3993817.

Williams, Henry, and Telis Demos. "Where Money Lives." *Wall Street Journal*, June 1, 2016. https://web.archive.org/web/20190428203429/http://graphics.wsj.com/where-money-lives/.

Wilson, Jonathan. "What Your Payment Method Reveals about You." The Hairpin, February 6, 2012. https://web.archive.org/web/20190323164832/https://www.thehairpin.com/2012/02/what-your-payment-method-reveals-about-you/.

Wolfson, Alisa. "This Is How Venmo Is Ruining Relationships." MarketWatch, July 15, 2018. https://web.archive.org/web/20190522171528/https://www.marketwatch.com/story/this-is-how-venmo-is-ruining-relationships-2018-07-15-288111.

Wolters, Timothy. "'Carry Your Credit in Your Pocket': The Early History of the Credit Card at Bank of America and Chase Manhattan." *Enterprise & Society* 1, no. 2 (2000): 315–54. https://doi.org/10.1017/S1467222700000550.

Women On $20s. "Why the $20?" Accessed July 19, 2018. https://web.archive.org/web/20180719050028/http://www.womenon20s.org/why_the_20.

Wortham, Jenna. "Braintree, a Payments Company, Buys Venmo for $26.2 Million." *New York Times*, August 16, 2012. https://web.archive.org/web/20190913174122/https://bits.blogs.nytimes.com/2012/08/16/payments-start-up-braintree-buys-venmo-for-26-2-million/.

Woyke, Elizabeth. "WePay: The Online Payment Start-Up behind Occupy Wall Street." *Forbes*, January 31, 2012. https://web.archive.org/web/20170908182844/https://www.forbes.com/sites/elizabeth-woyke/2012/01/31/wepay-the-online-payment-startup-behind-occupy-wall-street/.

Wray, L. Randall. "Introduction to an Alternative History of Money." Working paper, Levy Economics Institute of Bard College, May 2012.

Wu, Julianna. "A Surprising Number of Countries Now Accept WeChat Pay or Alipay." Abacus, December 7, 2018. https://web.archive.org/web/20190702164408/https://www.abacusnews.com/big-guns/surprising-number-countries-now-accept-wechat-pay-or-alipay/article/2176889.

York, Jillian. "@MsMaggieMayhem @melissagira @billclerico @WePay Wow, do they follow me around SF too to make sure I don't accidentally strip?" Twitter (@jilliancyork), May 17, 2014. https://web.archive.org/web/20190303163314/https://twitter.com/jilliancyork/status/467808457026859008.

———. ".@WePay's statement is bullshit. What someone does in their free time isn't their business to monitor. blog.wepay.com/post/86048891401/wepays-terms-of-service-as-it-relates-to-adult." Twitter (@jilliancyork), May 17, 2014. https://web.archive.org/web/20190303162736/https://twitter.com/jilliancyork/status/467806470482841600.

Young, A. Christopher, Jennifer L. Maher, and Katherine B. Puccio. "Loyalty Programs: All Fun and Games until Someone Wants You to Buy Them a Harrier Jump Jet." Pepper Hamilton LLP, May 16, 2016. https://web.archive.org/web/20190622212044/https://www.pepperlaw.com/publications/loyalty-programs-all-fun-and-games-until-someone-wants-you-to-buy-them-a-harrier-jump-jet-2016-05-16/.

Zeitlin, Matthew. "US Sanctions Mean Paying for Cuban Sandwiches on Venmo Is Complicated." Buzzfeed News, December 27, 2016. https://

web.archive.org/web/20170223111409/https://www.buzzfeed.com/
matthewzeitlin/be-careful-paying-for-cuban-food-on-venmo.

Zelizer, Viviana A. "Circuits of Commerce." In *Self, Social Structure, and Beliefs: Explorations in Sociology*, edited by Jeffrey C. Alexander, Gary T. Marx, and Christine L. Williams, 122–44. Berkeley: University of California Press, 2004.

———. "Payments and Social Ties." *Sociological Forum* 11, no. 3 (1996): 481–95.

———. *The Purchase of Intimacy*. Princeton, NJ: Princeton University Press, 2005.

———. *The Social Meaning of Money*. Princeton, NJ: Princeton University Press, 1997.

———. "The Social Meaning of Money: 'Special Monies.'" *American Journal of Sociology* 95, no. 2 (1989): 342–77. https://doi.org/10.1086/229272.

Zibell, Alan, and Brent Kendall. "Probe Turns Up Heat on Banks." *Wall Street Journal*, August 7, 2013.

Zook, Matthew, and Mark Graham. "Hacking Code/Space: Confounding the Code of Global Capitalism." *Transactions of the Institute of British Geographers* 43 (2018): 390–404. https://doi.org/10.1111/tran.12228.

Zuckerman, Molly Jane. "CNBC Fast Money's Brian Kelly: Bitcoin Is like the 'Internet in the 1980s.'" CoinTelegraph, April 15, 2018. https://web.archive.org/web/20190428213013/https://cointelegraph.com/news/cnbc-fast-moneys-brian-kelly-bitcoin-is-like-the-internet-in-the-1980s.

ILLUSTRATION CREDITS

INDEX

debit cards: history of, 35; and
transactional identities, 48, 54,
66–68, 73–74; and transactional
memories, 117, 121–22, 132;
and Venmo, 23
DEC (company), 38
Department of Homeland
Security, 134
de Recat, Olivia, 108, 110
Desan, Christine, 148–49
Deville, Joe, 17
Dewey, John, 6
digital currencies, 38–40, 114,
139–55, 168. *See also specific
digital currencies*
Diners Club, 35, 37, 56–58, 60–62,
107, 119–20
Discover, 48
Dodd, Nigel, 13, 110, 149–50
Dodd-Frank Wall Street Reform
and Consumer Protection Act
of 2010, 66
donations, 63, 76–77, 80–81, 96,
100, 103, 106. *See also* crowd-
funding
Do Thi Duc, Hang, 135–38
Drèze, Xavier, 159
due diligence, 88–89
Dunkin' Donuts, 150
DuPont, Quinn, 116, 129
Durbin Amendment, 66

EBT cards, 47
Economist on frequent-flyer
miles, 147
Ecuador: currencies used in, 11;
informal family banks (*cajas*)
in, 115
Edwards, Paul, 13
Electronic Frontier Foundation,
97
Electronic Funds Transfer Act of
1978, 66–67
Electronic Recording Machine,
Accounting (ERMA),
118
Ellison, Nicole, 21
emojis, 3, 21, 111–12

employers: Diners Club fees paid
by, 57–58; and frequent-flyer
programs, 62; and loyalty
programs, 158; and paychecks,
11, 69, 72, 74, 81, 84, 107; and
social media, 135
End Banking for Human Traffickers Act of 2017, 106
Enterprise Rent-A-Car, 167
entrepreneurs, 4–5, 95, 139, 141,
154
ERMA (Electronic Recording
Machine, Accounting), 118
Espeland, Wendy, 45, 104, 156
Eubanks, Virginia, 162
euros, 148, 151, 154, 173
Evans, David S., 63
EveryDNS, 80
exomemory, 131, 190n95
ExxonMobil, 167
E-ZPass, 2

Facebook: and data mining, 98,
155–56; Libra, 1, 20, 168–69;
Messenger Payments, 90;
payment systems in, 19–22; and
transactional memories,
112–13, 125, 128, 135
Fair Credit Billing Act of 1975,
66
Fair Credit Reporting Act of 1970,
101
FAO Schwartz, 59
Fargo, J. C., 33
FDIC, 80, 89
fear of missing out (FOMO), 111
Federal Bureau of Investigation
(FBI), 134
Federal Reserve, 3, 23, 33–35, 39,
55, 66, 74, 91
fees: Bitcoin, 141; Chase Sapphire
Reserve, 45, 52–53; Diners
Club, 58; foreign exchange, 43,
45; interchange fees, 53–54, 85,
91, 130, 165; and ISOs, 84–85,
87–88; loyalty programs,
156–57; money orders, 33;
online lenders, 99; overdraft,